The Architecture Annual 1997-1998

Delft University of Technology

The Architecture Annual 1997-1998

Delft University of Technology

Edited by

Prof. Henco Bekkering

Prof. Hans de Jonge

Klaske Havik

Marieke van Ouwerkerk

010 Publishers, Rotterdam 1999

Contents

6 Foreword
Prof. Cees Dam, Prof. Frits van Voorden

8 Introduction
Klaske Havik, Marieke van Ouwerkerk

Strategies

12 Research studios
Laura Kaper

16 Stylos Design Award
Jeroen Mensink

18 On re-reading Kafka
Deborah Hauptmann

23 River dynamics as design tool
Caroline Stegewerns

28 11 cities 52 plans
Peter de Bois

Landscape and urbanization

32 Urbanization & Haarlemmermeer
Mattijs van 't Hoff

35 Holland in transit
Joost van den Hoek

38 L'eautel à l'île perdue
Daniëlle Segers

41 Countryside as facility
Paul de Graaf

44 Utrecht: intense city
Merel Bakker

47 The final polder
Agnes Franzen

Shifting perspectives

52 Where does the architecture of the city originate?
Dieter Besch, Roel van Alst, Massimo Pauletto, Pascal Smits

55 Learning from The New Urbanism
Luisa Calabrese

62 Light urban development
Prof. Jon Kristinsson

64 Rotterdam: the enabling city
Dr Gerard Wigmans

68 U1 practice studio
Erik Wiersema

Mobility

72 Local traffic transferium for Amsterdam
Reshmi Oemrawsingh and Mark Westerhuis

75 Amstel Inter Modal Centre
Stefan van der Spek

78 The Arnhem-Nijmegen interchange
Christiaan de Wolf

81 Change at Delft
Ada Beuling

84 Interaction-model for concern and location synergy in the station environment
Gert-Joost Peek

87 Development in development
Paulien Eisma

90 Utrecht coronary
Alex de Jong

93 Rotterdam Grand Prix
Rico Zweers

Transformations

- 98 Optimization of land use on the Lelylaan in Amsterdam
  John Westrik, Thijs van Heusden, Sandra Rozemeijer
- 102 Advice regarding the ancient harbour of Byblos in Lebanon
  Prof. Frits van Voorden, Ron van Oers
- 110 Reflections on housing experts
  Kees van der Flier
- 114 An unsentimental journey
  Prof. Pi de Bruijn
- 118 D12 International renovation
  Leo Verhoef

Dwelling(s)

- 122 Supporting structures for density increase
  Julie-Anne van Gemert
- 125 Instant housing
  Annemieke Punter
- 128 Lake Shore Drive-in Apartments
  Simon van Amerongen
- 131 STAM + P: living in the suburbs
  Nynke Jutten
- 134 Viewmaster by the Maas
  Greetje van den Nouweland
- 137 Stacked villas in Middendelfland
  Margreet van der Woude

Interpretations

- 142 Sustainable housing in Europe
  Anke van Hal
- 145 IMPression
  Dr Rypke Sierksma
- 155 Managing corporate real estate
  Peter Krumm, Prof. Hans de Jonge

Culture, recreation and religion

- 162 'Through' - line transformer
  Marc Neelen
- 165 Dance and theatre college in Arnhem
  Nienke Ettema
- 168 Everyday temple
  Lidewij Lenders
- 171 Sports centre, sailing school and sports hotel in Hoorn
  Hans Konijn
- 174 Punto de Encuentro
  Huib van Zeijl

Techniques and technology

- 180 A design research experiment in brief: the Imaging Imagination Workshop
  Martijn Stellingwerff, Jack Breen
- 185 A strategy for the use of simulation tools in building design
  Pieter de Wilde, Marinus van der Voorden and Godfried Augenbroe
- 190 The quest for Zappi

Overview

- 200 Activities
- 204 Curriculum
- 206 Research programme
- 208 Acknowledgments

Foreword

Prof. Cees Dam, Prof. Frits van Voorden[1]

The Faculty of Architecture at Delft University of Technology has produced remarkable achievements in the 1997 - 1998 academic year. The architecture student association *Stylos* received the 1998 Rotterdam-Maaskantprijs, the most prestigious architecture prize in the Netherlands. The prize was awarded for the lectures, events and symposia that Stylos organizes, both for architecture students and lecturers as well as for the entire profession in the Netherlands and beyond. The lectures are attended by a total of about 7,000 people every year. Speakers in the recent past have included Rem Koolhaas, Peter Eisenman, Santiago Calatrava and Neil Denari.

The practical results of educational innovation are also remarkable. The coherence in the basic education (the first two academic years) has improved and space has been created for theory and methods of design. Furthermore, more attention was given to research, both in the basic and sequel courses.

In the field of scientific research, priority will be given to design projects with effect from this academic year. Outline drawings and plans have been rediscovered as products of scientific research. The graduation projects included in this annual show the fascinations of a new generation of designers/researchers. Research studios are being developed to further stimulate design research. The Architecture Research School of Design and Computation has been commissioned to implement the large-scale design and research project *De Architectonische Interventie* (The Architectonic Intervention), a cluster of multi-disciplinary projects by students, PhD students and staff that are based on design studios.

The position of architecture as a science has been probed by the committee that, under the authority of the Association of Dutch Universities (VSNU), has performed the International Review for Academic Research in Architecture, Building and Planning (VSNU Research Assessment of Architecture, Building and Planning, 1998). The report states:

"A fundamental problem in reviewing the research performance of architecture is that there are no clear-cut criteria for research in architecture. Architecture is neither science nor technology. It contains part of technology but it is not at all science. (...) Architecture depends on intuition, ideas, sometimes also on ideology. Some facets of art are present. (...)
 The central product (one might say "experiment") of architecture is design, but simply design is not recognised as research. This suggests that a core activity of a faculty of architecture does not contribute to scientific quality, productivity, and relevance. There is a systemic error in assessing the performance of a faculty of architecture since a large part and a most important part cannot be assessed by the rules (which apply to scientific research). (...)
 The Review Committee has felt that architecture is not adequately represented in NWO (The Netherlands Organization for Scientific Research) and that this situation should be improved."

[1] Prof. Cees Dam held the position of Dean until 1 July 1998; Prof. Frits van Voorden from 1 July to 15 November 1998; Prof. Hans Beunderman from 15 November 1998 onwards.

The Faculty is of the opinion that the claim must now be made for an autonomous field of study. Besides the scientific arguments, as outlined above, there are arguments of an economic nature – the total volume of the building production, the infrastructure and the land use within the national economy – and of a social-cultural nature. The latter concerns the importance of architecture for society as a whole.

Particularly the naturalness of the social function of buildings and settlements for society, for instance for living, working and meeting, makes it difficult to define the autonomy of architecture.
     Here as well, the VSNU report gives us something to go on:
     "Architecture, building, planning and policy comprise a wide field of activities, which are partly technological, partly social, partly artistic and more. The disciplines deal with the most primary needs of mankind, i.e. housing, but also with the environment, urban settlements, energy consumption, history of architectural design."

The overview of design and research projects by students and faculty staff that is presented in this annual is ideally suited to substantiating the claim for an autonomous field of study.

Introduction

Klaske Havik, Marieke van Ouwerkerk

Almost by definition, architecture courses are facing an identity crisis: between professional training and art academy; between technical (engineering) course and true university institute. This kind of identity crisis can be very productive if one is conscious of it, as the faculty has been during the past few years. It has resulted in the faculty being constantly forced to reformulate the aims for both education and research.

The development of knowledge is the main *raison d'être* of a university faculty. This development not only takes place in the form of research activities by the scientific staff: the training of students, and their contribution to the development of knowledge in general, is an essential if not absolutely paramount aspect. The faculty plays an important role in creating the conditions for a critical discourse to unfold – a discourse essential for the development of an independant stance.

The development of architecture, and, for that matter, of all technical professions, takes place in close connection with developments in society. This connection extends much further than the technical-instrumental field. Courses must therefore have a broader orientation than their own field of study alone so that the future engineers have the necessary tools to take up a position related to the context in which they will operate in the future. Courses must therefore be based on a new kind of certainty: the certainty that you will be continually confronted with unknown things, and will have to respond to them.

Being capable of forwarding one's knowledge is thus explicitly also a skill the engineer requires. The relevant field of knowledge is not only flexible, but also subject to permanent change. It is therefore important to go beyond the limits of one's own subject. There is an ever increasing trend towards an interdisciplinary approach in architecture, thus exploring the limits of and interfaces between the various fields of study. The exploration of these limits not only produces knowledge, but knowledge of a greater number of fields of study also makes it possible to form a perspective within one's own frame of reference.

In this respect, design research is of vital importance for an architecture faculty. Parallel to the question how education and research are related to one another, the relationship between design and research has been actively experimented with for a number of years already. The faculty has, for instance, set itself the task of bringing the research work of staff in closer contact with student work. This is partly realized by means of the creation of *onderzoeks-ateliers* (research studios). Graduates' design projects are part of wider research.

Design and research are no longer interpreted as two isolated activities. After all, the product of a design process can be regarded as a *research report*, even though it takes on a different form than usual. As a result, a questioning and subsequent redefinition of criteria for research becomes necessary: although the activities of design and research share certain features and quite often are performed in close interrelationship with each other, aims, methods and results differ thoroughly.

In the research studios, the aim is to achieve exactly this kind of integration of design and research. There is collaboration between lecturers, research assistants, students and professors, all from different professions. Exchange thus becomes a predominant feature of their work. A number of the graduation projects in this book originate from these studios.

In the light of the above-mentioned developments, the education in the earlier phases of the courses also takes on a new significance. For example, a new educational programme has been developed with attention being paid to *theory and method* early on, and activities like workshops, student-initiated projects, design competitions and experimental modules indicate that the courses are continually reviewed.

This is the situation that we have attempted to shed some light on in this annual. Not only is considerable attention devoted to the studios, but also the wide range of points of view and subjects relevant to the field of architecture is emphasized. The result is a summary of the 1997-1998 academic year. Particularly from the point of view of the development of knowledge by means of an exchange between fields of study – both in the form of interdisciplinary projects and in individual orientation – a structure has been chosen whereby articles from different perspectives are placed side by side.

Strategies

Research studios

Laura Kaper

Whereas vocational training focuses on designing as a skill and art academies on designing as an art, the Faculty of Architecture focuses on designing as an academic science. This means that when students choose to be taught at a university of technology, they make a particular choice as designers. Students can choose a graduation project that is part of ongoing research within the faculty, particularly of doctoral research involving a particular part of a professor's overall field of research. The name *onderzoeksatelier* (research studio) has been given to the partnership between final year students, PhD students and a professor, supported by a research assistant. The research theme is decided by the professor, who can take on PhD students. Final year students can choose a project connected to this theme. A practical advantage of the studio is that final year students are surrounded by various projects grouped around the same theme, enabling them to become familiar with the material quickly and participate in an exchange of information. The abundance and diversity of design assignments and solutions centred on the same theme provides opportunities for everyone involved in the studio to discover general rules in the variants, rules that are valuable for the total research project. The research studios all function independently, deciding their own working methods and the nature and frequency of meetings, excursions, sketching weeks or seminars. The exchange of ideas between studios is promoted by the monthly open studio lectures. Each studio organizes a discussion meeting once or twice a year on the theme of its work. One speaker from the studio itself and one outside speaker discuss the same subject from two perspectives: the practical side based on realistic assignments and the theory behind the graduation projects. The purpose of the research is to find relations – or in the case of design research, create relations – between phenomena that are apparently unconnected and random. The research studios and the open studio lectures help to ensure that this function of research also strengthens the personal and social ties within the Faculty of Architecture. In the 1997-1998 academic year, six research studios were in operation: *OVerstapMachine*, *Deltametropool*, *Buiten Plaats*, *Atelier NaOorlogseWoonwijken*, *Snel weg in Nederland* and *Netwerk-stad VROM*. Together they involved an average of 70 final year students, about 15 of whom have now graduated. The two oldest studios, *OVerstapMachine* and *Deltametropool*, have both produced a publication on their graduation project output, while other studios are preparing one. The themes of the research studios are described briefly below.

OVerstapMachine

Individual liberty and freedom of choice are central values in our culture. Freedom of movement is part of this, an aspect represented in fairly physical terms in the wide range means of transport and communication. Their use results in individual patterns of movement, which overlap at certain points, creating hubs where people transfer between two or more types of transport. These interchange points, including park-and-ride systems, are the subject of research and design in the *OVerstapMachine* (transport interchange) studio. The interchange points have a dual character: firstly they form intersections in a system of connecting lines and secondly they are a feature of the urban setting. The various fields of study focus on different aspects of research associated with these points. Architectural Design concentrates on the spatial optimization of the interchange point as a junction, with a view to minimizing distances and time spent inside it. Urbanism focuses on optimizing the transfer location as a concentration point in the urban fabric and the interaction with the urban context, while Real Estate and Project Management centres on the effect that the presence of an interchange point has on property values in the vicinity. The *OVerstapMachine* has developed various activities apart from the production of graduation topics and research. These included an open studio lecture on station areas and a lecture series from 9-11 March on the areas containing the five High Speed Line stations in the west of the Netherlands and the design of the High Speed Line in the south, as well as an excursion to interchange points in the Netherlands.

Deltametropool

The concept of the metropolis refers to an urban complex of social, economic and cultural activities that are part of the global system of major cities. The creation of the European Union has placed urban development in the Netherlands in a different perspective. The context of this development is no longer the relationship between the west of the Netherlands and the rest of the country, but between the *Randstad* conurbation and other population concentrations in Europe. This studio bases its work on the hypothesis that the *Randstad* conurbation will develop into a metropolis, the *Deltametropool* (delta metropolis). The design task here is tackled on various scales – international, interregional, regional and local – with international comparisons of design assignments and design solutions always forming part of the studies. The research in the *Deltametropool* studio took on up-to-the-minute significance with the appearance of the manifesto of the same name issued by aldermen in the four main cities in February 1998, in which they took the view that the cities should not adopt individual urban planning policies but instead a complementary approach designed to create synergy. This makes the development of design tools and methods for metropolis creation more realistic. This year's open studio lecture by the *Deltametropool* studio raised the question of how a metropolitan landscape could be organized and shaped. Two options were presented in this lecture: *Wilde Wonen* (catalogue construction of individual dwellings) and *Supermarktstedenbouw* (supermarket urbanism). The latter was researched and developed in the graduation project by Mathijs van 't Hoff, which appears elsewhere in this publication.

Buiten Plaats

Until the 19th century the shape of cities in the *Randstad* conurbation was closely connected with the landscape and its topography. The city was like an enclave of urbanism within the surrounding countryside. Dikes became streets and ditches became lanes. As a result of the increase in scale in the 20th century, the city's shape has become independent of the landscape. The urban network is spreading out over the whole of the *Randstad*, further severing the contact between the modern city and the landscape. The city and its reflection, the landscape, together now form a new metropolitan territory – a territory for research into new relationships between urban programmes and fragments of countryside, between living in the country and work, between buildings and landscape, and between infrastructure and horizon. The outcome of this research is the *Buiten Plaats* (country estate). Housing estates in the countryside are the concentration points where the topographical, spatial and programmatic aspects of the landscape (including the urban landscape) are interpreted and manipulated. They form striking urban "hallmarks", dramatizing the genius loci of the landscape in the west of the country. This makes them potential centres for a landscape of country homes, a public landscape on a regional scale, a "countryside" for the *Randstad* (or the city in general). In the studio the country estate serves as a model for the city's new countryside, for country living, for new woods in the city and new landscapes of water and cultivated land.

Atelier N.O.W.

The appearance of *NaOorlogse Woonwijken* (post-war residential neighbourhoods, 1950-1970) is a translation in spatial terms of the ideals of a specific generation of urban developers and architects. As such it no longer corresponds with today's ideas about and use of space in a neighbourhood. To enable space to be used in a different way, these neighbourhoods require reurbanization. This studio examines possible approaches to reurbanization, looking at the following research issues:
– How is the urban planning task formulated in the neighbourhood?
– What should be the new position of the town or neighbourhood in the region?
– What is the quantity and quality of new programmes?
– What urban planning tools can be used in the reurbanization process?

For Urbanism, the main task is to examine the current structure of the whole neighbourhood and produce a design for optimizing this structure, along with current and future use. Architectural Design focuses on the elaboration of certain sectors or a building in the neighbourhood, within the conditions laid down for optimizing the structure and use of the neighbourhood as a whole. Housing's contribution consists of studying the local residents' needs and behaviour, while for Real Estate and Project Management the main focus is on the feasibility of reurbanization in these neighbourhoods and their subsequent management.

Snel weg in Nederland

One characteristic of 20th century urban development is the problematic relationship between large-scale infrastructure networks and urban communities. It is difficult to realize positive interaction between urban and interurban elements at local level. Although they are essential to a city's existence and development, large infrastructure projects are often seen as a necessary evil, usually resulting in areas of a low urban quality and creating physical barriers at the local level. Where there is a confrontation between large-scale infrastructure and the city, the task is to shape these confrontations with integrated urban planning designs to give the infrastructure more than a functional significance and more possibilities for use.

Snel weg in Nederland (motorways in the Netherlands) concentrates on research into the significance of integration between the city and infrastructural elements. All the studies share a common aim: to use the introduction of large-scale infrastructure in the urban area in order to bring about a structural improvement in the urban area itself. The main areas studied are:
– The integration/reintegration of existing and new connections
– Transformation of the image and use of town and countryside via road, rail and water
– Reuse and reinterpretation of what were once extensive traffic areas

This studio's first experiment is a "travel landscape" in the form of a scale model. It consists of a collage of all the projects by students and tutors, in which various fragments of the Dutch urban landscape are placed side by side and various integration assignments are presented. These assignments require a multidisciplinary approach, therefore civil-engineering aspects feature very largely in the integration issue in this studio. The model will be discussed in a workshop at the conference *Town and motorway: sustainable investment in the future*. This conference, organized by the Municipality of Den Bosch in partnership with the Netherlands Institute of Land Use Planning and Housing (NIROV), is about spatial integration, intensification and structural reinforcement and is designed partly to develop a more widely shared view on the integration of new motorways.

Netwerk-stad VROM

Our society is increasingly dependent on information and communications technology (ICT). Developments in ICT involve new ways of working, shopping, learning and entertainment. Worldwide financial and economic transformations are also strongly influenced by ICT trends. Despite many potential and current changes, the relationship between ICT and the city has not been adequately taken into account. For instance ICT did not feature prominently in the discussion about the Netherlands in 2030. Prof. Paul Drewe carried out an exploratory study for the Ministry of Housing, Spatial Planning and Environment (VROM), which led on to the *Netwerk-stad VROM* (network city) studio. Ten students who are interested in ICT transformations are now working here. The main purpose of the studio is to draft possible scenarios for site-specific projects on various scales. There are plans to study alternative programmes of requirements in which ICT applications feature significantly. Five themes have been chosen:

- The conurbation of the future
- The rest of the Netherlands, past the periphery
- Mainports as hubs in logistical networks
- The Euroregion plus, over the Dutch border
- The office/home of the future

The graduation project by Paulien Eisma, *Development in development*, included elsewhere in this publication, provides a good impression of the type of research and design produced in this studio.

Stylos Design Award
Cities in transition

Jeroen Mensink

The origins of the initiative to organize the *Stylos Design Award* national students' competition lay in a unique collaborative arrangement between the *Stylos* student association, the *Stylos Bookfund*, the journal *De Omslag*, and Arie Graafland's architectural theory seminar group. The Town Planning and Housing Department and the Port of Rotterdam Authority provided assistance in the formulation of the assignment and the determination of the area for the competition's plan.

The assignment consisted of the development of a vision, in text and images, of the future of Rotterdam's Waal and Eemhaven regions. The gradual shift of large-scale port activities from the city in the direction of the Maasvlakte, the high levels of unemployment in the adjoining Charlois neighbourhood and the increasing trend towards containerization make a new interpretation of the world's largest excavated harbour necessary. The character of Rotterdam as a seaport is changing; the city and the port are growing apart. This is not a development unique to Rotterdam, as other large seaports have also seen their harbours disappear from the city. This development gives rise to the question as to how a new relationship between city and harbour should be given shape. The competitors were expected to prepare a scenario for the future development of the region, and to draw up a design that could be a possible interpretation of this scenario.

The competition was intended for students following a design education in the Netherlands. The competition was given the name *Cities in transition*, and was announced in a special issue of *De Omslag*. In the same issue, students of the architectural theory seminar group reviewed publications of authors whose work is related to the problem raised in the competition. The authors reviewed during the weekly meetings of this group are architects and town planners, philosophers and sociologists, such as Walter Benjamin, Richard Sennett, Manuel Castells, David Harvey and Christine Boyer.

The central theme of both the competition and the journal was the relationship between design and research on an urban scale. Rotterdam's location for the competition served as a test case. Architecture and town planning find themselves in the midst of an interplay of social forces. In order to get a grip on these forces architects and town planners will need to carry out an in-depth examination of the context – in the broadest sense of the word – in which they are active. If they remain within the confines of their discipline then this will result in inbreeding and autism. This is the reason why it is important that future designers become familiar with a wide range of subjects, and that they become aware of developments in areas such as economics, politics, philosophy and social science. There is little room for these subjects within regular education. It is obvious that these disciplines are important in an architectural education; however the role they play in design is uncertain. And parallel to the question as to the role of these disciplines the existence of architecture in the form of a scientific discipline is also a subject that is open to discussion.

The competition began at the end of 1997 with the publication of the journal. The material for the plan was made available at the end of a meeting in which Caroline Bos (Van Berkel en Bos) showed some of her office's projects and explained their design methods.

A symposium was organized in February with the objective of assisting the contestants in the development of their vision. During the symposium a varied group of speakers each gave their view of the port as seen from their discipline. The speakers included Arie Graafland, Han Meyer, Wouter Vanstiphout, D'laine Camp, Mariëtte Kamphuis and Donald van Dansik.

The results of the competition were announced at the end of March following a paper presented by a member of the jury, Winy Maas, who gave a personal vision of the future of Rotterdam. The chairman of the jury, Joop Linthorst, a former Alderman of the Municipality of Rotterdam, read the very critical report from the jury. The jury's criticism focused on the limited depth of the essays, and the inadequate relationship between research and design.

A conference was organized in November 1998 as a sequel to the competition, again with the title *Cities in transition*. And once again the city of Rotterdam occupied a special place, although on this occasion supplemented by discussions about more general theoretical subjects, other seaports and the broader Dutch context. The conference will result in a second publication in the 'Critical landscape' series.

On re-reading Kafka

Deborah Hauptmann

Introduction

In the recent past there has been an enormous amount of cross-disciplinary interest in the writings of Walter Benjamin. Benjamin's commentary on the modern metropolis – the activities surrounding growth and the effects of overpopulation both on the individual and society – remains significant for architecture as well as urbanism.

Of course Benjamin often delivers the image of the city through his *reading* of others' *writings*, through his *seeing* through others' eyes, thus in turn providing a valid model for subsequent *re-readings*.[1] He has produced an extensive critique through his recasting of perspectives offered by, among others, the philosopher Hegel, the modern French poet and prose writer Charles Baudelaire and the American writer Edgar Allan Poe. In *On some Motifs in Baudelaire*, Benjamin makes a distinction between those who internalize the crowd – seen as a *mass*, an entity in itself as opposed to a collection of individuals – and those who are able to stay aloft, to view it from the outside. He addresses the idea of man as a singular element set against, or placed within, the crowd – the individual in danger of being swept up and ingested by the (object) crowd consciousness.[2] The struggle of the *self* then becomes the resistance to the objectification of that same self. This resistance can be seen par excellence in the work of Franz Kafka.

Benjamin describes the city as having the capacity to be both a landscape which opens itself to the flâneur and a room which encloses him. Contemporary critiques within the disciplines close to architecture have focused heavily on reading the city as landscape (or *cityscape*), as exterior and thus urban. Kafka, however, operates within the enclosed space of the interior.[3] Moreover, it is a space of the fray, where the conflict between the experience of tradition and the experience of the metropolis resides. An attempt to explicate the resistance of the mystical framework to the thrust of modern progress forms both an immanent and imminent tension throughout the body of Kafka's work. It is perhaps Kafka's inability to resolve this tension which Benjamin refers to as "Kafka's failure".

It is an interest in this idea of "failure" that motivates my reading of Kafka. For it is precisely this irresolution that leaves open a door into a contemporary space where the discourse on resistance and relinquishment continues to be relevant. Moreover, it is arguable that Kafka's work poses itself as a model, a model that predicts (as it exhibits) conditions that have, over the past decade or so, been discussed in terms of reflexivity. Just now, however, this paper represents a heuristic exercise. In it I begin to re-read Kafka through some prevalent thematic filters. Included in these *re-readings* are a few sideways glances at some current architectural tendencies. These glances are not intended as an architectural critique (although they may certainly read as such) but merely as exemplars upon which these Kafkaesque readings have been superimposed.

1
This idea of reading and writing has occupied much space in literary analysis as well as cross-disciplinary investigations since the 1970s. Of course, this is not to say that Benjamin's descriptions of the metropolis only exist within the framework of literary analysis.

2
This very issue of individuality against collectivity, private identity versus social responsibility, is a concern that surfaces as peculiarly modern in the sociological and cultural writings of thinkers such as Georg Simmel, Siegfried Kracauer and Max Weber, to name but a few.

3
Deleuze and Guattari present an excellent model of Kafka's interiors in *Kafka: toward a minor literature*, London, Minneapolis, 1986 (translated from the original, 1975).

Through the eyes of the Crow

The function of *naming*

What is it to assign a name to a thing, to a person? Furthermore, what is it to *own* that name, to possess it or have it possess you? I suggest that the act of naming is an act of exhibiting power and ownership. Equally, and conversely, it is an action leading to empowerment and agency. To name an object, to signify a thing with a noun, is to give it a value, a value primarily of exchange. To name a place is to give it coordinates, to bring it forth from the ethereal matter of space. It is also to establish a limit, a line that can be crossed, transgressed or violated. To give a name to a living thing, such as an animal, is to convert it from an object into an essence, to endow it with life. In the book of Genesis, place is named before man. Eden gives name to the location, to the manifestation of the six days of work. Adam is named as the first man and is subsequently endowed with the power of naming, for he is given the task of naming all animals. In fact it is Adam, not God, who names woman: Eve. However, her name derives from an action, for she has, through the act of disregarding the word of God, become "the mother of all living" (Genesis 3:20).

In moving beyond this biblical domain to that of man and his formation of society, we find a similar power structure at work. Socially a name is a label which also indicates action and order, as well as identifying a person within a class structure. Without a proper noun (name) with its own history or genealogy, its own etymological meaning, a person cannot exist. Conversely, the common noun is seen only in abstraction as an a-historical condition, as a commodity as mentioned above. To possess a name is moreover to accept responsibility for values, which are incumbent on the proper noun ascription. In other words, to assign a name is both to take possession *of* and *to* issue agency to that person or thing.

It has been argued that this focus on the name or its absence, the *problem* of naming in Kafka's work arises initially from the circumstance of Kafka's own name. Kafka's surname is related to the Czech word *kavka*, which means "blackbird" or "crow". His given name in Hebrew was Amschel, a name easily associated with the term *amsel*, which in Hebrew also translates into "blackbird". Thus he was given not merely a name but a double name, or a doubling of the name of "crow".[4] This *action* imposed upon Kafka not merely a family history (common in all surname inheritance) and responsibility, but also an abstract identity – an identity manifested as a condition (both conditional and conditioning), which Kafka inevitably attempted to mediate within his literary work. This mediation of the imposition of history with the contemporary sense of self-identity brings us back to the idea of failure as it relates to the battlegrounds between tradition and modernity.

Anyone familiar with architecture will know the name of Le Corbusier or simply Corbu (Crow). The distinguishing factor between Franz Kafka and Charles-Edouard Jeanneret is that while the former was consecrated with a *given* name, the latter chose his name and was thus self-anointed. By virtue of *choice*, Jeanneret inverted the inherent position of culpability. Kafka's crow is caged, while Corbu's crow flies free. Thus we see the internalized conditioning of the one and the externalized positioning of the other through the respective frames of traditional man as reflective and modern man as visionary.[5]

The *disembedding* of meaning

Kafka operates fluidly in the field of proper noun displacement, a displacement that implicates an entity rather than a being. His stories are recognized as stories of Prague, yet he never names this city, never locates action within the limits of place. The characters in his novels are often identified by initials only. Anyone

---

[4] For a thorough etymological survey of the name of Kafka, see: Clayton Koelb, *Kafka's rhetoric*, London, Ithaca, 1989

[5] This aspect of the "serious" work as opposed to the "visionary" work of a writer is discussed by Walter Benjamin in correspondence with Bertolt Brecht. Kafka's visionary capacity was described by Brecht as follows: "Kafka saw what was to come without seeing what is." Walter Benjamin, *Reflections*, New York, 1986

familiar with Kafka will recognize K as an appellation that reveals the minimum necessary to identify the protagonist of his novel *The trial*. Kafka's characters, thus represented, do not however constitute an abstraction that reduces them to a state of sameness often associated in modernism with *everyman*. The "I" without a name does not automatically convert to the "we", the "us" – the automatons – who are defined by our similarities as opposed to our singularities. Kafka's characters are always presented through action, through the expression of individual needs and desires. In fact, they place themselves in the framework of relative possibility as *anyman*. In other words, Kafka does not revel in generalities of modern *consciousness* but presents conditions and particulars of action. Furthermore, Kafka confronts the ambiguity inherent in the absence of naming, inherent in anonymity, with the positioning of man as both productive and produced through his action.

A group of architects and theorists recently produced a conference series with titles such as "any one", "any way", "any where", "any how" (the 11-part series came full circle, concluding with another "any one"). With these titles, they simultaneously ascribed name and denied signification to the proper pronoun function of naming. In other words, they used the framing device of naming without allowing it the power to give meaning. They actively (and consciously – or perhaps self-consciously?) defined their domain in ambiguity, while diminishing their culpability through the non-appellate of *anonymity*. The conference results so far reveal a forum in which the possibilities of discourse are free, unrestricted by any singular imposing or self-determining agenda. This freedom of discourse is of course potentially very fruitful. Members of the conference can say anything, assert anything – anything, that is, as long as they do not posit a principle which infers a causal relationship, let alone a meaning. Arguably, questions of *meaning* are profoundly problematic in Kafka's work. However, what of cause and effect as expressed through a theory of action? The *free-for-all* forum produced by the organizers of the "any" series has resulted in a hermetically sealed framework. Yet have they not marshalled a system that is totally self-referential, one that imposes, or at the very least supposes, total freedom? Is not such freedom an illusion, a modern chimera par excellence? Furthermore, without action, without the particular determinants of the individual agent, is it not *everyman* that the "any-one" fraternity actually invokes? This inquiry about freedom naturally leads on to my next theme.

The formlessness of *The Law*

The Law must be *seen* as an ever-present force in Kafka's writing; equally and inversely, the law is that which can never be seen. We can witness the law only in terms of that which it produces. We are aware of its presence only through the limits which it imposes. Thus we often encounter the law only in terms of restriction and collision, and often of violence. We address it face to face, yet always and only at face value. As Kafka sees it, we can never know the law, for it is not only without form but without content. At best we can approximate it by gaining knowledge of *how* it works. However, to understand it in terms of the *why* of its workings is necessarily a futile endeavour. Kafka chronicles the irrelevancy of man's actions when he operates in a structure that is discordant with his own time[6] – a structure which, though obsolete, continues by the force of sheer necessity, for man must have laws, as Georg Simmel suggests, in order to be free. It is of course the essence of this idea of freedom that Kafka continually queries. Kafka's work is suffused with the distance between men and their institutions of government, the battle between modernity and tradition, as mentioned above. And what happens to the man who operates outside the law? He is in constant peril of moving beyond the frame of irrelevancy to futility and, in Kafka, subsequently to death.

[6] This irrelevancy is not necessarily a nihilistic negation of meaning for, like Nietzsche, he also assigns a positive value to irrelevance. On this idea of the positive function within seemingly nihilistic frameworks, see Friedrich Nietzsche, *Thus spoke Zarathustra*, Penguin Books, 1964 (translated from the original, 1883)

Trespass as an action beyond transgression

Just as the law can be seen as the system upon which all activity depends, trespassing can be seen as a violation of the nature of any such system. The impact of progress in the late 19th and early 20th centuries on *traditional* frameworks is an example of such trespassing. This concept establishes the position of the *outlaw*: the one who stands outside the world.

The protagonists in Kafka's work generally occupy this position of *outsider*. In fact they never ultimately recover from their confrontations with the law. The inability to recover is a consequence of their own inability to admit the framework in which they inevitably perform, the denial of culpability. This denial typically takes the form of either an active model of arrogant self-assertion (as in the case of Joseph K. in *The trial*) or a passive model of ignorance (the prisoner in *The penal colony*).

On the other hand, many characters seem to have found a method of coping. They have mastered the regulatory actions necessary to proceed within the system without trespass. Not long ago, at the Faculty of Architecture, during the Indesem workshops, a confrontation seminar between Adrian Geuze of West 8 architects and the writer/theorist Michael Speaks was arranged. Geuze took a firm stance against theory, arguing that his main task as an architect was to merely take the rules and requirements of the numerous different governing bodies and compile them into a model that could be built in terms of architecture. Hence Geuze operates within the law and in the process is extremely effective. However, just like the attorneys who operate *within* the system (inside the law) in *The trial*, it is irrelevant to consider whether he *understands* the system in which he is obliged to act. The only point is that he has learned to function within it. He has accepted the position of resistance by refusing to search for meaning. In the Kafkaesque system, irrelevance is inherent in the fact that man does not, cannot, understand it, for it is a system that is relevant (as opposed to self-referential) only in the act of engaging it. The act is thus the enactment and within this limiting and ordering framework, the architect is seemingly free. Within this reading it is therefore clear that Geuze, like practitioners with a similar approach, operates as a traditionalist.

The *distantiation* of time

The flâneur is caught up in the flow, the motion of the crowd, resisting yet becoming part of the movement. Kafka's portrayal of K does not in any way address movement, for it does not frame itself in time. Kafka seems to remain connected to one task, the task of describing action, of clarifying the relentless interrogation of the law, the neurosis of rational man. Le Corbusier produced models for living to meet the needs of modern man – environments that contain action as a rational necessity. Kafka created the essence of the productive forces themselves, the rationality of the law made irrational by its inaccessibility. The positive or teleological visionary still saw man as a rational agent. In Kafka, all agency is lost in the absence of flow, in the impossibility of discourse.

In the rush of progress, understanding has been displaced by knowing, while belief has been profoundly subjugated. And without belief man, for Kafka, is destined to operate in a system to which he can never belong. Modern man's sense of *being* in the world turns violently to a sense of *becoming*, as exemplified by the act of metamorphosis.[7] This produces a non-temporal condition where any sense of chronological sequence is disavowed, where there is no goal, no direction towards, and hence no sense of time. Le Corbusier's towards is totally annihilated in Kafka's here and now.

---

[7] This condition of *becoming* is highly complex in Kafka when one understands that the theory of action belongs more properly to the discourse on *being*. Deleuze and Guattari discuss this process in terms of de-territorialization. See Deleuze and Guattari, *Kafka: toward a minor literature*

Process as discourse

To *read* Kafka is to witness Kafka *writing*.[8] His gift consists of a method that in itself is both the expression of its structure and simultaneously an example of its form. If Benjamin chronicles the effects (psychological and moral) which the *progress* of modernization has on man, Kafka provides us with a glimpse of the system (physical and expressive) which produces these effects.

Kafka's model replaces meaning with function. He manipulates the predicative structure of language to an extent that no meaning can exist beyond the meaning inherent in his writing. The *content* of the work is simply the *as is* of the text. The face-to-face model proposed above returns as the condition of readability, not as a metaphor in want of decipherment. The Kafkaesque trope necessarily leads not to an external system of representation, but to an internal and self-referential structure of revelation. Of course the Kafkaesque frame of the self-referential operates differently from the one cited above in relation to the "a n y" series, and is in fact much more productive.[9] I would like to propose that with Kafka, the *self*-referential is replaced by the *inter*-referential. When the body (the self) no longer maintains a subject/object relationship but itself becomes the embodiment of an *inter-referential* and aesthetically assertive *reality*, it performs as a *reflexive* as opposed to self-reflective machine, as suggested in my introduction. It becomes a machine of both transcription and inscription within the breach that abruptly separates tradition and progress, functioning as resistance while simultaneously announcing relinquishment.

[8] For further reference on the idea see Adrian Jaffe, *The process of Kafka's Trial*, Michigan, 1967

[9] Self-referential frameworks such as the one created within the "any" series develop into an idiosyncratic system – a system which can only be monitored by its members (itself). This argument will be elaborated on in my continuing work on Kafka. For general reference, see Giddens, *Modernity and self-identity*, 1991, Cambridge: Polity

River dynamics as design tool

Caroline Stegewerns

1
Helmer, W. et al, *Toekomst voor een grindrivier* (Future for a gravel river), 1991
2
Desvigne, M. & Delnoky, C., "Michel Desvigne & Christine Delnoky" in: *Het landschap*: vier internationale landschapsontwerpers (The landscape: four international landscape designers), Antwerp, deSingel, 1995
3
Archiprix 1997: the best student plans, Rotterdam, Uitgeverij 010, 1997

Over the centuries the rivers in the Netherlands have been forced into a tighter and tighter straightjacket by embankment construction, river training and canalization. However, in recent years a change has been taking place; many plans for the development of nature in riverside areas have been arguing in favour of more space for natural processes such as river dynamics, vegetation dynamics and grazing. Ooievaar, Meinerswijk, Grensmaas and Millingerwaard are examples of this. The focus on natural processes in river areas illustrates the changing attitude towards nature. Efforts to exert rigid control are changing into an attempt to work with the dynamic environment at the margins of river management, a search for new ways of handling the uncertainty inherent in natural processes. Maybe the new approach to confronting the uncertainties of nature can serve as inspiration for urban planners and architects faced with the intractability of both individuals and society. In any case the dynamic river, as an ecological structure and as a representation of nature, forms an important counterpart to the growing urbanization of the Netherlands.

This article specifically examines river dynamics as a design tool, looking first at the transformations of nature produced by the dynamic river, and second at the way these transformations are manipulated in the tradition of hydraulic engineering and landscape architecture. The current plans for more natural rivers provide the context for this discussion.

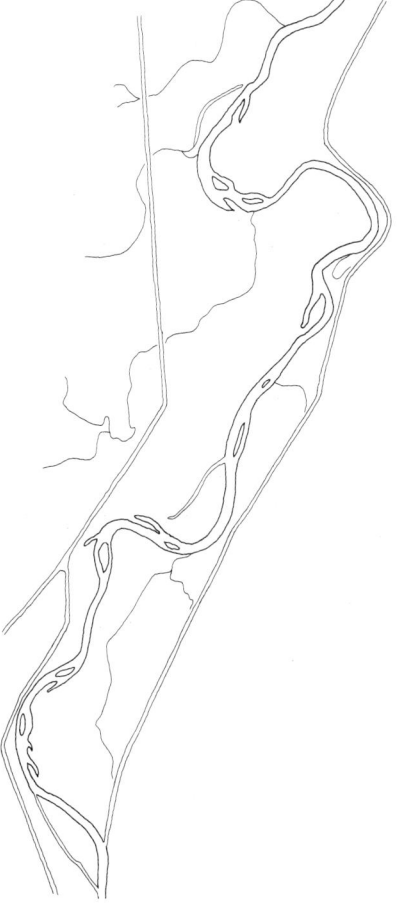

Buro Stroming: design for the Grensmaas. By widening the flow channel and lowering the ground by the river under a sloping bank, it should be possible to create a more natural gravel river.

Strategies

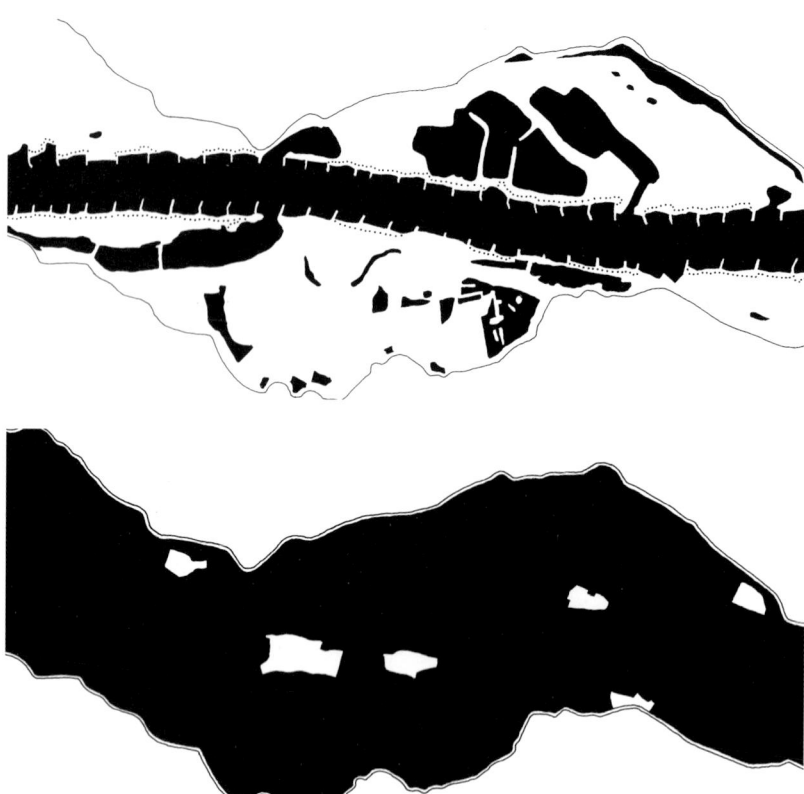

Low water shows how winding the river is; sandy shores with groynes, any sandbanks in the river and hollows in the water meadows also become visible. High water reveals a wide expanse of water with islands rising out of it.

Changing rivers

The strategy leading to more natural rivers involves taking advantage of river dynamics. A more natural river is subject to constant change. As the water level rises and falls under the influence of river discharge and tides, the water surface expands and shrinks. This periodic change in the shape of the water is known as hydrological dynamics. However, a river consists not only of water but also of sediment. Sand, clay and gravel are picked up by the current, carried along and deposited elsewhere. Water and sediment in the river exist in a constantly changing equilibrium, as a result of which the river bed, the river's path and the periodically flooded areas surrounding the river slowly but surely change shape too. This constant change in the shape of the land through erosion and sedimentation is known as morphological dynamics.

For centuries the Dutch have expanded their hydraulic engineering knowledge in order to control these natural processes. Winter dikes, summer dikes and weirs determine the water's room for movement. Groynes, dams and bank reinforcements help to contain the sedimentation and erosion. Would it be possible to convert these civil engineering management tools into architectural design tools – for a more natural river to suit modern requirements and ideas?

Hydrological dynamics: the periodical metamorphosis

It is a real metamorphosis: flood water transforming the narrow winding stream into a wide expanse of water in the space of a few hours or days. Isolated patches of higher ground containing brickyards or farms are transformed into islands. Some time later, when the stretch of water disappears, only the water in a few isolated hollows reminds one of the flood. Low water also produces a metamorphosis of the river, albeit on a smaller scale. Sandy banks, sometimes intersected by groynes, are exposed; sandbanks in the river become visible. Flood water and low water are irregular but recurrent phenomena. In principle every level of river discharge recurs after a shorter or longer period, changing the river's appearance in its own way.

The hydrological dynamics do not have the same impact throughout the river areas of the Netherlands. In the area downstream, the tide reduces the differences between high and low discharges, so the embanked floodplains are very narrow there, compared with the width of the summer bed. There is far less variety in the width of the river here. On the other hand, in the section upstream, with its very wide embanked floodplains, the river expands and contracts in a spectacular way. Weirs, such as those on the Maas and Lower Rhine, also

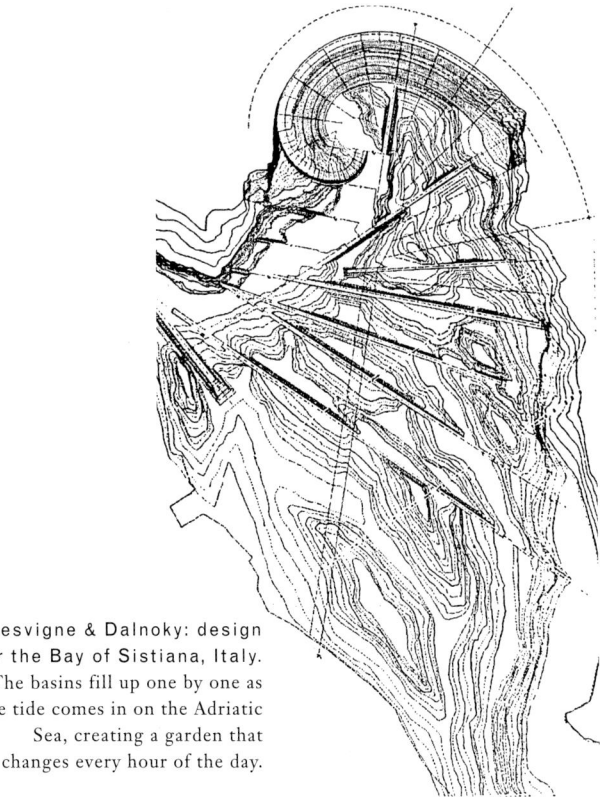

Desvigne & Dalnoky: design for the Bay of Sistiana, Italy. The basins fill up one by one as the tide comes in on the Adriatic Sea, creating a garden that changes every hour of the day.

Designing with water

By deliberately altering the shape of the bank, we can manipulate the metamorphosis of the water's shape. In other words, we do not actually need to alter the discharge volume or tidal movement (as a weir does) in order to achieve this. Assuming that the bank has a gradual slope, there are two kinds of bank transformations that will have a major impact on the river's appearance: the creation of transitions in several steps and the introduction of local differences in height. Both kinds of bank transformations have been used frequently in the history of Dutch hydraulic engineering. By constructing major dikes and summer dikes, sometimes combined with spillways, engineers have created a system with two or three compartments: the summer bed, the winter bed and where necessary a spillway area. The formation of basins that fill up one by one has a civil engineering purpose here. However, this change also has a major impact on the appearance of the river and the river landscape. The same applies to the creation of isolated high points and hollows in the embanked floodplains, such as brickyards on mounds and clay pits. However, such alterations to the bank may also primarily serve a design purpose. For instance the French landscape architects Michel Desvigne and Christine Dalnoky have designed a system of basins in a bay of the sea which fill up one by one at high tide, thus representing and revealing the movement of the tides in architectural terms. The water articulates the successive contours that are created, so to speak. An approach that is useful for the civil engineer as a management tool is here used by the architect as a design tool.

restrict the hydrological dynamics, keeping the river at a constant, fairly high level for most of the year. Low river levels no longer occur above the weir; only very high discharges can still change the appearance of the river. To sum up, interventions in the hydrological dynamics have the greatest impact on stretches of river with no weirs and no tidal flow.

How the shape of the water surface alters, in other words what we observe, depends on the relief of the bank. Where the bank has a gentle slope, the water surface will gradually expand and contract. This situation occurs with most of the natural lowland rivers. In places where the bank rises sharply, levels or compartments occur. When the river level rises, the water surface will remain the same for a long time at the rim, before spreading out (rapidly in some cases): the last drop that makes the cup run over. The rise and fall of the water will also reveal local differences in the height of the bank. Isolated high points and hollows may become particularly striking fragments in the river landscape at times of flooding or low water.

Design involving water and taking advantage of higher and lower water levels is in fact a traditional form of landscape architecture. You see this in parks beside rivers, where gently sloping banks are transformed into flights of steps that allow people to read the water level. The contours of high and low water are embodied in the topography. Only the time when the various stages will be revealed to onlookers is unpredictable and uncontrollable. Despite the natural dynamics of the water, such a design may be completely artificial in nature, mainly representing the management of nature.

Morphological dynamics: constant transformation

The river landscape is subject to constant transformation due to erosion and sedimentation. Although these processes take place continuously, they do not occur at an even pace. Erosion occurs when the current is able to pick up large quantities of sediment, which is the case when the velocity of the current is high, on the outside of a bend, where the river is constricted or with high rates of discharge. In the opposite situation, where the current has a low velocity, the river has a low capacity for sediment. The excess sediment (the heaviest part) settles on the bottom, as happens on the inside of a bend, where the river widens or with low rates of discharge. Erosion and sedimentation are processes with an evolutionary effect. The shape is constantly changing and, in principle, the original shape never returns.

The river shape that emerges from this constant process differs in various stretches of the Dutch rivers. First, there are variations in the extent of erosion and sedimentation. The Waal, which has a high discharge and carries a great deal of sediment, has a more powerful erosional and sedimentary effect than the other river branches. Second, there are differences in the patterns made by the river under natural conditions. Thus broadly speaking, as one moves downstream, one finds the following sequence in rivers in the Netherlands: first twisting or winding or zigzagging, then twisting gently, and finally flowing in a straight line. Interventions in the morphological dynamics can take advantage of this.

Just as the hydrological dynamics have an impact on the shape of the water, so the morphological dynamics have a (direct) impact on its counterpart, the shape of the land. To observe morphological dynamics one needs a keen eye; here there are no rapid metamorphoses but gradual processes. What can be observed is not so much the change itself as its consequences in the shapes of the river. The scale of these may vary; think for example of meanders and islands, banks and river dunes, steep banks and beaches, natural levees and basins – telltale signs of present or past dynamics. The morphological river dynamics produce land shapes that reveal the flow of water and wind, shapes that we appreciate as "natural" (i.e. self-created).

Designing with sediment

By manipulating the morphological dynamics, we can create an interplay of the river's changing shapes and deliberate design interventions by human beings. Assuming a situation where the morphological dynamics are autonomous, two types of interventions are conceivable.

On the one hand there are permanent interventions that divert, speed up or slow down the current, causing a change in the pattern of erosion and sedimentation. Groynes in the river are a good example of this. Such groynes create a contrast and confrontation between the rigid, fixed shape of the structure and the dynamic and changing shapes of sediment and water. Interventions of this kind are an example of one-way traffic between the engineering structure and river morphology: the structure changes the river morphology but itself has a fixed shape and effect, because it is permanently managed. In landscape architecture, Michel Desvigne has used such interventions as design tools in his "elementary gardens" where a pattern of weirs and canals contrasts with and has an impact on the sedimentation and erosion in a mountain river. The landscape architect Nikol Dietz, winner of the Archiprix 1997, uses similar tools in her design for the *Grensmaas* (the section of river which forms the border with Belgium). Dams, weirs, narrow and wide sections provide the choreography for a river alternating between flooding, forming interweaving streams and drying up.

On the other hand there are non-permanent interventions that have a temporary effect on the morphological dynamics. A low dike constructed in the embanked floodplains which is no longer managed will gradually change shape as a result of the morphological dynamics and will lose its ability to divert the current. Interventions of this kind involve an interaction between man-made structure and river morphology, with each influencing the other's shape and impact. As a result of the slow pace of morphological processes in rivers, the shape of the low dike, softening and blurring, lingers on for a long time in the landscape. In practice the lingering of created shapes is often an unintended effect of changing land use. However, it is also used deliberately in landscape architecture and art, for example in the earth art projects by the artist Robert Smithson, where created land shapes gradually fade into the water.

Desvigne: jardins élémentaires.
Experimental gardens in a constantly changing context, where the elements of water and wind are collected, miniaturized and intensified. Here: manipulated erosion and sedimentation in a garden in a mountain river.

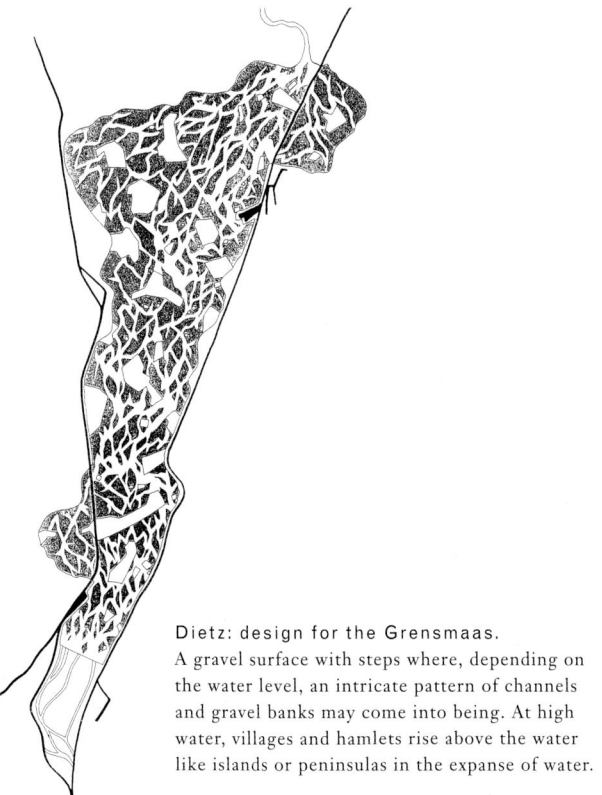

Dietz: design for the Grensmaas.
A gravel surface with steps where, depending on the water level, an intricate pattern of channels and gravel banks may come into being. At high water, villages and hamlets rise above the water like islands or peninsulas in the expanse of water.

Between these two extremes lie interventions that are managed periodically. The original shape of the structure is restored after a certain period; in the meantime the interaction between created shape and natural dynamics is allowed free rein. Examples in practice are the periodic deepening of main or secondary channels and the cutting down of osier beds every four years.

Unlike with hydrological dynamics, where water can be used to articulate a designed land shape, with morphological dynamics the natural shape creates its own structure, in contrast with the designed shape. By providing scope for the morphological dynamics in a design project, you introduce uncertainty in both time and space. The innovative element in designs for more natural rivers consists mainly of the space given to morphological dynamics. The straightforward manageability of topography, space and image is renounced in favour of a complex interplay of designed and natural shape.

Conclusion

There is a long tradition of managing river dynamics in the Netherlands. The fact that this has also meant shaping the water and land has usually been an unintentional side effect. Now that there is more scope for river dynamics and greater awareness of the design of the river landscape, the hydraulic engineering tradition is turning out to provide starting points and inspiration for new design tools in the play with water and sediment.

Hydrological dynamics and morphological dynamics each have their own potential for changing the river landscape. Hydrological dynamics only creates uncertainty about the time when a particular water level will occur. The contours of water and land remain manageable in principle, also as the object of design. Once morphological dynamics are also given more scope, a genuine interaction can occur between the designed and the natural, self-regulating shape. The river landscape will then become a garden of the elements.

11 cities 52 plans

Peter de Bois

In response to an invitation from the construction company Feikema in Friesland, 52 students produced plans for 11 well-known towns in Friesland. The work took place under the supervision of the Urban Design section and in collaboration with the student association for urbanism Polis. The book containing all the plans is called *11 cities 52 plans*[1] and is a joint publication of the Urban Design section and Feikema BV.

Despite its impressive landscape and historic towns, Friesland finds itself in a difficult situation these days, with high unemployment, vacant properties in certain residential areas and a marginal position in relation to the *Randstad* conurbation. The disappearance of the internal borders in Europe is hastening the process of economic and cultural change, necessitating a rearrangement of existing structures. It is already clear that large-scale intensive agriculture and horticulture are having a major effect on farming production, the cultivated landscape, water quality and water management. The discussion within the EU member states about individual contributions towards the costs on the one hand and payments to disadvantaged regions on the other shows that there are still difficulties with the system of financial and economic settlement. All this is having a significant impact on the spatial and functional characteristics of European districts.

At the same time these functional and spatial changes are bound to strengthen the cultural identity of these districts. Individual identity in the cultural sense, i.e. a combination of climatological framework and urban landscape culture, will take on additional meaning. After all, that is the source of the distinctive features which are only present – or only absent – in that place.

Friesland exists in infrastructural isolation. The lack of infrastructure, the great distances between settlements and the vast openness and transparency of the landscape provide plenty of scope for wind and weather, making the rural space into a real space. That is one reason why the old town centres have a very pronounced private, condensed nature. This is an exceptional feature, a relationship that needs to be preserved as an identifying pattern, making it necessary to disperse new housing development over all the available centres rather than concentrating it in a few. At the same time it will be necessary to apply the rules for construction more strictly to the preservation of individual physical spatial characteristics, so that the manner of building derives its quality from the very way it reinforces identity. This provides an alternative to what is sometimes called the 'creeping blight' of new development. The fear that this dispersal of housing development will take place at the expense of the necessary level of services is a characteristic *Randstad* doctrine. Dispersal of housing results in a concentrated level of facilities. At the same time it can be a stimulus for people to create small-scale facilities at local level. This can have a laboratory function in the context of the current unemployment.

Friesland's isolation has yet another exceptional feature in the physical spatial sense. The dispersal of economic functions over the various urban centres operates almost as though Friesland were an island. That is virtually what it was in the past. The access routes over land had all the characteristics of bridges. And the land access can still be called austere, which is how it should be allowed to stay. This isolation is one of the distinctive features of Friesland. And it was this that formed the starting point for the students developing new concepts for the 11 towns in Friesland. The terms of reference for the 11 towns project was to use a design study to create new perspectives for the towns in question and the countryside around them.

1
11 cities 52 plans, Delft University of Technology, Faculty of Architecture Urban Design section, Peter de Bois and Ciska Verhoef (ed.)

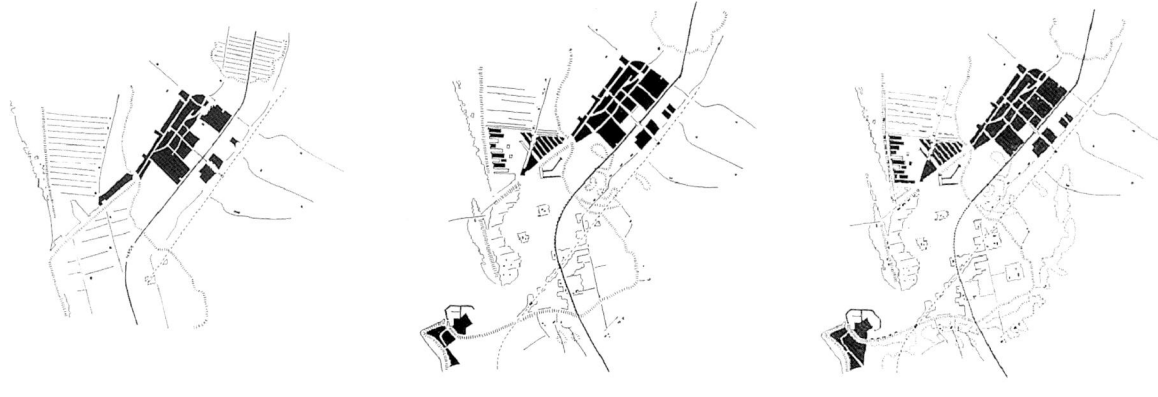

Present Workum Workum 2020 Workum 2040

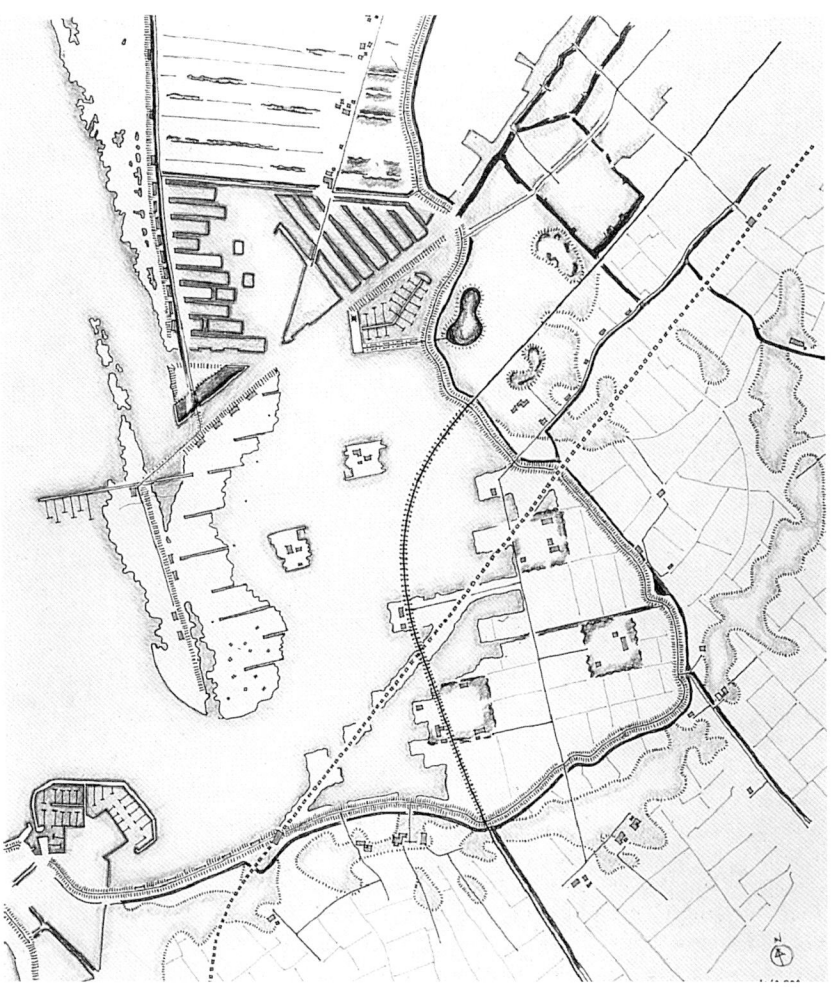

Masterplan

One of the plans in the book is the project *Workum Waterstad!* (Workum, a Town by the Water) by the student Joost Degenkamp. In the distant past Workum was a town by the water but with the silting up of the harbour mouth, it lost contact with the water. Everything changes when Workum is restored to its position by the water. The old dikes, which are now merely a reminder of the past in the centre of the landscape, take on the function of water-control structures again. At the same time this creates an opportunity to enlarge the nature reserve, which is isolated at present. The existing dikes and the creation of a new line of windmills act as connecting elements between various areas and facilities. The extension and reinforcement of existing structures strengthen the identity of Workum and its surroundings functionally and visually, creating country estates and private islands which can be traced back to the original allocation of land in blocks, while the housing developments by the water follow the allocation of land in strips in the northern landscape. At the same time the dike house regains its traditional status. Other (smaller) differences in height found in the landscape inside the dikes can start to function as wet-dry elements (osier beds) between the new wetlands and the existing meadows.

Landscape and urbanization

Urbanization & Haarlemmermeer

Mattijs van 't Hoff
graduation project Urbanism

mentors
Prof. Dirk Frieling, Dr Wouter Reh, Dr Luuk Boelens

The Haarlemmermeer is currently one of the most dynamic regions in the Netherlands: national and international companies are seeking a location for their business here; an equal number of new and different types of infrastructure, from high-speed rail tracks to an Underground Logistics System, are being built; and the average Dutchman can find his or her paradise on earth: the single-family dwelling with garden and parking space for two cars. The spatial growth and dynamics find expression in increasing spatial claims on the natural environment. These conflicting interests will have to be reconciled in a new urban development strategy.

Towards a New Urbanization

The growth is not caused by a central city in this part of reclaimed land. The Haarlemmermeer has been situated on the periphery of Amsterdam, Haarlem and Leiden for more than a century but the change only started in the past decade. A major part of the growth can of course be explained by the presence of Amsterdam Schiphol airport. But more factors play a role in the new urbanization processes that have led to a different mode and morphology of the urbanization. In order to explain and utilize this as a controlling design tool, the underlying social system will have to be examined.

We can think of the social system as being divided into three sub-levels: the economic and technical, the social-cultural, and the political.[1] The greatest changes have taken place within the first level and the consequences are also the greatest. The development of new technologies has led to a fundamental change within management and economy.[2]

The consequences of this are perceptible at all levels in society. The use of information technology aims to accelerate and improve the processes of management and control. The global network within which this knowledge and information circulates is the *space of flows*. Besides the *space of flows*, the *space of places*, the spatial reality, continues to exist. The influence of the *space of flows* nevertheless has a hold on the *space of places*. These two worlds together form a *dual city* where analogue coexists beside digital, and locality beside globality.[3]

Increasing globalization by the *space of flows* results in a world of time-space compression in which only the *present* is important. Experiences become more superficial and the space and time horizon come closer to the observer. The rapid decision-making that this requires means that ad-hoc politics is increasingly becoming the order of the day. A simultaneous universalization in the social-cultural level results in the 'Generic', where it is no longer the identity of the location which is important, but the 'event' of the location.[4] Here, the individual tries to give expression to his individuality. Politicians and those involved in urban development will have to be aware of and deal with the various forms of scale and time that result from this. On account of this time-space problem, the spatial structure changes in character. Time-space must be structured to include the aspects of parallelity and continuity. This structure should be simultaneously multidimensional-dynamic and real-space-covering.[5]

1
According to Castells, M., *The informational city*, Cambridge Mass. & Oxford, Blackwell, 1989, p. 2; and description of Althusser in Boelens, L., *Stedebouw en planologie*: een onvoltooid project (Urban development and planning: an incomplete project), Delft, Delftse Universitaire Pers, 1990, p. 57

2
Sassen, S., *The global city*: New York, London, Tokyo, Princeton N.J., Princeton University Press, 1991, ch. 9

3
Castells, M., *The rise of the network society*, Cambridge Mass. & Oxford, Blackwell, 1996

4
Koolhaas, R., "The generic city", *S.M.L.XL.*, Rotterdam, Uitgeverij 010, 1995, pp. 1239-1267

5
Boelens, L., "De planologie en het tijd-ruimte-vraagstuk" (Planning and the time-space problem), *Archis*, no. 10, 1991, pp. 40-45

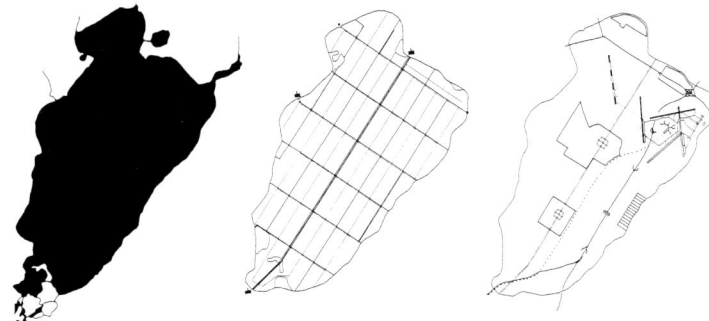

Landscape transformations in the Haarlemmermeer: natural, technical and urban landscape

'Supermarktstedenbouw' (supermarket urbanism) in a transformation landscape

The consequences of the changes in society can be placed in the trend of landscape transformations through the centuries. The natural landscape was transformed into the existing urban landscape in four stages. [6] The cultural transformation passed by the Haarlemmermeer since the land reclamation of the area in 1852 was part of the technical transformation: the industrialization of the landscape. Following the separation of functions in the functional transformation and the fragmentation in the economic transformation, which have together created the urban landscape, a total annexation of the landscape is now taking place in the current transformation.

The city has exploded like a fragmentation bomb with its splinters searching for a new spot in the landscape. In the resulting metropolitan landscape the various social processes and programmes regroup into new environments. The multidimensional character of the various processes results in a concurrence of programmes. Structures with different scales and speeds lie on top of one another and form new landscape images and elements. The metropolitan landscape should therefore be thought of in terms of processes and events linked to space and land use.

With the method of supermarket urbanism a visualization can be made of the creation of a metropolitan landscape in the Haarlemmermeer. By typologizing the metropolitan landscape in a catalogue of landscape architectonic elements, programmatic environments can be made visual. Analysis of the force fields and conditions of the Haarlemmermeer can indicate potentials and restrictions, and can result in a catalogue of sites. The relationship between sites and elements can be shown by means of a land value matrix.

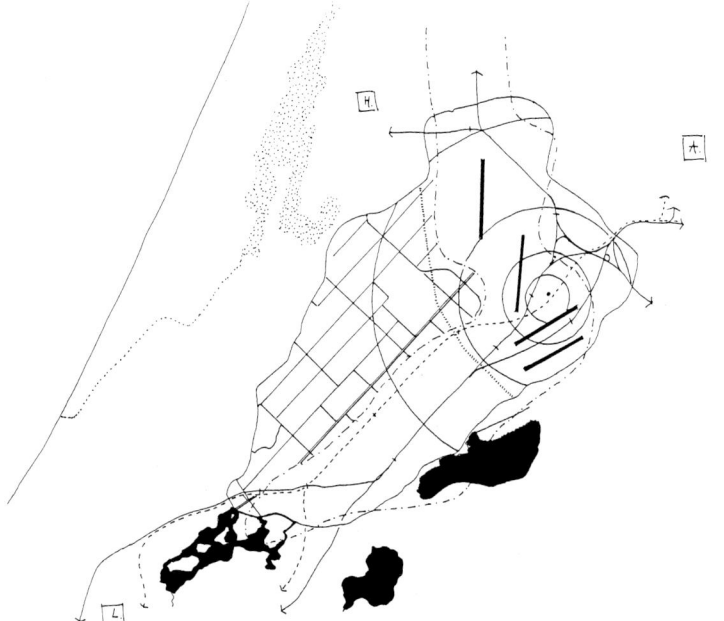

Metropolitan landscape sites

6
According to Reh, W., C. Steenbergen, P. de Zeeuw, *Landschapstransformaties* (Landscape transformations), Delft, TU Delft Bouwkunde, 1995

The Haarlemmermeer as metropolitan landscape

The elements are assembled on the sites of the Haarlemmermeer in an architectural landscaping tradition. The assembly focuses on conditioning the programme and reinforcing the structure. The relationship between the processes and the landscape produces a visual representation of the metropolitan landscape.

The *techno-Arcadia* is the technical no-man's-land of Amsterdam Schiphol airport that, with the coming of the fifth and sixth runway, has monopolized a large part of the Haarlemmermeer. In this Arcadian moment of fascinating scale and size, the connection between nature, technology and art is given a new experimental expression. A strip across the closed Buitenveldert runway clarifies the length and scale, while a number of *artificial rubbish hills* stage-manages the emptiness.

In the *nature reserve* along the west side, high-quality living and working environments are linked to the natural décor. Existing and newly created ecological and recreational connections change into a network of delightful landscapes in which private and public properties alternate. This 'copy-paste' of the inner dune edge onto the ring canal is interrupted by *landscape theatres* of the emptiness of the polder. New working environments are concentrated in the *coral* of brain parks attached to the hubs of the *flow landscape*: junctions and stations.

In combination with other elements like *metropolitan plantation* and *circus*, the Haarlemmermeer is transformed into a metropolitan landscape;
a landscape which is built up of layers of scale and time;
a landscape with urban mutants beside the long-term networks;
a landscape in which the processes take place,
s i m u l t a n e o u s l y !

Supermarket urbanism
in the Haarlemmermeer

Holland in transit

Joost van den Hoek
graduation project Architectural Design and Urbanism

mentors
Prof. Henco Bekkering, Prof. Carel Weeber, Dr Wouter Reh, Prof. Cees van Weeren

This study examines the integration of the A4 motorway into the landscape between Vlaardingen and Schiedam. The choice of this subject was determined by the following topical factors:

A
Urban growth consists more and more of redefining existing urban territory. Here, the spatial reserves in this urban territory consist chiefly of the spaces around large-scale motorways and other infrastructure.

B
It is desirable in spatial planning terms, as well as economically feasible, to introduce intensive urban programmes for these zones, which are the blind spots of spatial planning.

C
We are now seeing the development of urban corridors, as a result of which locations for new urban development are no longer chosen in relation to a town centre or historic centre but rather on the basis of potential for infrastructure in the regional context.

Thus: how can the construction of new motorway infrastructure be combined with new programmes in the immediate physical vicinity? The construction of the A4 between Vlaardingen and Schiedam was chosen as a case study. The construction of this road has been in an impasse for the last thirty years due to poor decision-making and a lack of imagination. The existing plans, to build the A4 in the traditional way, based on a dike body with 12-metre-high noise barriers, have attracted a lot of criticism because of the environmental pollution and the failure to integrate the road into the surroundings. In addition it is impossible to make more intensive use of this interesting spot.

Situations involving buildings and large-scale infrastructure in close physical proximity can usually be described as urban planning road accidents. But other approaches are possible, as examples from Barcelona show. There the ring road is integrated into the existing urban fabric in an exemplary way. We can formulate the integration assignment in terms of the need to produce an integrated design for the A4 and new development

Construction of the A4 between Vlaardingen and Schiedam in the traditional way: after 30 years of administrative impotence there is still no asphalt!

Landscape and urbanization

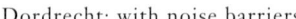
Dordrecht: with noise barriers

Kleinpolderplein: without noise barriers

Buildings in the immediate physical vicinity of motorway infrastructure: urban planning road accidents!

on both sides of the motorway. The new buildings comprise a mixed programme of neighbourhood-based housing, amenities and motorway-related businesses.

An important feature of this assignment is the fact that the presence of the infrastructure forms the basis for the spatial-programmatic organization of the area – indeed, the design is an individual response to the contemporary problem of integrating large-scale infrastructure into a more closely knit urban environment. A good Dutch analogy is the integration of urban design and water management.

In the area of the plan, the infrastructure is built in two layers, with local and regional traffic stacked on top of each other and connected on the edge of the area. The cross-section comprises a tunnel construction, which is located at ground level, partly for financial reasons. The area of the plan is now subdivided into zones at right angles to the infrastructure. In alternate zones the sand that for years has been awaiting the construction of the A4 is used to bridge the differences in height.

This creates an artificial landscape of sand bridges and connecting strips, interspersed with "cul-de-sacs", between the neighbourhoods on both sides of the road. The differences in height determine the use. The development of existing housing continues in the cul-de-sacs with increased density. The sand bridges provide a location for programmes with a larger-scale significance, such as parks, amenities and motorway-related businesses. The new buildings are organized in bands parallel to the infrastructure.

The urban development plan does not provide a picture of the final situation. In the first instance it determines the mainframe of sand, water and infrastructure. The next step is to decide on a regulator, consisting of specific programmes, a modular curved grid and a number of housing capacity studies. To conclude the study, an architectonic study of motorway-related businesses is produced within the framework of the urban development plan, examining the conditions created by Holland in transit.

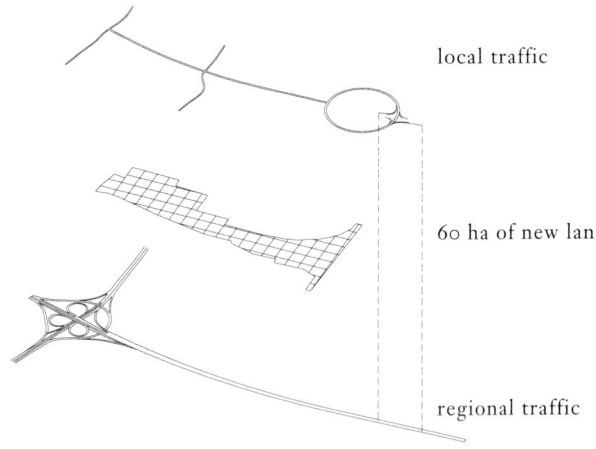
local traffic
60 ha of new land
regional traffic

Local traffic is stacked on top of regional traffic

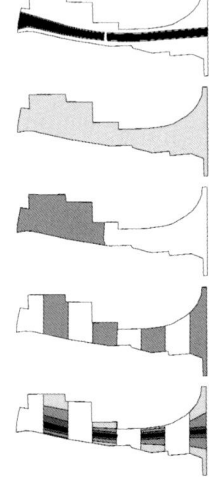
New topography by moving sand already on site

Framework of sand, water and stacked infrastructure

New topography
Holland in relief

New lots
cul-de-sacs:
– housing
sand bridges:
– amenities
– green spaces
– motorway-related programme

Possible development
organization parallel to stacked infrastructure

Park strip

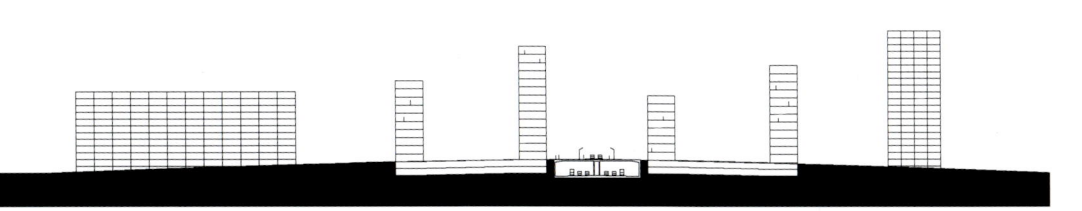

Motorway-related businesses

Landscape and urbanization

L'eautel à l'île perdue

An urban area development plan for the nineteenth century dockland area *Het Eilandje* (The Island) in Antwerp and the architectural design of an Apartment Hotel on the bend in the River Scheldt

Daniëlle Segers
graduation project Architectural Design and Urbanism

mentors
Prof. Henco Bekkering, Richard Foqué, Dr Wouter Reh, Rogier Verbeek

The 19th century dockland area *Het Eilandje* lies on the edge of the old town, the river and the modern port. Although many of the port's activities have moved away, they still define the character of the location. However, this situation is undermined by the isolated position of the area and the state it is in today. The island therefore awaits new stimulus. This should be provided by a spatial programme which springs from the present situation, explicitly preserving the area's character while at the same time incorporating it into the city. The purpose is not to impose a style but to create the conditions for a new vitality by making the area part of the urban network.

Existing elements, such as buildings, ships, bridges and docks, will be retained in their original situation, while at the same time they acquire new meaning. These elements conceal a firm grid pattern, created by the tradition of loading and unloading in the port, with its rational organization. This grid is extended over the entire site and then transformed under the influence of the existing elements, directions from the surrounding area and the connection with major urban lines and adjoining parts of town. Finally the grid is shaped in response to the programmatic layer. The site is divided into five thematic zones in east-west direction: *under the ring's spell*, *waterworks*, *the inner city*, *the shelter of the Kattendijk Dock*, and *the vitality of the river*. The grid is given increasing freedom as it moves west. At the same time it undergoes a transformation starting from the city centre. The dense mediaeval building structure changes from large buildings with narrow lanes to blocks in open spaces. At the spot where the elastic of all these transformations is stretched furthest the Apartment Hotel is situated.

At the bend in the river the winding dike presents the greatest contrast to the grid of the docklands. The building mass of the Apartment Hotel conforms to this strict pattern; its size suits the large scale of the setting. The building consists of two sections: a strip that reacts to the horizontalism of the river landscape and a landmark that creates connections with various strategic places in the city.

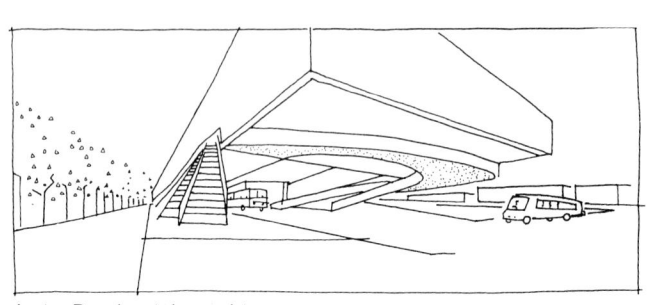

Asia Dock with parking

Water works in the Kempisch Dock

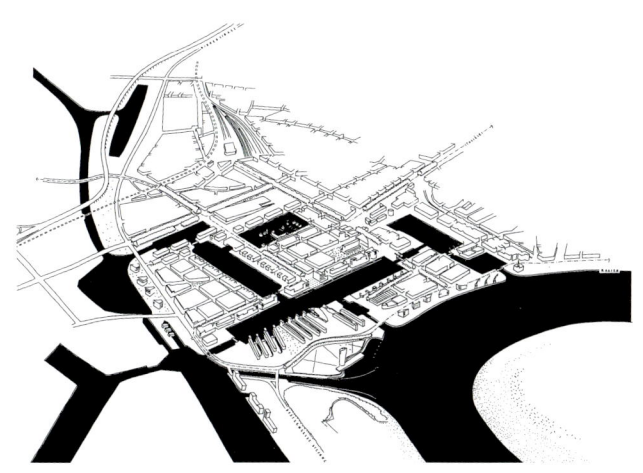

Bird's eye view

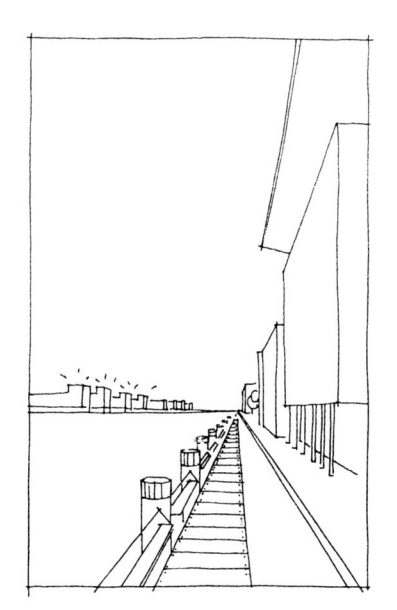

The sheltered
Kattendijk Dock

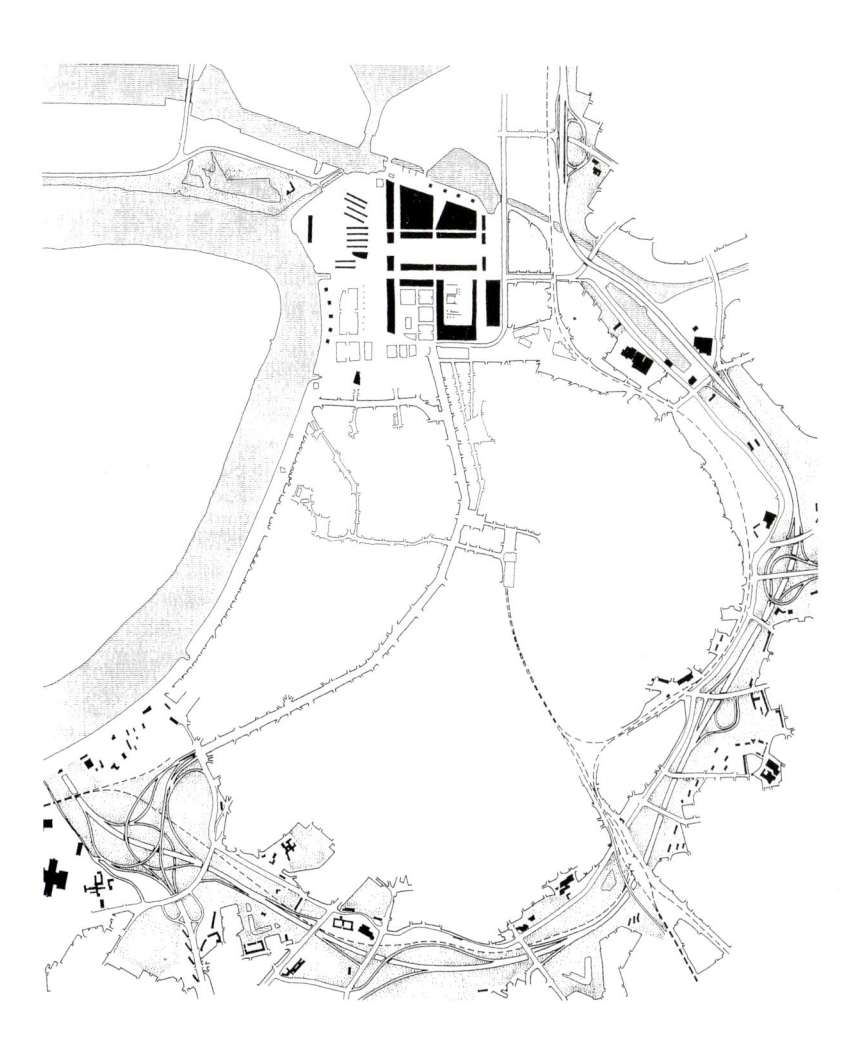

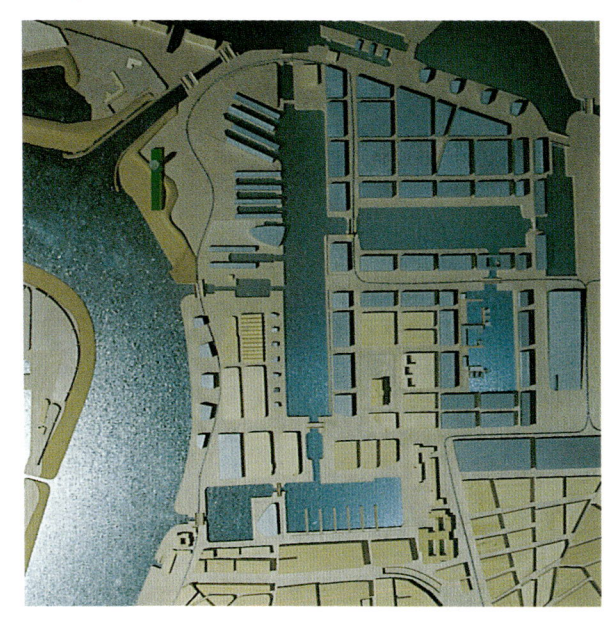

Top view of model

Landscape and urbanization

L'eautel à l'île perdue

View from the water taxi

Inspired by the diversity of residents and visitors that has characterized the dockland area for centuries, the goal is to attract as many different types of people as possible: not only business people, tourists and students, but also the residents of Antwerp. This is achieved firstly by the relationship between the building and the landscape. The building volume is raised to a height which does not encroach on the route over the dike and the view from the dike. The building is partly on dry land and partly on the mud flats of the tidal river. The grass-covered roof creates a green area high above the river, thus extending the landscape. Secondly, a wide variety of people are attracted by the diversity of the programme. Various amenities have been included in the strip, while the tower contains hotel rooms and apartments. The whole structure is organized in such a way that staff and visitors do not meet. In the wide guest area, stairs lead to the different floors, while the slopes and voids invite the visitor to discover the various activities.

The building is characterized by a strong pattern of moving floor planes in the strip and *fenêtres-en-longeur* in the landmark. On the land side the various ramps play with the lines of the dike, the river and the horizon. On the water side the slopes are less dominant; here a void of varying height and a loggia provide the view and tranquillity that do full justice to the panorama of the meandering river.

Outline of landmark and strip

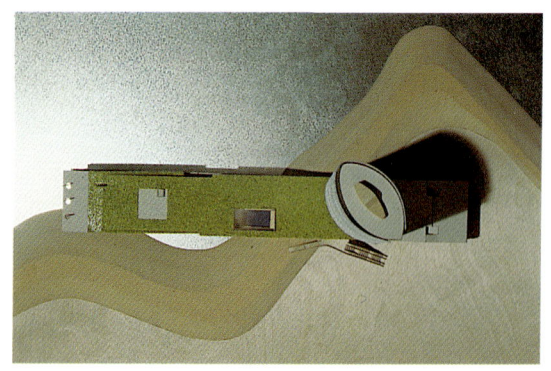

The green area on the roof

Countryside as facility

Paul de Graaf
graduation project Architectural Design

mentors
Prof. Wim van den Bergh, Prof. Jon Kristinsson, Prof. Dr Clemens Steenbergen

Why this house is in this place: the role of architectural design in this project

This project zooms in from the scale of the Netherlands as a geographical unit to focus on a specific location with a specific architectural design. I would like to take responsibility in this project for the fact that this building is present at all on this particular spot. The role of architecture lies just as much in its place and presence as in its final manifestation. It is the most specific result of a series of considerations on various scales concerning the future of the countryside.

Rural renewal: the countryside as facility

The project started out as a study of the implications of the term *new country estate* in relation to the problems of the countryside. The countryside is undergoing major changes: agriculture, nature and recreation are attempting to find a new balance in a landscape that is in a process of urbanization. The new country estate could take advantage of this in a specific, location-related way. The countryside is being developed into a high quality country amenity.

Keukenhof in the bulb-growing area is an inspiring example of an earth-bound identity in a landscape-architectural shape. The product – the tulip – is not only the logo but also the material used to give the world-famous visitors' centre its appearance.

The overlap between various policy maps provides potential locations. One of them is developed into Streek Rijnwaarden, a new rural estate. This area is geographically unique because it is where the Rhine enters the country. It is famous for the Lobith waterlevel radioreports. The characteristic dikes divide the region into three areas parallel to the river. Each of these has been given its own function, while complementing the others programmatically. The result is an attractive recreational area with its own regional identity.

One of the three areas is named *Rijnstrangen*, after the former river arms that run through it. Here, so-called *stranghouses* provide an exclusive type of landscape perception. These buildings – available on a limited scale as head offices or conference centres – take advantage of the growing demand among businesses for a green working environment as well as a green image. Apart from the existing farmhouses, the distributary houses are the only architectural properties in the area. The *strangen* themselves become a water purification system for the houses in the area.

cultural nature   +   makeable nature   =   potential locations

Rijnwaarden

Architecture and landscape: the *stranghouse* concept

The *stranghouse* is built on a terp or man-made mound, an island in the swampy countryside, and is only accessible via a stylish drive. The landscape is experienced from this architectural structure. The house provides a solution for the paradox that nature implies the absence of human beings, while the perception of nature requires their presence. The assumed aspects of the outdoor life, such as space and fresh air, are made perceptible – in a sensory, artificial way – in the indoor world of the house.

Water plays an important role in the building. The Living Machine, an ecological internal water purification system using eco-technology, creates an indoor tropical garden. The bath has been placed by the outside wall, so that the landscape and nature can be enjoyed in an intimate way. By way of thanks for the presence of an audience, the layout of the new landscape conforms to the building and its visitors. The bath water appears to flow into the landscape and the corn spells "GO". As a result of this manipulation, the building enters into a reciprocal relationship with the landscape, without this affecting its functioning as a nature or water purification area.

The development of the distributary houses contributes to the sustainable development of the cultivated landscape, thus becoming part of a strategy that may place this region, and possibly others, on the map as a unique example of countryside, meeting the demand for a fulfilling country experience, now and in the future.

43

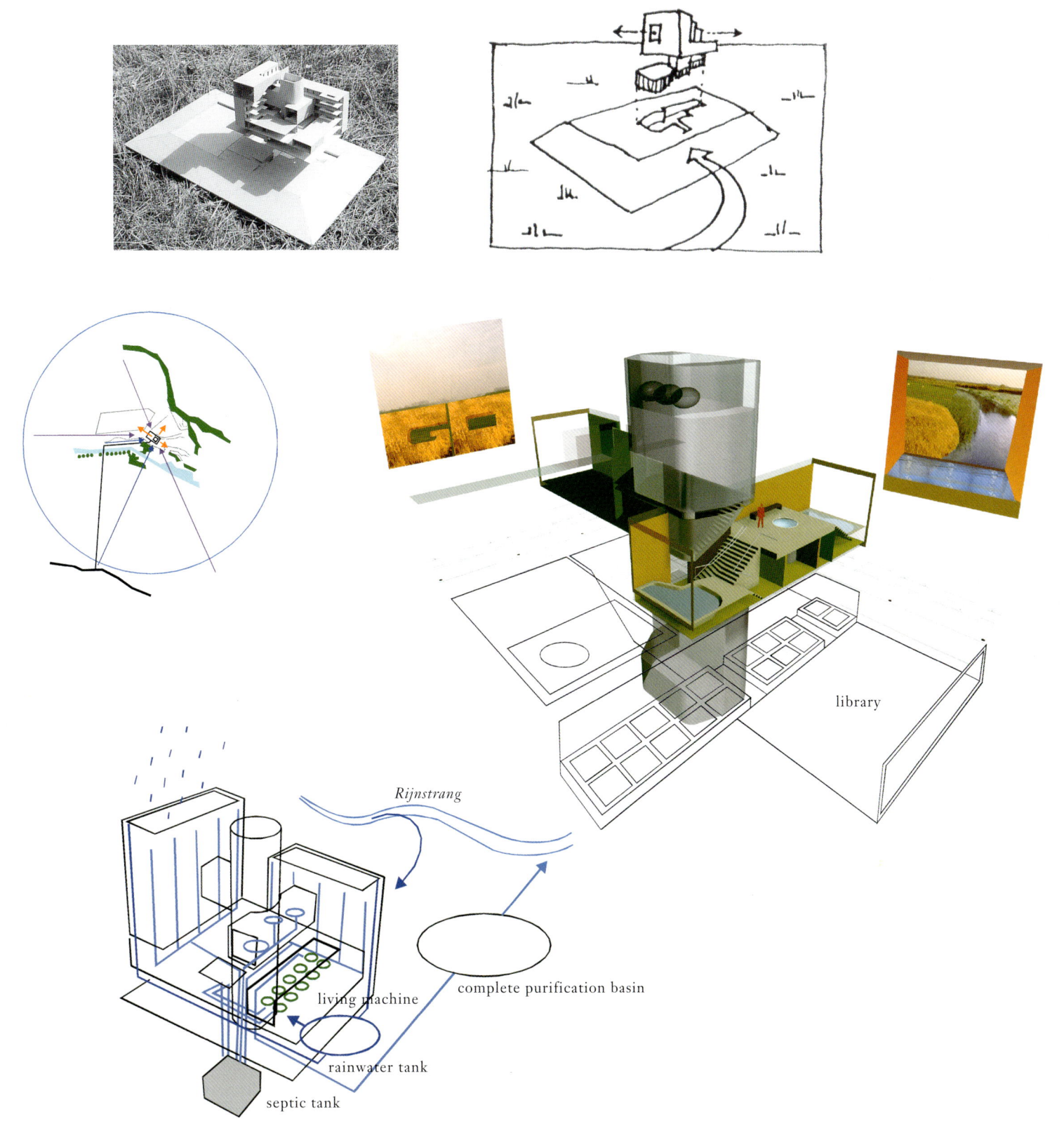

Rijnstrang

living machine

complete purification basin

rainwater tank

septic tank

library

Landscape and urbanization

Utrecht: intense city

Merel Bakker
graduation project Urbanism

mentors
Peter de Bois, Christian van Ees, Hein de Haan

Utrecht: intense city looks for an alternative for the large-scale expansion locations on the outskirts of the city. The VINEX (Supplement to the Fourth Memorandum on Physical Planning) building specification for 30,000 houses near Utrecht should offer major opportunities for the existing city. With a concentrated urban development it is easier to support facilities and public transport, thus creating a greater variation of images and activities. In order to find strategic locations for intensification an analysis was made on the basis of the coherence between form, structure and function at various scales.

Form

The Utrecht urban area is bounded by major infrastructural works. The motorways and waterways that are connecting elements on the regional scale have a dividing effect on the scale of the agglomeration and the city. Two peripheral strips are created on the east and west side of the city. The western strip will be urbanized in the future due to the planned connection between Leidsche Rijn and the existing city. However, there are still no specific plans for the eastern strip, while there are considerable opportunities here.

Structure

Based on the existing urban structure a logical opening up principle has been sought with the historical radial pattern serving as the basis.

Two other important structural supporters in the city are the public transport system and the open space structure. The open space structure must form a counterbalance for the densely populated urban area. In Utrecht, there are a number of very valuable nature reserves and recreation areas along the Vecht and the Kromme Rijn. By connecting the fragments together and making them accessible from surrounding districts the physical spatial void can become a programmed fullness.

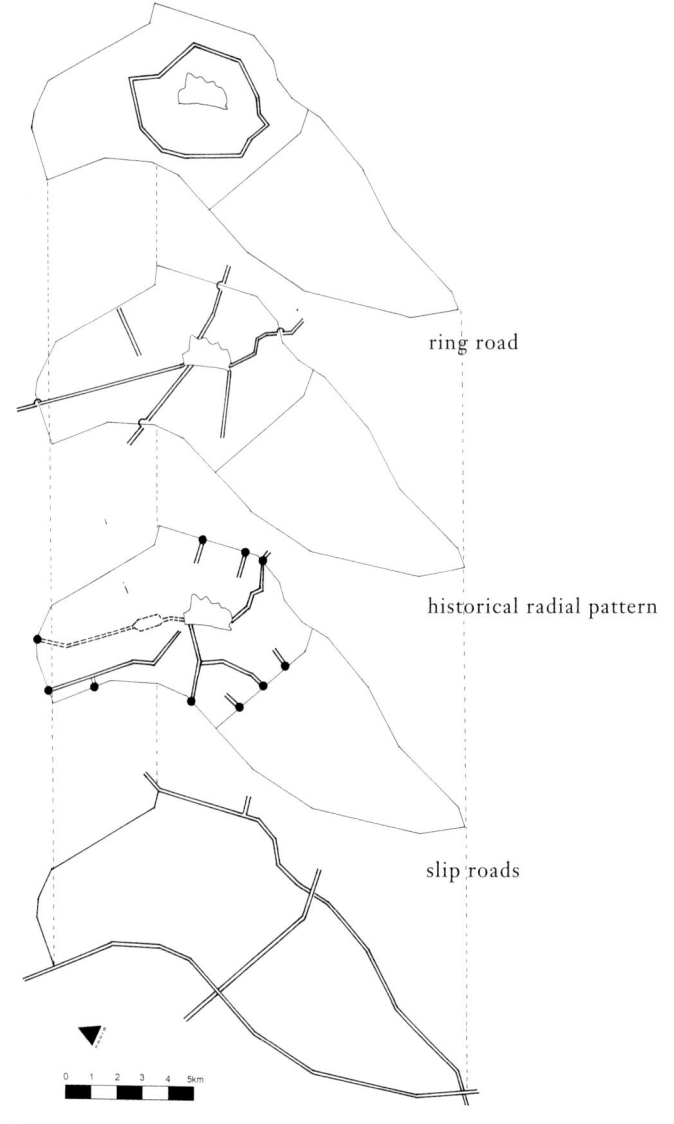

Structure plan Future situation

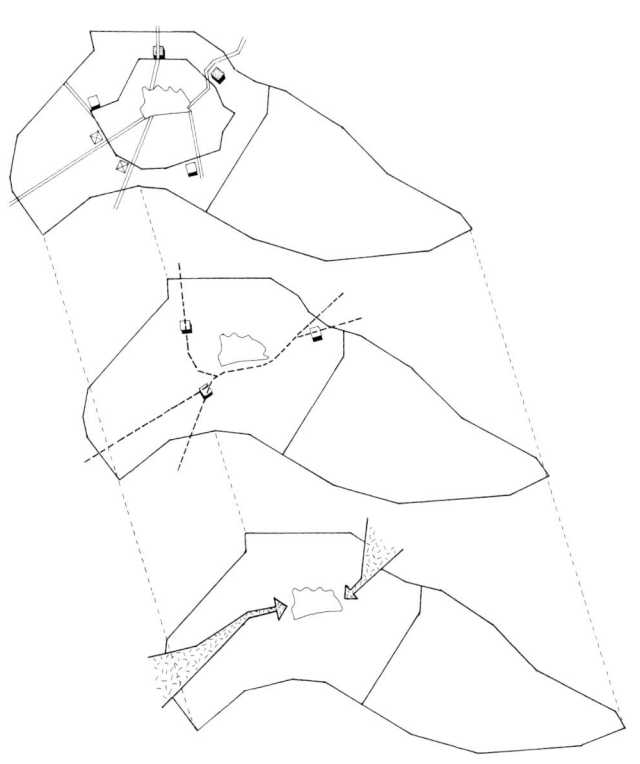

Structure plan Subcentres in the city centre

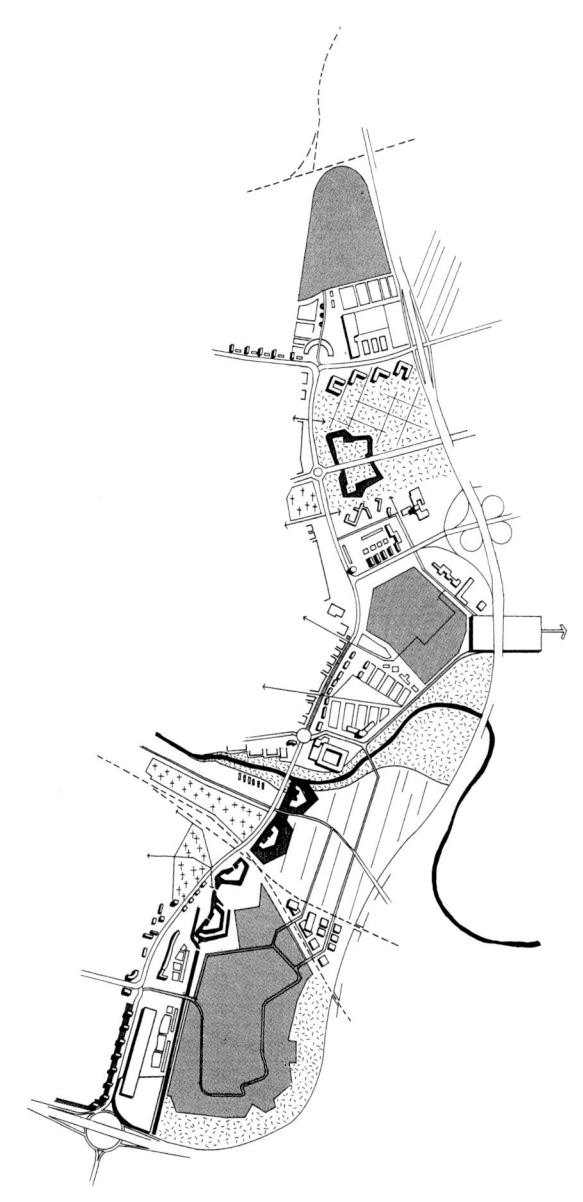

Eastern outskirts of Utrecht

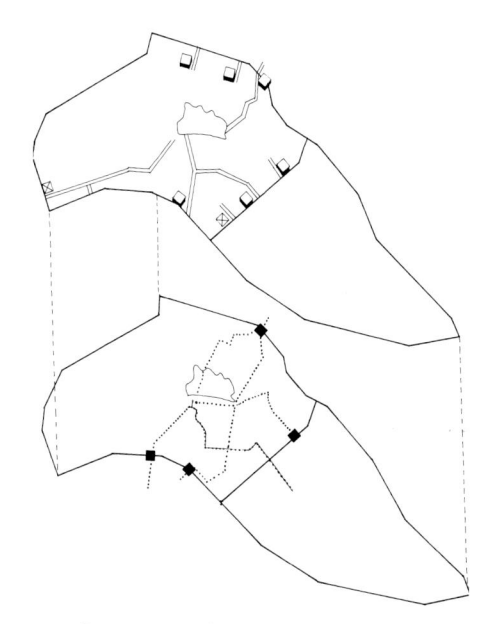

Structure plan
Subcentres at the motorway

Function
- access road
- high-speed tram
- tram
- green structure
- transferium
- subcentre with high development potential
- subcentre with poor development potential
- subcentre for recreation

Landscape and urbanization

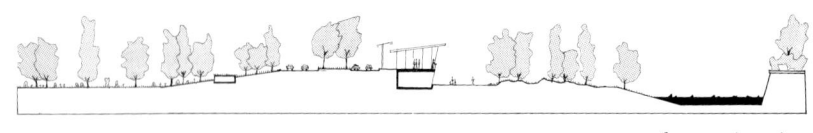

future situation

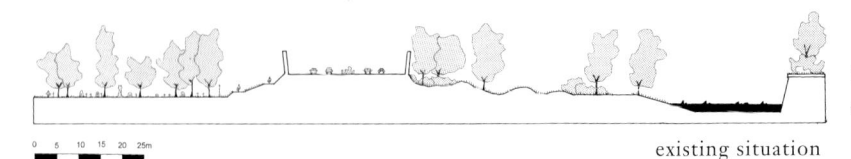

Cross-section of eastern ring road

existing situation

Function

Strategic locations to intensify the city were determined on the basis of the new structure. Densely populated, very varied subcentres where motorists park their cars in a transferium and continue their journey with public transport are created. The transferium must not only be a transfer location, but should also have a high staying quality and have a relationship with the adjoining residential districts. It is, for instance, possible to include a cinema, a supermarket or places of entertainment. These strategic locations are situated at spectacular sites in the city, for example on the open areas along the Vecht and the Kromme Rijn.

Eastern ring road

One of the structural problems on the eastern outskirts is the lack of a connecting element on the scale of the city. The old motorway forms a barrier so that districts in the eastern strip become very isolated. By locating one transferium at Lunetten, the traffic intensity on the motorway decreases considerably. As a result, the road can be transformed into a parkway so that the transverse relationship across the road receives a lot of attention. On account of the elevated aspect, it runs through the eastern outskirts like a linear platform.

As the road will be used less intensively, the construction of a transferium will make it possible to further intensify on this point. There is a possibility to create a subcentre near the Lunetten exit. Eight hectares of land are available for the building of high-density services, offices and houses.

Conclusion

Subcentre Lunetten is just one of the five subcentres on the eastern outskirts. If all these intensification locations were to be optimally utilized, a quarter of the VINEX capacity could be realized in the existing city. These inner urban transformation areas can improve the connections between the surrounding districts so that functions in the districts reinforce one another. This graduation project has shown that building within the walls of the existing city not only produces extra homes and services, but also that these locations can make a positive contribution to a more varied image of the city.

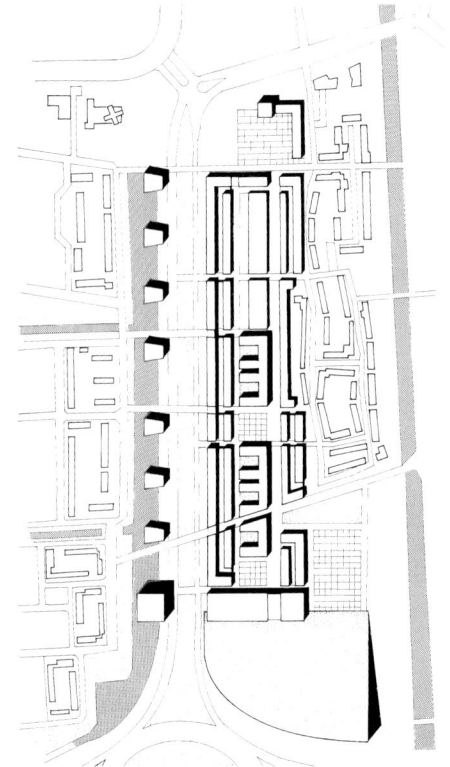

Subcentre Lunetten

The final polder
Rearrangement of the Netherlands

Agnes Franzen
graduation project Architectural Design and Urbanism

mentors
Prof. Dirk Frieling, Prof. Carel Weeber, Inge Bobbink, Henk Mihl

This project makes a proposal for a rearrangement of the Netherlands. The rearrangement consists of the relocation of Schiphol, the Westland and the flowerbulb area from the inland edge of the dunes to the Markermeer. This rearrangement provides an answer for the problem of lack of space in the Randstad and the current problems of capacity, noise and congestion around Schiphol. The relocation of the airport can be regarded as a strategic intervention with which the Netherlands focuses on the economic developments in Eastern Europe. The airport is linked to a high-speed train line in the direction of Scandinavia and the eastern part of Germany.

Besides its favourable location with respect to Eastern Europe, the Markermeer offers a number of other advantages. The area is centrally situated within the Netherlands, a large part of the necessary infrastructure is already available and development of this area would provide a good economic impulse for the north of the Netherlands. Since it is possible to fly above water, the noise nuisance above populated areas is lower and safety is higher compared to the existing Schiphol. Land reclamation can be limited to 13,000 hectares so that 59,000 hectares of the Markermeer still remains for recreation, water management and fishing.

By relocating the airport (Schiphol closes in the future), it is possible to take advantage of the most recent developments in the aviation field, such as the increase in the number of passengers, alliances, the increased capacity of new aircraft and the professionalization of the aviation industry. In order to give the airport sufficient growth potential, to limit the congestion and noise nuisance and to retain optimum accessibility, space will be reserved at Lelystad for the airport's economic spin-off.

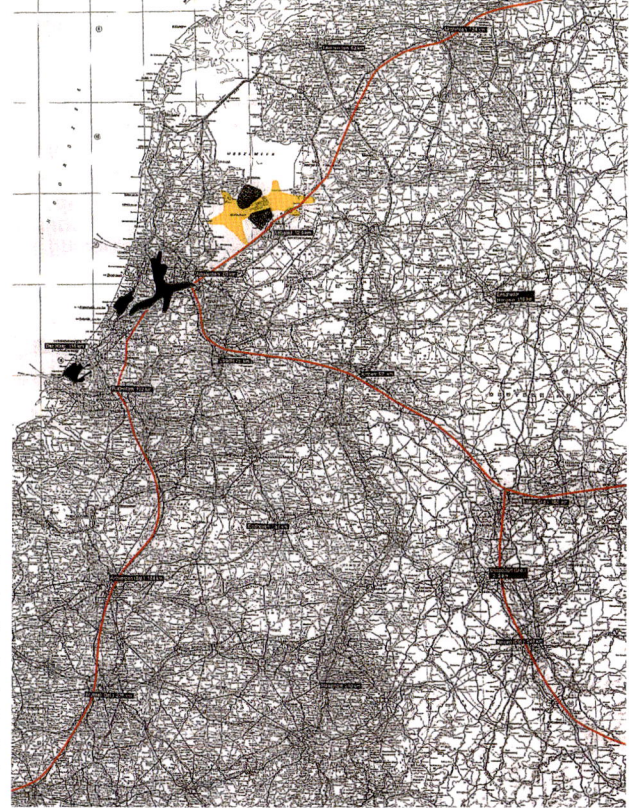

Rearrangement of the Netherlands
The elements of the rearrangement in black, the high-speed train line in red and the noise contour of the new airport in yellow

The total realization costs will be reduced by including other functions besides the airport. In addition, the area offers considerable potential for the flowerbulb sector and cultivation under glass. The flowerbulb sector can benefit from the presence of 'Enkhuizerzand' (very good soil for bulbs), good connections to existing cultivation centres and the possibility of realizing a concentrated area with large plots of land. For cultivation under glass, the proximity of the airport and the German hinterland is very attractive. As a knowledge and capital-intensive complex, the latter sector can fulfil a laboratory function.

The airport as transit machine

Schiphol originally only consisted of a field with a runway. During the past few years, however, the number of flights has increased dramatically. Holidays are becoming more and more exotic and the average Dutch person likes to go on holiday (by plane) twice a year. To satisfy the ever-increasing demand, an initial capacity of 80 million passengers is assumed for the new airport. A linear concept is chosen in response to the professionalization of the aviation industry and the ever longer walking routes and the associated complexity of existing airports. Repeatable units, a clear arrangement and short walking routes are the basic principles. The airport can thus easily be extended and time spent at the airport kept to a minimum. The terminal consists of 48 units grouped around the access road that is situated on the same level as the arrival and departure hall. With arrivals and departures on the same level, space is saved and rapid clearance of passenger flows is promoted. A people-mover connected to the high-speed train station in Lelystad is situated one level lower. Baggage clearance and services are also located on this level.

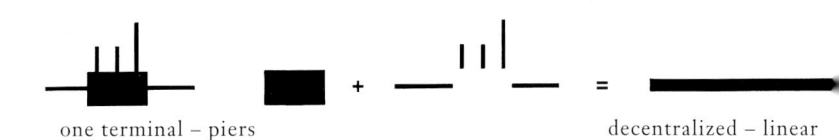

Draft rearrangement

one terminal – piers   decentralized – linear

Transit machine

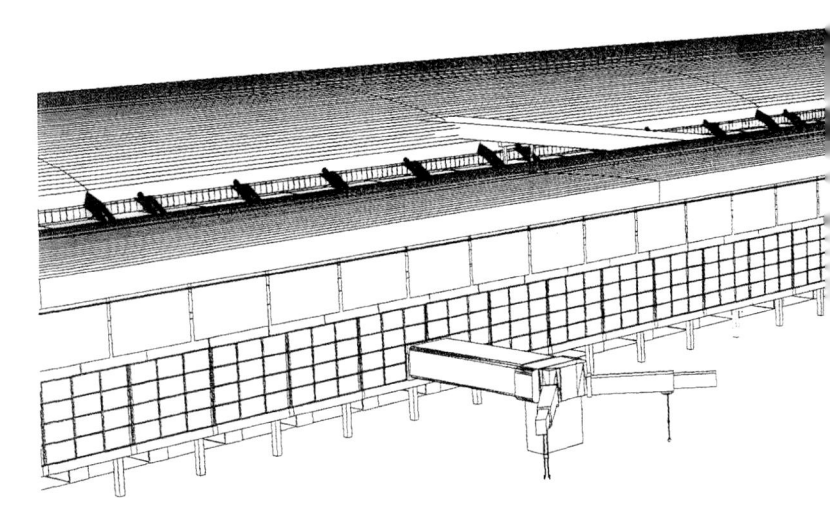

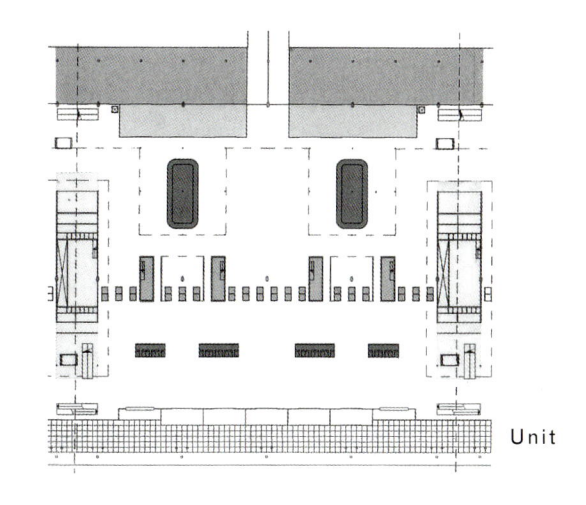

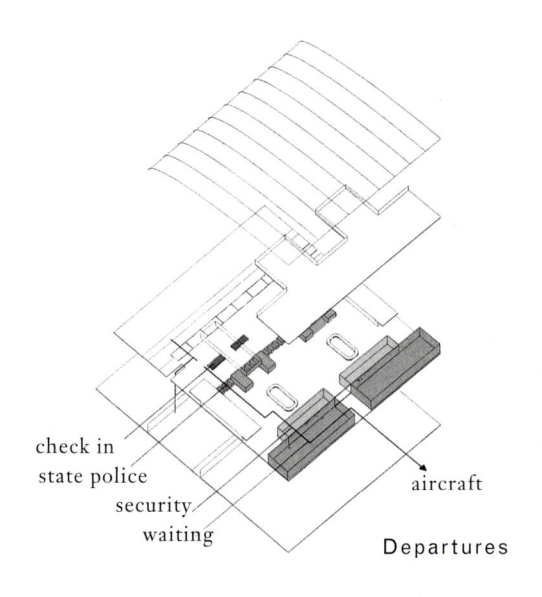

Unit

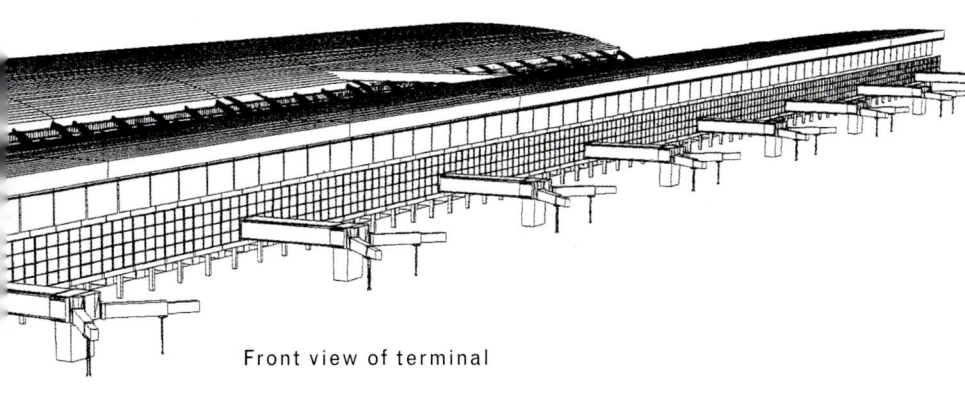

Front view of terminal

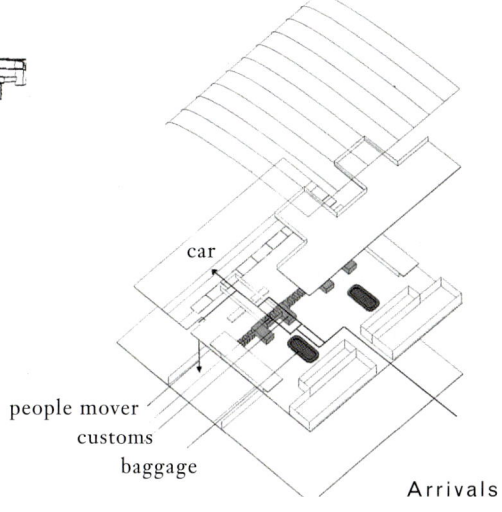

check in
state police
security
waiting
aircraft
Departures

car
people mover
customs
baggage
Arrivals

Landscape and urbanization

Shifting perspectives

Where does the architecture of the city originate?
The ideology of architecture, a student-initiated project

mentor
Dieter Besch

In the construction boom in the future German capital Berlin, three clearly distinguishable design practices are emerging in the reconstruction of public urban space. Kollhoff, Libeskind and Kroll are the main protagonists of these practices, which were studied against the background of the *Planwerk Innenstadt* formulated by the *Senator für Stadtentwicklung*. The central question in the research section of this project was: **can any one of these three practices be described as more contemporary or modern than the others, or is there no difference between them?**

The City of Bits
A redefinition of architecture in the reunited Berlin
Pascal Smits and Roel van Alst

The idea that infoculture is rapidly becoming bodiless, that our technology is leading us into a post-corporeal world order, has become almost commonplace. Places in cyberspace – like architectural and urban places – have characteristic appearances, and the interactions that unfold within them are controlled by local rules. Sharing a virtual place is not quite the same as sharing a physical place. The crucial factor is simultaneous electronic access to the same *information*. Many of the places in cyberspace are public, like streets and squares; access to them is uncontrolled. Others are private, like mailboxes and houses, and can be entered only if you have the key or can prove that you belong. You move from place to place in cyberspace by following logical links rather than physical paths; this is the new architectural promenade. The network is the urban site before us, an invitation to design and construct the City of Bits.

Architects of the twenty-first century will still shape, arrange, and connect spaces to satisfy human needs. They will still seek commodity, firmness, and delight. But commodity will be as much a matter of software functions and interface design as of floor plans and construction materials. Firmness will entail not only the physical integrity of structural systems, but also the logical integrity of computer systems. And delight will have unimagined new dimensions.

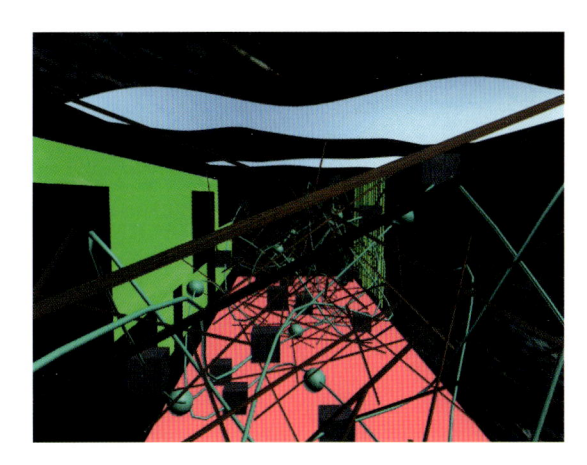

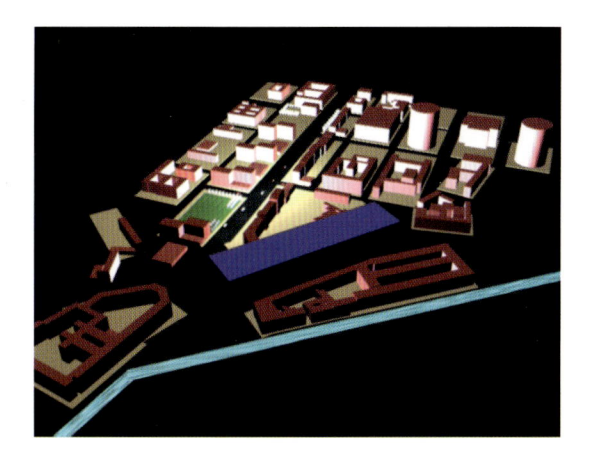

Imagine an architecture which is capable of absorbing and strengthening the sensibility of humankind. In order to reintroduce corporeality, *sublime* buildings must be created. It is not easy to define the formal characteristics of the *sublime*; it is an experience, a process of perception, where the initial threat dissolves in the delight of the moment. The aesthetics of the sublime find their tension field between on the one hand the threat, which is the result of the impossibility of linking the perception back to the familiar, and on the other hand the delight. For Lyotard it is important that this tension is experienced in an attempt to visualize the image of the world in an object. Through the strangeness of an object (the threatened body), a related tension field can be conjured up. We want to use this contrast to underline the essential quality of architecture, the fact of its own expression.

Historically speaking, architects always understood movement as the voyage of the moving eye in space. In this view, architecture is seen as static, fixed, ideal and inert. Buildings were not only constructed as invariable forms but, more importantly, architecture was conceived and designed based on models of stagnation and equilibrium. Computer animation software adopted the assumption that architectural design exists in a Cartesian context, waiting for the animation of the moving eye. Instead of designing space as an invariable and motionless form, we visualize it as plastic, flexible and variable in its dynamic evolution, evoked through motion and transformation. There is, however, a distinction between the design phase and the execution phase. In order to construct the fantastic results of the first phase, the *blobs*, traditional constructive means must be used.

By using interfaces which introduce tactility in virtual surroundings, one can design on a more intuitive level. The totalitarianism of *perfect* visualizing will be replaced by the development of a vision. Design environments will be organized so as to create the greatest potential for unforeseen relationships.

The interior of our building is conceived as a symbol for cyberspace. Both can be compared with the rhizomatic system of Deleuze and Guattari. The rhizome is a structure without a centralized, hierarchical organization, a structure that reflects the more *natural* pattern of geo-organic development. According to Deleuze and Guattari, we are taught to act like trees and forced to think like trees, although we more *naturally* think like rhizomes (grass not trees).

Some of their statements about rhizomes can be compared with features of our design. Any point in a rhizome can and must be connected to any other. This is very different from the tree or root, which plots a point, fixes an order. The rhizome is an anti-genealogy. The rhizome is an acentric, non-hierarchical, non-signifying system without an organizing memory or central automaton. The rhizome offers some hope of bringing about a kind of liberation from structures of power and dominance.

Generations of architects have worked on the *language of building*. We find that this language of metaphors is no longer applicable. We try to show a new form of architecture, based on the notion of dialogue. This interactive, virtual architecture responds and agitates; it literally calls for dialogue with users and spectators. Architecture no longer is an object of perception to be interpreted, but rather a system of communication.

Shifting perspectives

The bridge in between
Massimo Pauletto

The design location is a point representing a break between different fragments of the same city originating from different schemes and periods in history. The project was expressly designed for a very strong impact in this situation, based on a concept of changing scales between urban design and architectural typologies (ways of living). It had to be strong enough to restore to the area a meaning that was lost in the emptiness created by the bombardments of World War II and the post-war reconstruction. Therefore the primary goal was necessarily to define the spaces (on the assumption that a building would be able to give order to different spaces just because it was there) and secondly to organize the hierarchy within (directions, priorities, functions and meanings). Through the *building*, a strong and stable space is defined; the *strips* (public spaces) are using it, floating in it and under it, and finally re-establishing the lost connections in the city.

The bridge in between contains the exact virtual meaning of this design. That is why the direction of the strips is derived from the position of the buildings in the socialist city. And now we can see that the design of the post-war buildings is based both on the block structure of the old Berlin and the large-scale reconstruction of the socialist city after the war.

Learning from The New Urbanism
A semiotic reading

Luisa Calabrese

[1] An article recently appeared on this magazine about New Urbanism; see Shannon, K., "The great leap backwards", *Archis*, March 1998

[2] Over the past five years, a movement to reform America's urban growth patterns has emerged. The individuals at the forefront of this movement have organized themselves into a group known as the Congress for the New Urbanism (cnu). A series of congresses has been convened where members of the group have discussed the principles, policies and techniques of The New Urbanism. The first CNU I attended was held in Alexandria, Virginia (USA) in the Autumn of 1993.

[3] Harvey, D., "The New Urbanism and the communitarian trap", *Harvard Design Magazine*, Winter/Spring 1997

The New Urbanism is an American planning movement officially founded in 1993 by leading city planning and design practitioners, educators and developers. The different groups were united by a commitment to reform urbanism in the USA by countering the current car-dominated forms of development with a model based on mixed-use towns accessible by foot and mass transit.

This article describes the relationship between The New Urbanism (TNU) and the development of a professional language for city planning. It explains how the principles of TNU have been developed through intense debate in successive congresses and through the production of their own Charter at the fourth congress in May 1996. The Charter represents the first attempt of the Congress for New Urbanism (CNU) to lay down a coherent set of principles for review and debate of city planning beliefs, as set out in the 1933 Athens Charter produced by the Congres Internationaux d'Architecture Moderne (CIAM).

There is a rich literature[1] on the subject of what is called The New Urbanism (TNU). While some authors are in favour of this American movement, most are against its 'traditional' programmatic and formal statements. Nevertheless, despite all the criticism, TNU is an internationally known movement that can be quantified in terms of hectares of built environment and hundreds of written pages of theoretical statements, design guidelines and concrete data. Even more significant than this, with the CNU[2], a group of American architects and planners legitimized their status with a manifesto that is reminiscent of the Charter of Athens' idealistic adrenaline rush to defend the Holy Grail of urbanism. But still, for somebody interested in understanding what lies behind the seeming simplicity of the new urbanists' approach and the apparent naiveté of their plans, it is very difficult to find a way through all the readings and interpretations. David Harvey[3], for instance, warns us about "the false hopes of design" and describes the negative social implications of the neo-traditional neighbourhood model. "In the absence of employment and government largesse, the 'civic' claims of TNU sound particularly hollow" he writes. On the other hand, he praises the attention paid by this movement to the thorny problem of what to do with the automobile-based urbanization and suburbanization that has characterized the American landscape since the Second World War.

In all probability the problem lies in the one-way solution they propose rather than in the substance of their intentions. Nevertheless, as mentioned above, there is already sufficient literature to illuminate the debate. What I wish to highlight, instead, is an interesting aspect of TNU I discovered while studying their design lexicon. The notion of language applied to urbanism relates not only to the skill of understanding the urban substance, but also – and mainly – to the development of knowledge to design it. As we have learnt from previous planning mistakes, to make cities sustainable we must base decisions about them on a more secure understanding of their substance than we do at present. What is unclear is what we mean by "a better understanding", for there are enough interpretative theories of the contemporary city. If we try to shift from the mere programmatic aspects of TNU planning philosophy to an analysis of its linguistic structure, we might discover something really 'new' in the urbanism it defends: the use of language as a design tool and the consequent importance of codification in the planning process.

Learning from The New Urbanism

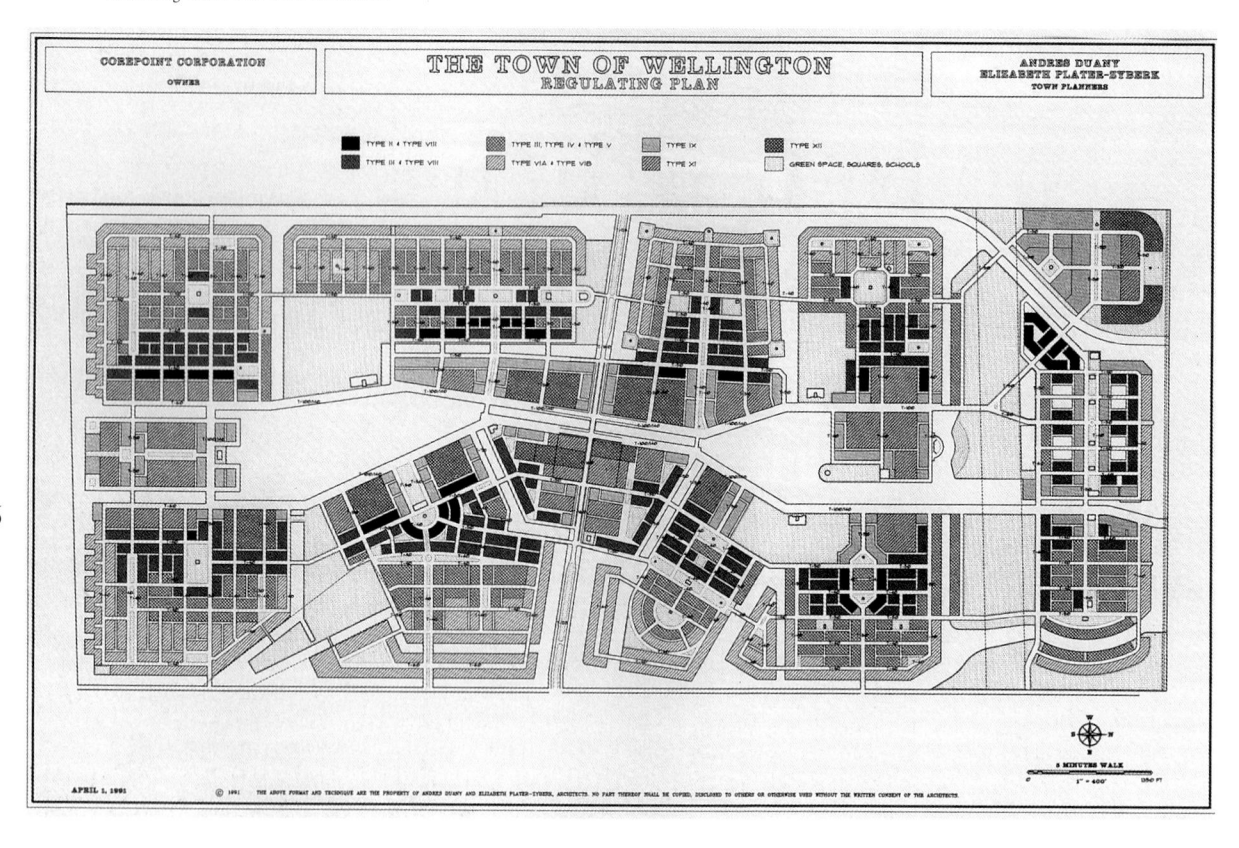

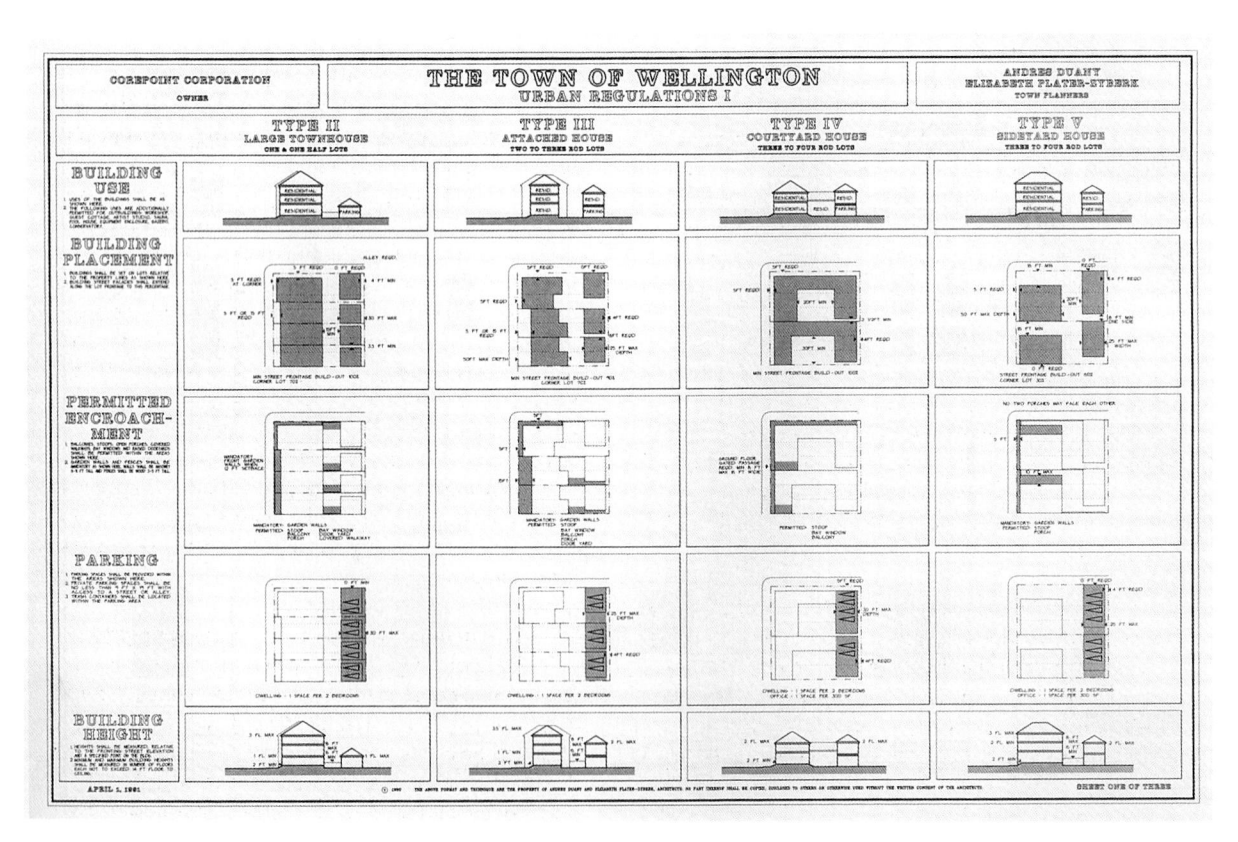

Why is language so important? And why a semiotic approach to TNU?

At a time when the complexity of the built environment has almost led the discipline of city planning to collapse under the pressure of previous serious mistakes, there is an urgent need to understand the meaning of what we are dealing with. We all agree on the fact that the planner/architect, and the profession in general, urgently need to redefine a position within the chaos of the clash of interests involved in the planning game: politics, money, social identity (or identities), ecology. And new urbanists have understood that need very well.

To combat suburban sprawl, they re-invented an idiom; in other words they codified a language. I say re-invented, because the ingredients of this design language are well known to all of us. Key concepts such as neighbourhood community, public space, street, boulevard were catalogued at the beginning of the century, when the discipline of city planning was born.

From this perspective, I agree with Kelly Shannon[4] that there is nothing 'new' in the movement's vocabulary. Nevertheless, the syntax and the codes have surely changed. Furthermore, in the absence of a really challenging response to the general silence on the questions posed by the built environment, TNU has the merit of going one step forward: from theory to practice, from general statements to precise design guidelines.

In exploring the extremes of contemporary theories of urban form we find, at opposite poles, the generic city of Rem Koolhaas and the neo-traditional neighbourhoods promoted by Andres Duany and his movement. Both icons frame a society desperately occupied with the search for identity and its symbolic representation.

Usually, to the extent that identity is derived from the physical substance of a place, from its memory and from the tradition, we somehow cannot imagine that something contemporary – made by us – can contribute to it. I wonder if this need for social reassurance belongs more to the citizen or to the city planner. In any case, it is definitely a symptom of the growing uneasiness of the latter.

What is missing in the profession is not a theoretical construction on the city, but a 'scientific' language able to articulate a debate.

The reading of the city as a text has a long tradition and it might seem as old-fashioned as the ideas of The New Urbanism, but indeed this linguistic analogy might be useful in explaining why it is worthwhile positively considering this aspect of TNU. The reference for their discourse on the city is the American metropolis, the result of a constant application of modernist principles. A patchwork of repetitive spatial clones with no defined boundaries, which changed the American landscape (and not only that) in the last decades. The absence of spatial signs in the suburbs generated what Europeans call periphery, and TNU defines as suburban sprawl. The nomenclature may vary but the concept is the same: a place that could be everywhere or nowhere[5].

If the loss of identity is at the heart of the debate on the contemporary city, a semiotic reading of the built environment could help clarify why signs are no longer representing it.

Semiotics underlines the fact that signs are related to their signifiers by social conventions; however, we become so accustomed to such conventions in our use of various media that it might be difficult for us to be aware of the conventional nature of such relationships. When we take them for granted we consider the signified as unmediated, as when we interpret

4
Shannon, K., op. cit.

5
On this subject see Kunstler, J.H., *The geography of nowhere*: the rise and decline of America's man-made landscape, New York, Touchstone Press, 1993

television or photography as 'a window on the world'. A semiotic approach can make us aware of what we take for granted in representing the world, reminding us that we are always dealing with signs, not with an unmediated objective reality, and that sign systems are involved in the construction of meaning.

The central core of the new urbanists' argument is that urban living can be radically improved by a return to meaning. They define meaning as the re-evaluation of archetypal city planning concepts. In other words they suggest that one solution is to go back to the time when utterances such as "placeless" or "lost space"6 were not part of the city planner's vocabulary. A magic time when collective memory was still represented by the physicality of the built environment and social identity was a reality. But how far back in time do we have to travel to resurrect this idyllic image of the city? And, as architects and city planners, what responsibility do we have in interpreting collective memory? This is not a rhetorical question if we talk about TNU, and more generally, about the essence of city planning.

The problem is that the long-lasting split between different forms of knowledge involved in city planning (planners, urban designers, architect, engineers) has resulted in a fragmentation of meanings of the built environment. We are no longer able to read and understand the city. More than that, we are not able to find solid planning answers to its growing complexity. Why? One of the reasons is that what was originally a design language with very precise rules of application and interpretation turned out to be incapable of keeping up with the frenetic growth it promoted.

Too busy to build and exploit a taxonomy of growth, city planners and architects found it easier to establish regulatory frameworks in which zoning laws and modernist utopias could develop freely. Zoning prescribed the activities that could take place on a plot of land: the size of the building that could be erected; dimensions for front and back yards and requirements for functional aspects such as parking. This mechanism did not propose any particular design typology, but surely it imposed an impoverishment of the city image and, as a consequence, of our ability to represent it. We are faced with a major dilemma: on the one hand the level of uniformity of suburbs/periphery implies banality and simplicity, but on the other the inner spatial and social relations within the built environment are so heterogeneous that complexity is the key word.

One of the main problems of contemporary planning practice is the loss of knowledge to express this complexity. From this point of view TNU has a lot to offer, not in terms of content perhaps, but in terms of the technique used to put it forward. TNU did not invent a language; it simply revised a forgotten grammar whose roots date back to the beginning of this century by re-compacting it with neologisms derived from the American experience.

As Todd W. Bressi7 remarks, the TNU approach to planning and design revives principles about building communities that have been virtually ignored for half a century. What Modernism has really forgotten is the hierarchical and detailed articulation of planning codes into different ranges of scale. New urbanists criticize the fact that, following the ideas of functionalism, urban blocks neglected the traditional urban form aligned with the street (the original icon of the American suburb) and stood as isolated elements surrounded by parking lots. We all have that picture in our minds. So what is wrong with that? What is new in criticizing that image is the way in which TNU organizes the arguments of its theory.

6
Trancik, R., *Finding lost space*: theories of urban design, new york, Van Nostrand Reinold, 1986

7
Bressi, T.W., "Planning the American Dream", P. Katz (ed.), *The New Urbanism*: toward an architecture of community, New York, McGrawHill, 1994

8
Guiraud, P., *Semiology* (trans. George Gross), London, Routledge & Kegan Paul, 1975

9
Andres Duany and Elizabeth Plater-Zyberk are the founders of the firm DPZ and were among the first to theorize TNU. Since its foundation in 1980, DPZ has designed over eighty new towns and revitalization projects for existing communities. These designs have had an influence on changing the practice and direction of town and urban planning in the United States. The firm's early project (1981) of the town of Seaside, Florida, is the first traditional town to be built in the United States since World War II.

Originally positive spatial signs such as the single-family detached house of the first suburban expansions, or the highway developments in the 1950s, become empty models that were replicated in countless communities, often with little modification to take account of local conditions.

Modernism's legacy was a series of detached icons without any syntagmatic structure or linguistic code. What is a linguistic code? In each text signs are organized into meaningful systems according to certain conventions which semioticians refer to as codes (or signifying codes). Such conventions represent a social dimension in semiotics: a code is a set of practices familiar to users of the medium operating within a broad cultural framework. A range of typologies of codes can be found in semiotics literature. These can be divided into broad categories such as social, textual and interpretative codes. Understanding such codes, their relationships and the contexts in which they are appropriate, is part of being a member of a particular culture. Codes are not static; they are dynamic systems that change over time, and are thus historically as well as socio-culturally situated. Giraud[8] calls the way in which such conventions are established codification.

Regulatory codes are at the heart of Duany and Plater-Zyberk's work[9] as well as that of their colleagues. With the codification of planning ordinances they started an on-going planning and theoretical process towards the elaboration of a specific design language for city planning. This process started a decade ago with the Seaside project – a modestly scaled resort community situated in northern Florida.

Early on in their work they realized that by using the existing set of zoning ordinances it was almost impossible to fulfil the aspirations of The New Urbanism to create urban neighbourhoods and to develop an alternative to suburbia. In this sense the use of language serves The New Urbanism to articulate a

Shifting perspectives

discourse about the built environment that finds direct application in design practice, bypassing metaphor. Indeed, their strength lies in the efforts made, first to reveal the poverty of suburban sprawl semantic structure, and second, to dismantle its syntax by demonstrating the environmental inefficiency of that planning language.

What they propose with The Charter for New Urbanism (1996) is a linguistic grid supported by a layering of codified signs hierarchically ordered in scale. The charter for The New Urbanism is a sort of *dictionnaire raisonné* of this planning language, unique in its genre. It is structured around the idea that a codification of rules is necessary to produce urbanism.

Starting from the three central concepts of Neighbourhood, District and Corridor, this semantic code is articulated into five main categories (according to a tree structure), the aim of which is to explore the largest, middle and smallest scale of planning. These categories are:

– The regulating plan
– The urban regulations
– The architectural regulations
– The street types
– The landscape regulations

Each of them is sub-divided into a set of definitions (linguistic signs), and graphic representations (semantic codes) that lead to standardized design guidelines. If architectural and urban design theory can be regarded as meta-languages (as semiotics suggests), the use of codes becomes necessary for the development of a comprehensible planning process.

In the complexity of city planning language the interaction between different codes (social, economic, political, ideological) other than planning rules, is impressive. As Umberto Eco[10] remarked, architecture starts from existing design codes, but it always depends on others (social, cultural, economic codes, etc.) to communicate meaning.

To clarify the concept I will use an example Eco cites.

It is obvious that when a planner/architect designs an urban street, he/she borrows from the traditional lexicon (set of rules) which classifies the 'urban-street' model. She/he may change the aesthetic content, according to local conditions, the proportions of building height to street or the sidewalk width, but the street will, generally speaking, be conceived at ground level, because this is the archetype idea of the code.

When instead Le Corbusier proposed the elevated street, he combined the original typological code (street) with another one (bridge); nevertheless, common sense was still able to associate this hybrid image with the original function. According to Eco's reading, this happens because the architectural operation was preceded by research into possible functions created by the new exigencies of the modern city, but not yet codified by traditional architectural codes. In other words, first he codified a set of possible desired functions, and then he elaborated a formal code of their denotation. These 'possible functions' or desires, as we might define them, go beyond the field of architecture and urban planning; they belong to sociology, politics and economics. They embody the meaning of the physical object (beyond form and function) and the possibility of interrelating different original codes into new settings. *An architect, therefore, must add a fourth dimension to the Cartesian space, that of culture and its codes.*

This is what Modernism forgot, and TNU criticizes, in planning suburban developments: the ability to understand the needs of contemporary cities and translate them into design codes. This loss of expertise

10
Eco, U., "La funzione e il segno: semiologia dell'architettura", *La Struttura Assente*, Milano, Bompiani ed., 1980

11
Nöth, W., *Handbook of semiotics*, Bloomington, Indiana University Press, 1990

12
On this analogy see, among others, Collins, P., *Changing in Modern Architecture*, London, Faber and Faber, 1965

exposes the most critical point of the planning profession, that of the 'responsibility' of the city planner/architect in the decision-making process.

Another TNU criticism of the modernist tradition is that planners found it easiest to fossilize in general regulatory frameworks instead of working towards a more detailed scale. In other words sprawl is the by-product of the absence of an innovative professional planning and design language capable of interpreting the local needs and characteristics of the built environment.

The original meaning of zoning rooted in Garnier's industrial city turned into a meaningless and over-simplified mechanism of planning. The inconsistency of the 'dead codes' applied made suburbs express a fragmented language in which no professional knowledge, either architectural or civic, could ever be expressed. Above all, one of the reasons for this semantic poverty is the absence of principles and articulation in a range of different scales that formed the basis of traditional city planning language.

The term articulation, as used by semioticians with reference to 'code structure', was derived from Martinet's structural linguistics. A semiotic code which has 'double articulation' can be analyzed at two abstract structural levels: a higher level called 'the level of first articulation' and a lower level – 'the level of second articulation'[11]. At the level of first articulation the system consists of the smallest meaningful units available (e.g. morphemes or words in a language). These meaningful units are complete signs, each consisting of a signifier and a signified. Where codes have recurrent meaningful units (such as the regulation pictograms in The New Urbanism), they have first articulation.

Without going any further into technical details with the linguistic analogy[12], we can easily evince from what has been said until now that the attention paid by the new urbanists to the re-invention of a professional language for city planning is praiseworthy and fruitful.

TNU, however, fails to capture important features of contemporary cities, especially the need for the integration of large-scale infrastructure. Indeed the spatial syntax of TNU reveals one of its limits in not being able to pick up the evolutionary process of urban phenomena by translating those 'less desirable' urban elements, such us ring roads, railways, etc., into design codes. In any case, TNU stands as a challenger in the international arena in which solo theories on the future of the metropolis are whispered or shouted for all to hear. Far from defending the contents of the message they promote, I am arguing that the merit of TNU is to have raised the thorny question of the professional role in contemporary planning processes from the right side, that of a missing professional language of city planning. And, by doing so, this American movement stimulates us to re-invent our alternative between the speechless suburban space and the neo-traditional neighbourhood it promotes.

Light urban development

Prof. Jon Kristinsson

The term light urban development is used to describe an intelligent, sustainable 21st Century settlement. Light urban development knows when it is time to come and go – and like a good traveller does not leave any traces. Infrastructure designers are developing a new integrated technology using a backcasting approach based on the year 2050.

In the light of the Brundtland report 'Our Common Future', our grandchildren will have only one twentieth of the present environmental capacity at their disposal. This will lead to a radical change in existing technological concepts.

In the first instance light urban development is made possible by the highly compact development in noise pollution zones, cutting out noise pollution at its very source.

Light urban development is a reaction against expensive and unnecessary infrastructure. It is possible to use the increasing self-sufficiency of buildings, for example through new recycling technologies and ecological insights. In my view these will take some 5 to 10 years to develop, depending on the amount of money available, and the general commitment. A number of factors will have direct and a variety of indirect effects on the built environment: fewer metalled roads and public utility mains, new types of transport and new concepts of individual/collective transport, changing social structures.

The concept of light urban development is gradually getting off the ground, but apart from the aspect of ecological and economic advantages, current legislation and traditions in the building industry do not favour overnight changes. Light urban development without infrastructure is not desirable unless there is also building within the pollution zone *with* infrastructure.

Light urban development largely follows the data contained in the statistical yearbook relating to where people would like to live: 71% of the Dutch population wish to live in a rural setting and 24% in a city environment. This would mean 10 dwellings per hectare in quiet areas and over 100 dwellings per hectare in busy urban agglomerations, rather than the 30 to 35 dwellings per hectare for nearly all the Vinex sites (locations referred to in the Fourth Report on Physical Planning).

Light urban development is mainly low-rise; it is known that people on low incomes do not do well in high-rise flats. Allotments and vegetable gardens are well-suited to the concept, but the grey economy that results for example from second-hand and scrap trade requires some structuring for environmental reasons. Light urban development must be able to withstand the undesirable effects of possible negative economic growth.

Light urban development can grow up around an 'inframedion', i.e. a cluster of central facilities, but a farmstead can serve equally well as a catalyst for the gradual development of a settlement. Costly site preparation as an initial investment is no longer needed.

Automobility as we know it could be far more efficient and cheaper. The individual/collective transport concept "Icarus" is a realistic concept for 24 hour door-to-door transport. The huge success of the car may be likened to the yeast used in wine making, which becomes inactive at an alcohol content of 12%.

My own car – love it – is a fine piece of industrial perfection. But beware! It may well be likened to a combined heat-and-power principle on four wheels, using an energy efficiency of 2 % to carry just its driver. In other words: our heavy 'bumper cars' with combustion engines are the mammoths of today's animal kingdom.

The use of the ground as thermal mass enables us to build much lighter structures with an equable and pleasant indoor climate in summer and winter. All thermal insulating materials are very light in weight. Natural building materials to be considered in this context are timber, fibre materials, cork, flax, hemp, acid clay etc. and reusable materials such as metals and glass from demolished buildings. Lime sandstone, brick and concrete are heavier and more difficult to dismantle when they have to be removed or replaced. Repairability and a long useful life-span usually justify a greater environmental load during construction.

For the present, integrated design based on constructional physics and urban development physics would seem to be the most likely means of developing sustainable light architecture within light urban development.

The term light urban development is used in certain quarters, including the Netherlands Ministry of Housing, Spatial Planning and Environment with reference to the long term. The persons using the term recognize the possibilities but do not take into account the aspects still to be resolved.

The Environmental Design Section is in the process of completing the notes for the lecture series Introduction to Integrated Design, to which is to be added sustainable urban development, i.e. light urban development, illustrated by a number of examples.

Rotterdam: the enabling city

Dr Gerard Wigmans

Many cities in western industrialized countries are undergoing a major transformation. This process of urban transformation is often described as a transition from an industrial city to a post-industrial, postmodern city. The prefix "post" suggests a new situation, one in which the city fulfils a different role and function within a different social and spatial framework. The city is reorienting and repositioning itself. In the Netherlands, this phase has coincided with an increasing focus on land use policy. The way land policy is defined, applied and adjusted in the Dutch situation is connected with the approach adopted by local politicians towards the city. In the doctoral thesis "De facilitaire stad"[1], an analysis of land policy is used as the empirical basis for assessing changes in the conception of the city. The study focuses on the situation and policy in Rotterdam.

Central to this study is the question of how the land policy of a local authority – in this case Rotterdam – evolves in circumstances where firstly the city is confronted with a network of factors which are uncertain and unpredictable, secondly the reference points for management are increasingly difficult to determine in view of the ongoing postmodernization processes, and thirdly there is a growing shift towards management on the basis of land policy. The changing perspective on management is examined in the light of the modernization and postmodernization processes. This changing perspective is interpreted in terms of a shift from classical governance to contingent governance.

Authors who have considered postmodernization processes (Rorty, Lyotard, Guèhenno, Harvey, Frissen) have all shown that the perspective on management is changing. Postmodernization is interpreted as an attractive concept, leaving open the possibilities of continuity with modernization while at the same time indicating areas of change and new trends. Castells and Harvey, two other authors known for their work as urban theorists, have concentrated on the processes of postmodernization in their recent work, Harvey in his study "The Condition of Postmodernity"[2], and Castells in "The Rise of the Network Society"[3]. Castells follows up some of the insights that Harvey explored in his study of postmodernization. The relationship that Castells and Harvey have established between postmodernization and urban theory makes their work an ideal foundation to build on.

Repositioning

In the first period, during the Seventies, the city was a preserve of political intervention, where public services determined the principles of city government. Local government policy was characterized by a normative approach based on a vision of the ideal future for the city and society. Land policy was used as the preferred instrument. Local politicians had a clear vision of the city and how the municipal territory could be developed. Local government's bureaucratic mechanisms were familiar (or relatively so).

During the Eighties, a discrepancy arose between the familiar concept of the city and the dynamics of society. Local government policy became disoriented, its relationship with the municipal territory evaporated. The uniform concept of the city was no longer tenable. A second period started with the publication of the policy document "Renewal of Rotterdam" (1987)[4]. This period involved a change in thinking about the city, which was related to a number of social developments, such as globalization of the economy and the impact of information and transport technology. The limits of rationality and the conception of governance came into sharper focus when the main orientation of bureaucratic mechanisms shifted more expressly towards the vagaries of market forces, which under

---

1
Wigmans, G., *De facilitaire stad*: Rotterdams grondbeleid en postmodernisering (The enabling city: Rotterdam's land policy and postmodernization), Delft, DUP 1998

2
Harvey, D., *The condition of postmodernity*: an enquiry into the origins of cultural change, Oxford, Blackwell 1995

3
Castells, M., *The rise of the network society*, Oxford, Blackwell 1996, Volume 1 of: M. Castells, *The information age*: economy, society and culture, Oxford, Blackwell 1996-1997

4
Municipality of Rotterdam, *Vernieuwing van Rotterdam* (Renewal of Rotterdam), 1987

Aerial photograph of Kop van Zuid

postmodernist conditions were deserting the city. Local government policy shifted and deliberately increased its focus on levels of scale beyond the municipal territory.

Against the background of the dynamics of market forces, the Rotterdam Real Estate Department (Grondbedrijf) received a new lease of life. The internally oriented Real Estate Department became a Real Estate Development Company focusing on external market forces. The creation of the Rotterdam City Development Corporation (Ontwikkelingsbedrijf Rotterdam) was intended to revive the urban economy under central direction and restore primacy to urban policy. The services sector emerged to compensate for the one-sided orientation on the port economy. The task of land policy was reformulated on the basis of this structural reinforcement, becoming subordinate and subservient to economic policy. Urban policy started to expressly focus on and adopt an enabling approach towards the services sector as the driving force in the modern economy.

Information technology

The new spatial planning strategy brought a shift in focus to major projects involving substantial public investment over a long period of time and great uncertainties about the market situation. The development process for a prestigious urban renewal project (Kop van Zuid) clearly demonstrated the need for a new method of budgeting in the area of land exploitation. The priority shifted to risk assessment in a market-driven environment. The traditional method of budgeting was outdated, so a different method was introduced. This eventually led to a new method of budgeting, where market information, processed using advanced information technology applications, was incorporated into the land exploitation process, representing a qualitative break with former budgeting methods. This change in budgeting methods mirrored the change in planning, from the certainty of the plan to the uncertainty of the unknown business environment. As part of this change, the myth of control was given yet another new meaning, thanks to the advanced application of information technology.

Shifting perspectives

The utilization of information technology in land exploitation calculations creates transparency in land policy. Certain developments and trends can be identified more easily and quickly. This transparency meets the need for integration at urban level under central control. A further aspect is the realization that information technology has the scope to create new information. This is not the simple calculation of policy alternatives as presented by city politicians, since the initiative there lies with the urban politicians themselves. It involves generating policy alternatives based on the current possibilities of information technology. In this way, the Rotterdam City Development Corporation (RCDC) has become responsible for the development and initiation of policy – a policy that is based on strictly functional technocratic rationality.

The advanced use of information technology in the form of computer simulation models introduces a new complexity which cannot be clearly encapsulated. The effectiveness of the parameters, the degree to which they are taken into account, is impossibly complex in the simulation model; the hierarchical pattern has disappeared from the results. So the RCDC creates its own virtual reality as it were, involving an impervious, uncontrollable and obscure chain of computer-controlled information. Large-scale and complicated combinations of databases create an entirely new political reality, which becomes an increasingly realistic competitor for our traditional forms of decision-making. The suggestion is created that you can simulate the market. For local politicians this seems to meet the requirement that the government should develop a market attitude.

The conclusion is that information technology, with its properties of calculation and transparency, is more likely to increase the complexity and obscurity of the modernization and postmodernization process. The black-box nature of the Real Estate Department seems to have given way to the RCDC as a virtual fortress.

The enabling city

The contraction of space means that the various communities around the world have been forced into competition with each other. This has resulted in localized competitive strategies and a growing awareness of what makes a place special and gives it a competitive edge. Such a reaction is far more concerned with the identity of the place, with reference to its unique qualities in an increasingly homogeneous but at the same time increasingly fragmented world. It is against the background of the qualification of time and space[5] that Rotterdam too has started to position itself as a place with its own identity. Going to considerable lengths to secure the position it desires, Rotterdam is becoming an enabling city.

The study revealed various types of essential facilitating conditions:
– The positioning of Rotterdam as a city focusing on the services sector makes it necessary to offer different types of sites to meet the differentiated demand and expectations in the office market. By providing a differentiated range of locations, where various features are on special offer as it were, the city hopes to increase the likelihood of sites meeting the requirements of businesses looking to move there.
– A wide and flexible range of plans needs to be available.
– The design and quality of the surrounding area (the conditions to attract new businesses) need to be upgraded by injecting capital.
– Rotterdam's position as an information technology interchange (telecom city) means investing in order to offer the business community all kinds of facilities and support. This means taking over investment that would otherwise have to come (or might come) from businesses.
– There needs to be support for site developments by injecting know-how not available to the private parties (financial engineering) and support based on far-reaching risk participation.
– The RCDC's open structure can be seen as a model at the administrative and innovative level, enabling market preferences and requirements to be translated into changes in the city in the facilitating sense.
– Steps are needed to promote network development involving companies, research and education institutions, etc. within certain clusters of economic activities.
– It is vital to create and provide various support services in fields such as data interchange and information technology for the business community.
– It is important to provide land for nothing or for a relatively low or significant contribution towards the price of land.

5
Compare Harvey, *The condition of postmodernity*: an enquiry into the origins of cultural change, Oxford, Blackwell 1995, pp. 201-323

– Another important factor is the significance now attached to the use of ground leases as a way of responding rapidly and flexibly to the demand for greater scope for commercial activities.

The RCDC has taken on a pioneering role in the enterprising city. As a public body it is beginning to observe market logic, with an investment strategy driven by potential demand from the market and various risky participating interests in private real estate development initiatives. The RCDC is acquiring an increasing vulnerability to market fluctuations. The logic of the market mechanism is becoming intrinsic to its structure.

The enabling city focuses on the market's flexible laws of motion and responds to that market's desire for flexibility. The enabling city makes risky investments in order to continue playing a role in the network society. Competition is intensified by the enabling attitude of cities. Existing flexibility in terms of freedom of movement is stimulated. There is a danger of an acceleration in the turnover rate of public investment in production factors seen as necessary for a continued role in the modern economy. The process of flexible accumulation and the vulnerable pattern of urban investments are becoming interconnected, reinforcing each other. The enabling city is therefore the label for the postmodern city, which provides the ideal support for this accumulation process.

The above arguments have consequences for theorizing about the city. The city as a collective consumption unit geared to social considerations has been replaced by the enabling city which must quickly and flexibly create favourable conditions for production. The study's results lead to the conclusion that the specific background to Castells' theory of the urban, as set out in "La question urbaine" in 1972[6], coincides with the high point of the welfare state. In other words, the relative constraints on cities in time and space are giving way to a qualification of time and space where cities or the places within them disappear or are created. The volatile and changeable nature of this development is associated with the process of flexible accumulation (in Harvey's terminology) and/or a chain of flexible networks (in Castells' terminology). The city supports a flexible network economy, within which links are established between the categories time and space. The notion of the city as the motor of the modern economy is giving way to a postmodern reality: the city as the enabling choice of location within a network economy.

Steering mechanisms

Instead of the traditional centralist model of government, based on the rational agency which plans and directs everything from a single point (the classical model), we have a model which takes differentiation, variety and diversity as its basic principles. The outcome of the steering mechanisms is no longer the planned result of a single actor, but the fragmented outcome of social developments and intelligent responses to them. The new steering mechanisms are characterized by great openness and variety, firstly to do justice to pluralism and secondly to prevent possible outcomes, in the sense of connections, being all-embracing.

Governance takes the shape of meta-management, i.e. remote, high-level government, while actual control is divided among a number of actors. The level of government moves to society, an unprecedented development. This means that local politicians are more likely to try to direct the decision-making procedures in an interdependent process where the ultimate determination (political or otherwise) of the goal has a contingent character. In other words, the goal is unpredictable and impossible to determine in advance. The result of management by government and other parties is coincidental and contingent. Contingency, coincidence and improbability become fundamental aspects of management.

Following Rorty[7], it is postulated that politicians under these conditions have to adopt an ironic position, irony here being the realization that views (even your own views) are contingent, products of a coincidence of circumstances. This means doing justice to the variety of decision-making possibilities, not imposing a choice. The quality of government resides precisely in the contingency of outcomes.

6
Castells, M., *La question urbaine*, Paris, Maspero 1975, pp. 295-304

7
Rorty, R., *Contingentie, ironie en solidariteit* (Contingency, irony and solidarity), Kampen, Kok Agora 1992

U1 practice studio
Students examine motorways in a commission from the Haaglanden metropolitan district

Erik Wiersema

The Faculty is presently designing a new curriculum with the intention of reserving more room for student's individual choices, and to offer an opportunity to provide other forms of education. An experiment carried out within the scope of this new curriculum consisted of a special educational project organized during the fifth period of the 1997/98 academic year. This involved what is known as a 'practice studio'. For a period of 8 weeks a group of 20 students worked on a real assignment under the supervision of 2 lecturers. The client was the Haaglanden metropolitan district, and the assignment was to carry out a study of the region's motorway network.

Sample

The project was given the name U1.

It was no coincidence that the letter U was chosen to designate this experimental form of education. The name was derived from what is known as the 'Unit' system offered at the Architectural Association (AA School) in London. In this method the lecturer is personally responsible for the decisions as to the content of 'his' unit, and the way in which the unit will work on the subject. This imparts each unit with its own very specific character, and it enables students to make a very conscious choice of the study they wish to follow. Project U1 also exhibited these features. The subject was specific to this project, and the method of working in U1 was also new.

Concentration

In principle each module at the Faculty is comprised of a number of components (design, lectures, examination, practical classes), which in combination should form an entirety. The consequence of this approach is that the student has to divide his or her time amongst a number of different assignments. In contrast to this, in the U1-project students devoted their time to one single design assignment during an 8-week period. This is the essential difference from the existing units and modules.

Symbiosis

Project U1 linked education to a real question.
The project was based on two simple observations:

Firstly, there are many questions in our daily practice that require a great deal of study, but for which no funds are available since the questions involved are not of a sufficiently high priority.

Secondly, our Faculty possesses a potential of more than 2 million extremely cheap (student) man-hours per year.

Simulator

In addition to this symbiotical link between education and practice two other characteristics also imparted project U1 with an experimental nature: it was full-time, and it was in the form of a studio. Space in the building on the Mijnbouwplein was made available especially for this studio, where the 20 students were to work full-time on the project. Each student supplied his or her own computer and printer. During the 8-week period the studio was in effect a fully-equipped architectural office with drawing boards, an area for model-making, reproduction tables, lunch and conference areas, etc. Sub-assignments and continual mutual criticism amongst the students were used, which resulted in a substantial increase in the efforts, motivation and concentration exhibited by the students. The student's performance was stimulated further by the interim presentations that were held for the clients. The fact that the results would be of practical use resulted in the student's adoption of an extremely positive and critical attitude.

Assignment

The client for project U1 was the Haaglanden metropolitan district. For some time the client had felt a need for a study of the position and significance of the motorways in this region. Increasing urbanization has resulted in motorways becoming transformed from a network of road connections between cities, into the main roads inside a continual urban landscape. These new main roads are now used daily by hundreds of thousands of people, and as a result they have become some of the most public places in the city. The streets have become a location from which the city is perceived, and consequently a feature that (jointly) contributes to the identity of the city. This is a transformation that the Haaglanden region, in particular, will encounter during the coming years. The new position and significance of the motorways offers new opportunities for buildings along these roads. A study of these opportunities will enable the Haaglanden metropolitan district to draw the attention of the all municipalities in the region to this transformation, and to take the initial steps towards formulating a joint regional vision for the development of the areas along the motorways.

Result

The final result was of a high quality. The use of the full-time studio made it possible to create a finished product of unprecedented value. Each student was required to complete his or her project in the form of pages to be supplied in digital form, including illustrations, text, and photos of models in a individual lay-out, to be used for the publication of a joint book. This book contains some 200 full-colour pages with a complete spectrum of possible suggestions that may be of assistance to the client.

Mobility

Local traffic transferium for Amsterdam

Reshmi Oemrawsingh and Mark Westerhuis
graduation project Architectural Design

mentors
Prof. Pi de Bruijn, Prof. Arie Krijgsman, Willem Hermans

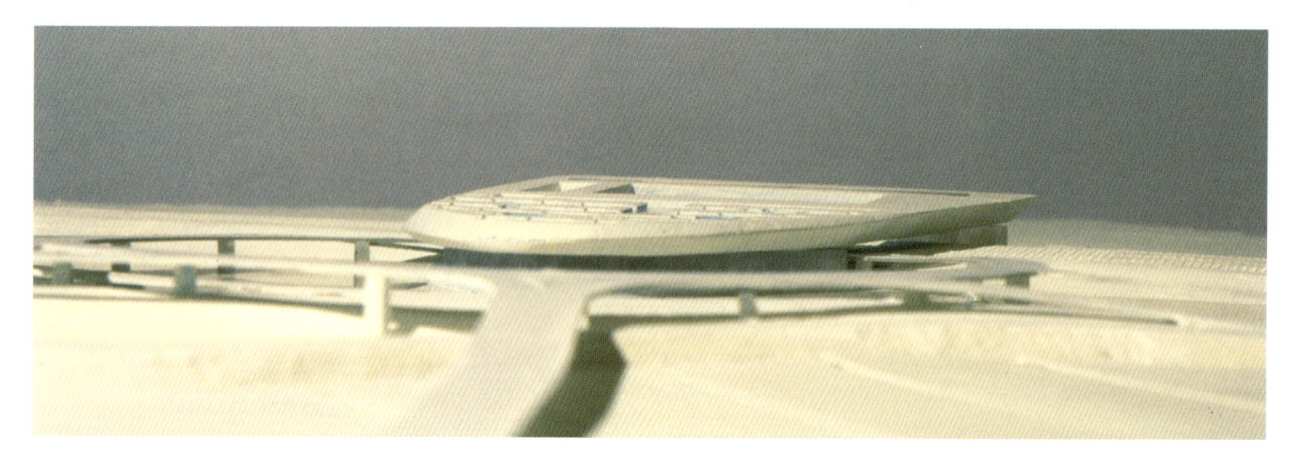

The government is striving towards a general reduction in car use. The goals are to improve the environment and to improve the accessibility of economic centres. For the realization of the environmental goal, cleaner technology should be considered in particular. The reduction of car use can only be achieved where the potential of public transport is present as a worthy competitor. This is the case in areas with high densities and an existing high-quality public transport system. Only these strategic locations are eligible for investments in public transport. 'Transferia' open up these areas – with public transport as the main transport system – for the car user. A 'transferium' should entice car users to swap the car for public transport. A ring of 'transferia' form the *trait d'union* between the town centre and the periphery, improving the accessibility of the town centre and shifting the parking pressure. On account of the expected impulses that such infrastructural intersections can deliver, it is proposed to link transferia to large-scale programmes that do not fit in town centres. Hereby the transfer process can take place in luxury accommodation.
The spatial differentiation in the region can be reinforced by programme themes. Large-scale programmes which otherwise lie in the periphery are now combined and opened up with public transport.

Ring of transferia around Amsterdam

Lattice girders form a framework within which variable functions can take place

Three types of transferia can be distinguished within the Randstad. *Origin transferia* intercept the car users almost immediately, and subsequently enable them to travel by public transport. These are relatively small transferia, distributed throughout the entire Randstad. *Green belt transferia* lie between the area of origin and destination. Within the Randstad these transferia will mainly lie between the four major cities. *Local transferia* are situated close to the destination and have the greatest chance of success, as the quality of public transport is the highest within and around the cities.

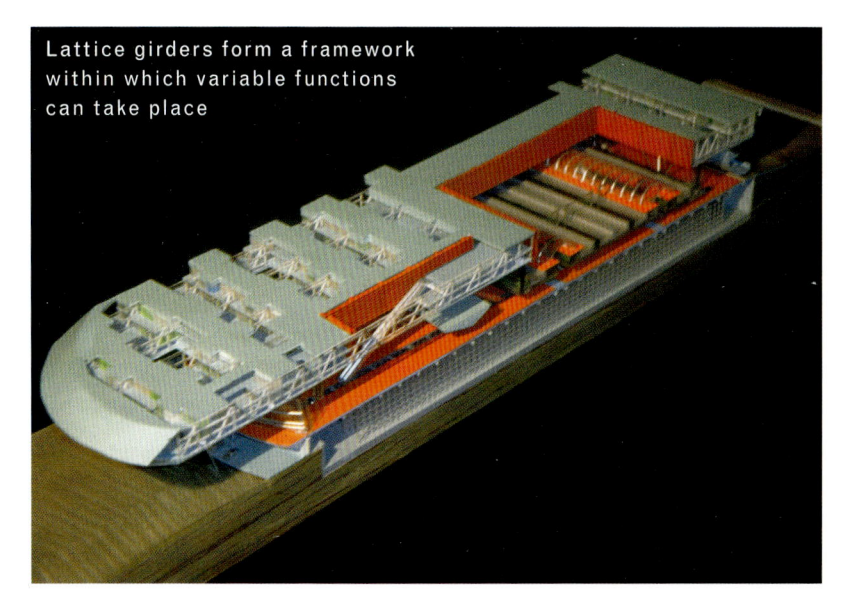

The plan area is situated in the green outskirts of Amsterdam-Zuidoost and the future IJburg. The concept for the new landscape aims to intensify the existing dual structure, i.e. the infra(structure)landscape and the polder landscape.
The intersection has been redesigned with a connection to the new IJburg exit so that a link is created between rail, road and programme. The large-scale trotting and race track will also function as economic carrier for the polder landscape.

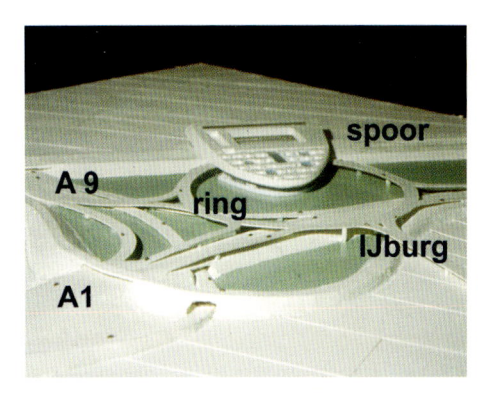

New junction: separation of through traffic and local traffic

Mobility

Local traffic transferium for Amsterdam

Local traffic transferium

The new Diemen intersection separates through-traffic from local traffic. A ring-road is created above the intersection of the A1 and A9 motorways, which provides access to IJburg and the transferium. The size of the ring makes it possible to actually connect the motorway with the railway line. Traffic jam-free access to the transferium (re-use of the carpool lane), car garaging by means of a mechanical parking system and air-conditioned waiting rooms ensure that the transfer is a pleasant experience. The central space in the transferium is the transfer hall, which not only regulates the transfer from car to train and bus, but also serves as entrance for the remaining programme. The constructive and spatial structure provides for a fixed programme core around which variable functions can take place. The fixed functions include the transfer machine with an underground car warehouse and the trotting and race track. The variable functions are situated on a plane, suspended above the railway line and the ring-road. The construction of this plane consists of lattice girders that form a freely divisible framework. The patio hotel and the conference centre have been designed to test the possible functions. From the intersection the transferium looks like a boulder which has been polished by a pedestal of infrastructure. The panorama to the polder opens up on the other side. The most generous space is created in the intersection under the boulder. Unprogrammed but indispensable, this space provides a view of the infrastructure: a meeting point.

Amstel Inter Modal Centre

Stefan van der Spek
graduation project Architectural Design

mentors
Prof. Pi de Bruijn, Pieter van Drongelen, Prof. Dirk Frieling, Wim Kamerling

Transport interchanges have become the subject of growing interest in recent years. When stations and station areas are redeveloped, property development and commercial functions often dominate the thinking, while the optimum interchange between the various modalities is a secondary consideration. The work of the *OVerstapMachine* studio involves the search for compact, functional and integrated designs for transfer points.[1]

In the existing situation the Amstel Station[2] is situated beside the railway embankment and the tracks can be reached via a *low tunnel*. *Three exits* from the station hall provide access to the other modalities: the main exit leads to the taxis, bikes and Kiss&Ride, another exit leads to the parking area and international coaches, and a tunnel leads to the trams. The *city and regional buses are scattered around the station*.

The location is characterized by *extensive use of space* and *confusion* for travellers due to the absence of *visual relationships* between platform, hall and public space. The high quality of the distinctive hall is largely cancelled out by the *quality and functioning of the interchange*. In the next few years the *pressure* on this transfer point will increase due to growth in nearby offices and homes, and growth of the number of passengers.

The design is based on the following principles:
– The optimum transfer mechanism is achieved by combining all modalities compactly under one roof.
– A transfer point is the most public building in the city.
– The identity and accessibility of a transfer point should not disappear behind the additional commercial programme.
– The number of level crossings and conflicts between transport flows (interface) should be kept to a minimum.
– connection, assembly and distribution function, and the concentration function[3] should be maximized.

As well as an increase in density in the surrounding neighbourhoods, a comprehensive and varied programme is introduced in the immediate vicinity[4], in order to improve not only safety but also the attractiveness of the interchange.

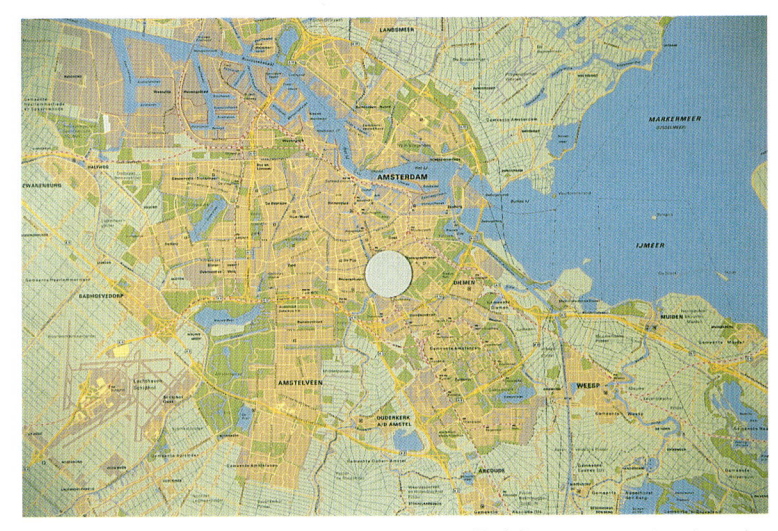

Public transport network

1
See also *De OVerstapMachine*, TUD, 1998
2
Amstel Station, Van Eesteren, 1938
3
Interchanges in public transport networks, RvVW, 1996
4
See drawings of cross-sections

Amstel Inter Modal Centre

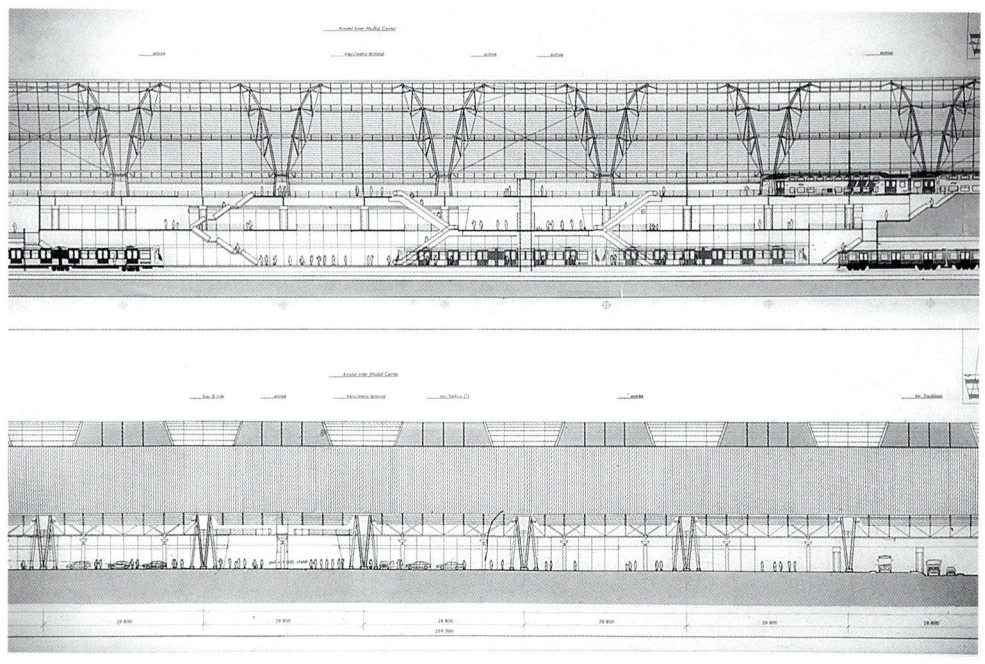

Longitudinal sections

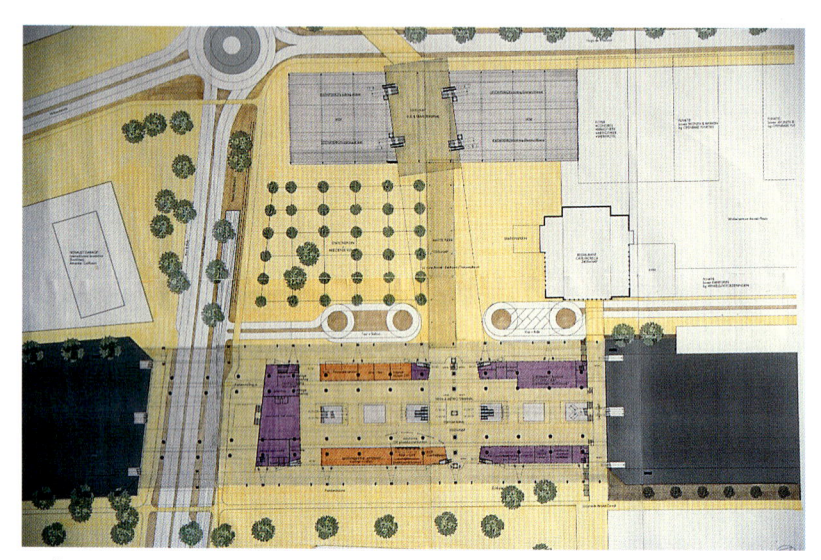

Programme intersection

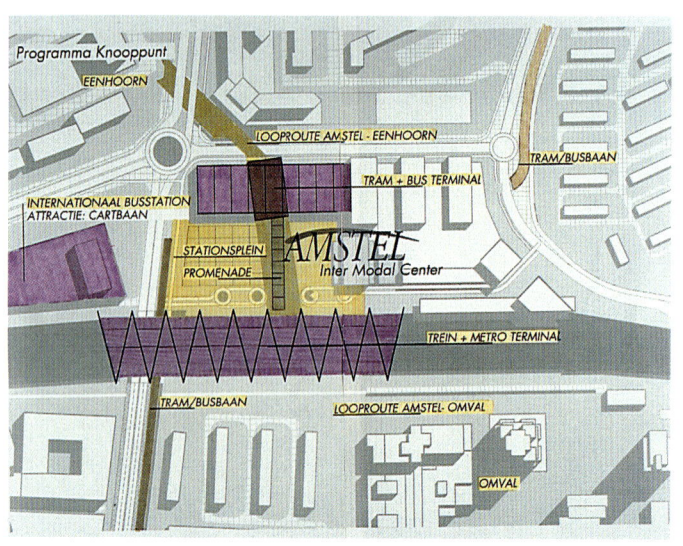

Programme context

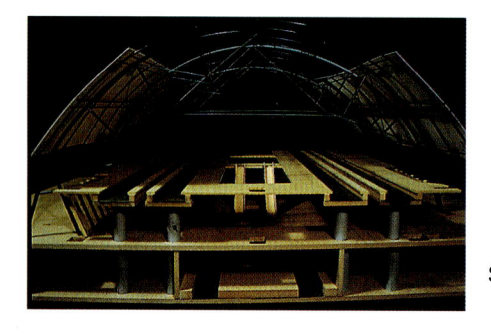

Scale model

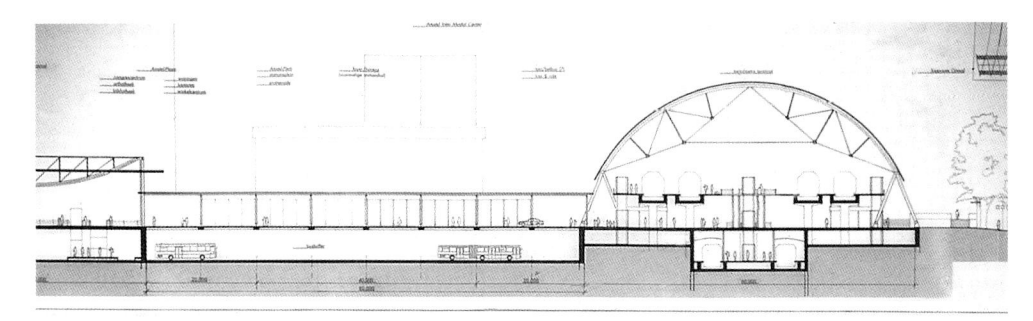

Cross-sections

To transform Amstel Station into an Inter Modal Centre, the old roof has been removed and the railway embankment replaced in some places by a bridge over a continuous square[4]. The old station hall has been retained for its spatial quality and forms the pivot of a new centre with commercial and service functions. The transfer mechanism consists of three elements: two parallel terminals, linked by a square with a covered route. The ground level and square together form the interface.

The bus/tram tracks carry on like a moving river beneath the interface. To make the transfer process smoother, there are separate platforms for getting on and off. This also makes it possible to design them differently. Special entrance and exit doors have been used at the metro and the tube is separated from the platform by a glass wall.

The metro is one level below the surface in the new situation, enabling the largest transport flow to move through quickly, compactly and efficiently. The trains travel one level above the surface. The central Intercity platform has a direct link with the metro. There are a large number of openings to provide the central metro platform with daylight.

The public nature of the terminals has been developed in terms of accessibility. The public spaces are large, logical and conveniently arranged, and contain plenty of information. The main principle is the transport function and facilities are of secondary importance. The materials and design are both durable and geared to the human scale.

The structure is built up of Polonceau trusses on A-trestles, spanning an area of 60m altogether. These have been rotated, creating a dynamic and unique picture. The trusses are linked by three-dimensional girders, on which the roof trusses are fixed. The roofing consists of closed KALZIP bands and transparent panels.

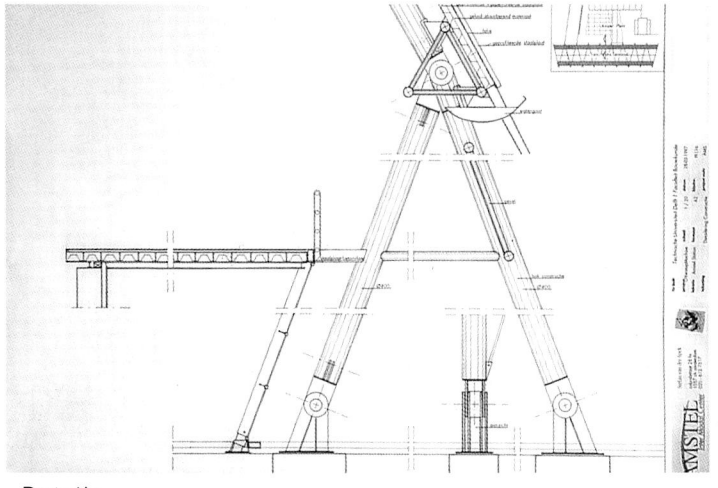

Details

The Arnhem-Nijmegen interchange

Christiaan de Wolf
graduation project Architectural Design and Building Technology

mentors
Prof. Cees Dam, Prof. Ab Trotz, Prof. Arie Krijgsman, Prof. Dirk Frieling

The graduation project involves the design of a transport interchange, in this case located in the Arnhem-Nijmegen region. It creates a link for various types of local and regional traffic: pedestrians, cyclists, motorists, bus passengers, cable railway passengers and train passengers. The design covers a large number of scales. It includes proposals for the urban planning of the region, the suburbs and the city square, and proposals for the facilities for the various types of traffic. Some of these facilities have been worked out in detail, with proposals ranging from the use and shape of the space, via the main design of the structures, down to details of shop fronts, wind breaks and parapets, adding up to a very comprehensive project. The various elements, the different scales, and the space and materials have been largely integrated in the final plan. The design provides a picture of an important phenomenon that will in reality need to be developed in the near future.

Region

In view of the complexity of both the area and the assignment, an outline of the region was designed as the starting point, based on three themes (types of landscape, models of urban planning principles, mobility). A typical three-dimensional effect is the exceptional clash and contrast between the closed nature of the high lateral moraines and the openness of the low-lying basins and the river/water meadows landscape. The model is the linear city, a theoretical polycentric structural principle, with high-quality public transport providing the link between the two urban concentrations. With economic development concentrated mainly in the Overbetuwe region, the housing/labour market areas of Arnhem and Nijmegen merge and cross-river traffic increases.

These themes result in an outline of the region characterized by a number of high-density centres, specialized in function and connected by a subsidiary motorway link, and a centrally located, high-quality rail link, which can carry a large number of passengers quickly and directly, thus creating the basis for spatial developments.

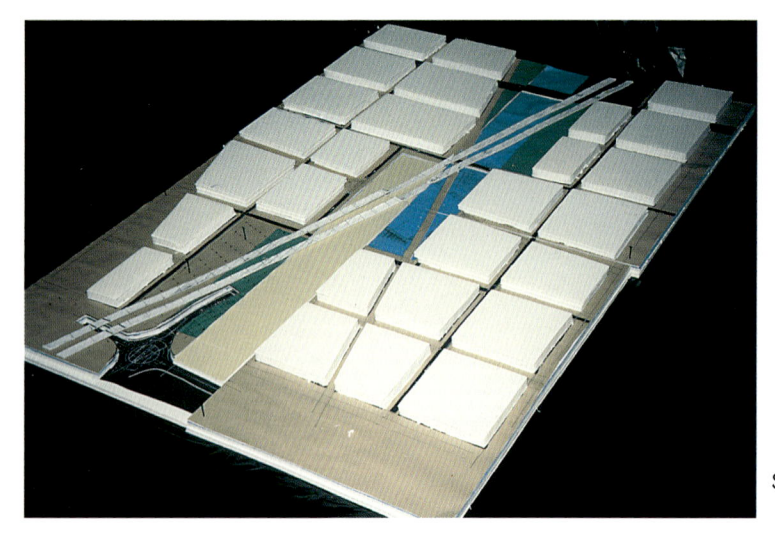

Scheme of urban situation

Suburbs

The Waalsprong is a site for fifty thousand inhabitants on the edge of a compact metropolitan region. The presence of various types of landscape and water makes this a characteristic green/blue attraction for the public. The location between large urban concentrations creates an environment suggesting a sub-centre, with a strong mix of commercial and public functions. Internal access routes are based on the grid structure, creating a central area that is flexible with shifting boundaries.

Freedom for programmatic and architectonic details makes it easier to manage urban transformations. Clustering in enclaves and urban ensembles increases the density in favour of the landscape surrounding the Waalsprong. The central location gives the transfer mechanism a connecting and central role. The station area with its small-scale 24-hour businesses functions as part of the city centre for the public. The daytime/evening functions are directly related and promote symbiosis.

Model

Section

Transport interchange

In spatial terms the station area is characterized by three main directions (transport corridor, main shopping route, historical axis), forming the basis for a grid. This is used to determine the positioning of architectonic and building technological elements on various scales. As a result the various modalities independently cross each other and run parallel.

The composition is also based on good access and short walking distances. The transport corridor is the regional link and crosses the main shopping route, which functions as a local route for slow-moving traffic between the two parts of the centre. The historical axis provides the link with the old village centre. The openness of the transport corridor with respect to the urban fabric minimizes the barrier effect. The canopy roof functions as an element linking all the urban movements and forms the public space.

Change at Delft

Ada Beuling
graduation project Architectural Design

mentors
Prof. Pi de Bruijn, Arie Krijgsman, George Hotze

In the current situation at Delft station, the trains travel through the town on a viaduct, which has room for two tracks. On most of the section from Rotterdam to The Hague there are four tracks. This makes Delft a bottleneck. When this section is widened, the best solution would be to place it entirely underground and remove the viaduct. Studies of interchanges show clearly that trains account for the largest number of passengers. It is noticeable that many travellers use a combination of bike and train. The provision of bicycle sheds is a problem at many stations in the Netherlands and bikes carelessly parked all over the place are a familiar sight.

Bearing this in mind, the following objective was formulated:
To design a new station for Delft, with four railway tracks below the surface, based on the following principles:
– the transfer between the different systems of transport should take place as smoothly as possible
– the station should be successfully integrated into the town
– there should be an attempt to solve the problem of providing bicycle sheds

The following criteria also played a role:
– short walking distances
– convenience and simplicity
– no time-wasting features

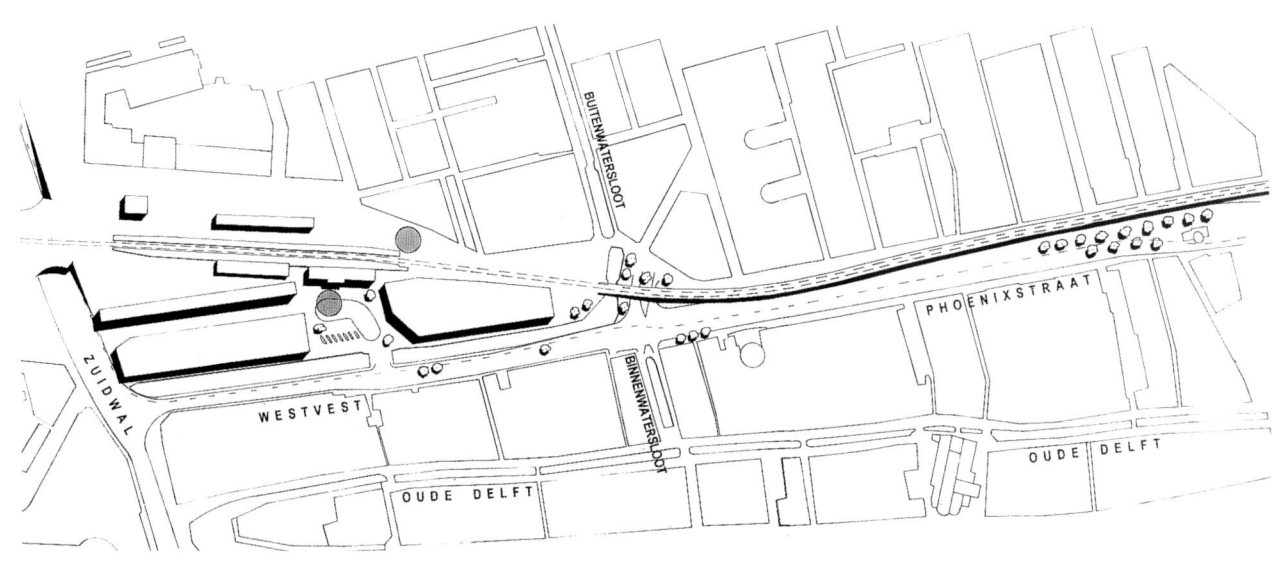

Delft, present situation

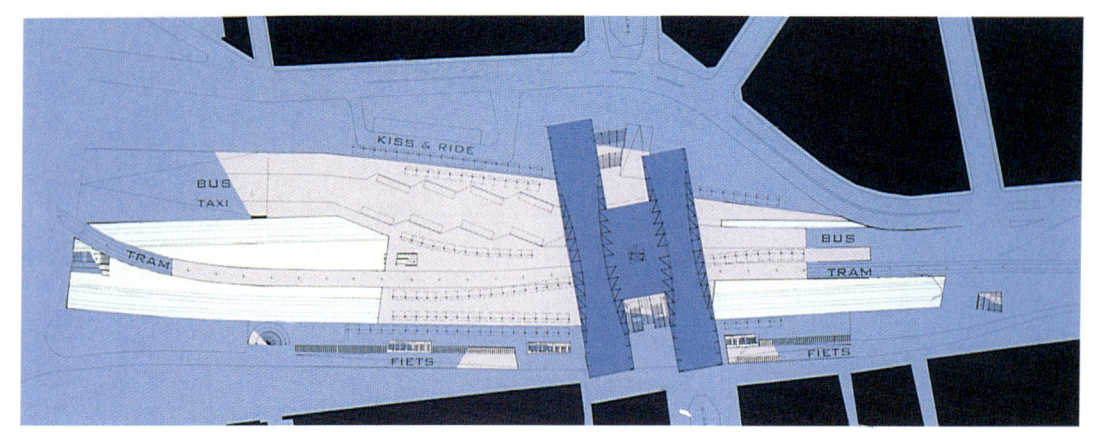

Plan at ground level Traffic flows

Level −2, ten metres below the surface, is intended for trains. There are four tracks with a central platform. Trains that stop at Delft travel on the central tracks, while through trains use the two outer tracks. This creates a straightforward situation for travellers. Stairs and escalators have been placed at the end of the platform. As level -2 is only half under cover, the train platforms are clearly visible from the upper levels.

Level -1, four metres below the surface, provides space for tram and bus stops, taxis, and an underground car park. From here people can transfer to another means of transport. The station facilities, restaurant facilities, ticket offices and shops are also situated on this level. There is a pedestrian zone, created by a disproportionately large zebra crossing.

Level 0, ground level, is constructed as a bridge over the various transport combinations. The surface is made of sand-blasted glass, illuminated from below at night. The whole structure comes across as a crystallized sugar confection. The bridge is designed to catch people's eye; it is the only section extending above ground, making it a distinguishing feature.

Section through mega-parking for bicycles

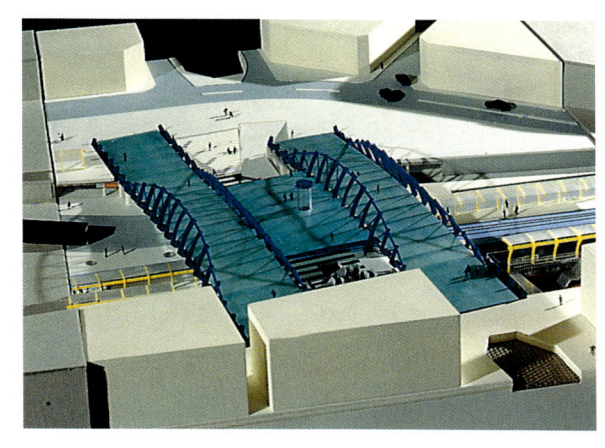

The square as a bridge over
the various traffic flows

The parking of bikes is a problem at every station, despite the Netherlands' reputation as a cyclists' paradise. The problem has been solved in this design by providing proper facilities for cyclists: sufficient spaces and room, convenience, avoiding wasted time. In principle the system works like an underground car park. The ramp in the station is also the through-cycle route. This ensures that the cycle sheds are close by the station and walking distances are kept as short as possible. The sheds have room for 5800 bikes, some in a secure area. For extra convenience a special cycle stand is used, with sensors to indicate whether or not the space is already occupied.

Delft station has become a dynamic interchange and a vital feature of the urban scene, partly because it has been moved closer to the centre of town. Transport routes that create barriers are now underground, providing extra space for the urban theatre to flourish. The station itself is designed to function as efficiently as possible, to be convenient for travellers and to minimize the time needed to find the way. All this helps to make the use of public transport more attractive.

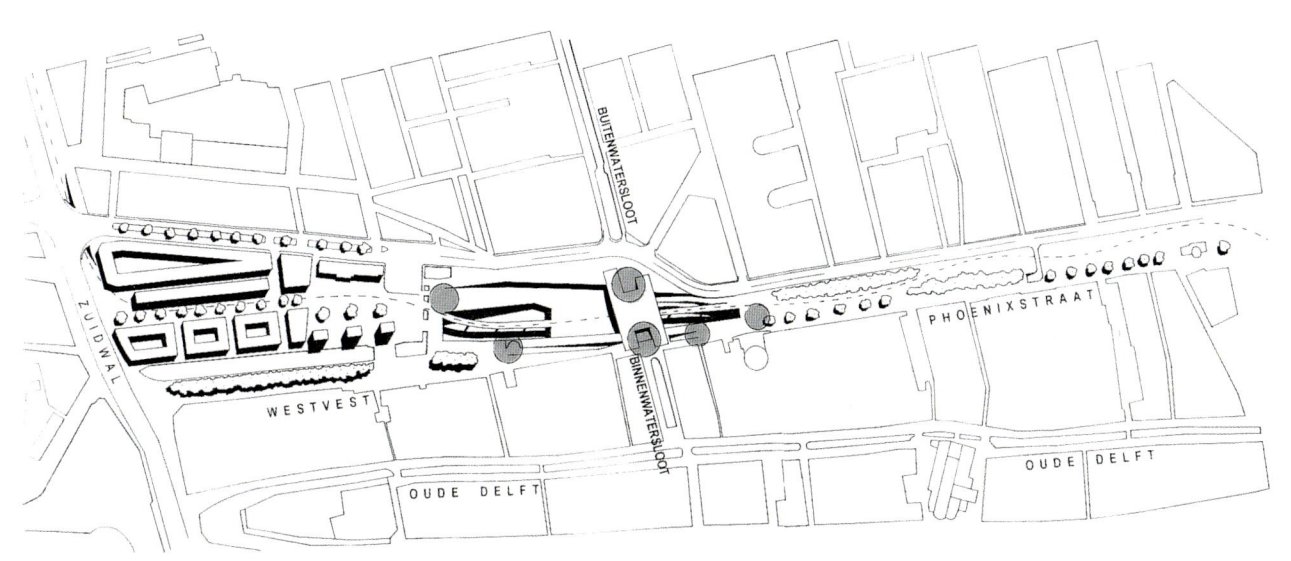

Delft, new situation

Interaction-model for concern and location synergy in the station environment

Gert-Joost Peek
graduation project Real Estate and Project Management

mentors
Prof. Hans de Jonge, Jo Soeter, Prof. Dirk Frieling

Virtually every large or medium-sized city in the Netherlands has seen major changes in the station environment in the recent past or will experience such changes in the future. Efforts are being made to find a new design for many of the station locations in order to meet the growing demand for accommodation and travel facilities. The causes of this demand include the government's spatial planning and mobility policy, the development of new transport systems and the expansion of existing ones, and the changes in the organization of urban areas.

Station locations tend to be redesigned under pressure from the property and transport markets. As a result of the dual nature of the station location, conflicting interests are often involved: a station location functions both as a node in a network and a place in the city. [1] Redevelopment can therefore be defined as the problem of integrating node and place.[2]

With the privatization of the Dutch railways, the conflicts of interests between node and place have also become evident within the concern itself. *Node* is represented by the business unit *NS Reizigers*, responsible for passenger transport, while *place* is represented by the business unit *NS Vastgoed*, which concentrates on developing and managing property in the vicinity of stations. But the combination of these two core activities also provides scope for the creation of horizontal concern synergy. This type of synergy occurs when added value is achieved between different units of the same concern, without the decentralized responsibilities of the units in question being significantly affected. [3]

This graduation project provides insight into how the activities of *NS Reizigers* and *NS Vastgoed* can reinforce each other. A model describing the effect of location synergy in the station environment has been developed. The model was then applied in a study of the relationship between closeness to a station and the level of investments in office space in Amsterdam.

The model consists of three components: the station environment, the local property market, and the local collective transport market. *The station environment* is composed of static and dynamic elements. The interaction of people with this environment creates the conditions for its perception. The total area containing a station can be divided into the *transfer area*, the *station environment* and the *station area*.

An examination of the market position of *NS Reizigers* and *NS Vastgoed* provides a good starting point for examining the scope for concern synergy in the vicinity of stations. *NS Reizigers* is a player on the (local) collective transport market, while *NS Vastgoed* operates on the (local) property market. The two markets can be represented within the location-specific context of a station

concept of quality		definition	interconnections
stay	travel		
morphology		*static elements*: buildings and infrastructure	accommodation for dynamic elements
place	**node**	*dynamic elements*: accommodation and travel functions	use of real estate by businesses, institutions and individuals
perception		*experience*: complex of static and dynamic elements	perception of environment by individual participants in dynamic functions

Definition of four features of the station environment

designation	area	qualifying feature	indication of size
transfer area	... which is used by transfer functions	node	circle with radius of 100 m, with the stations focal point as centre
station environment	... which is determined by perception of the transfer function	perception	circle with a radius of 300 m, with the stations focal point as centre
station area	... within walking distance of the station	place	circle with a radius of 1000 m, with the stations focal point as centre

Spatial layout of station environment

environment as a succession of niche markets. A plot of land bypasses these niche markets and is eventually used for transport or property functions. Buyers and sellers take joint decisions in both these niche markets. These decisions lead to the construction of buildings or their use and thus have an impact on the four features of the station environment.

NS Vastgoed operates in the local property market as the owner of the land and buildings. Thus the results of its property investments are determined by the decisions taken in two of the niche markets within the property market: the *land use designation* and the *building use decision*. The latter decision is taken in the building services market. The land use designation and the building use decision affect the feature *place* and are in turn affected by the four features of the station's vicinity: *morphology*, *place*, *node* and *perception*. I have concentrated on the impact of the synergy between two features, *place* and *node*, on the land use designation and the building use decision.

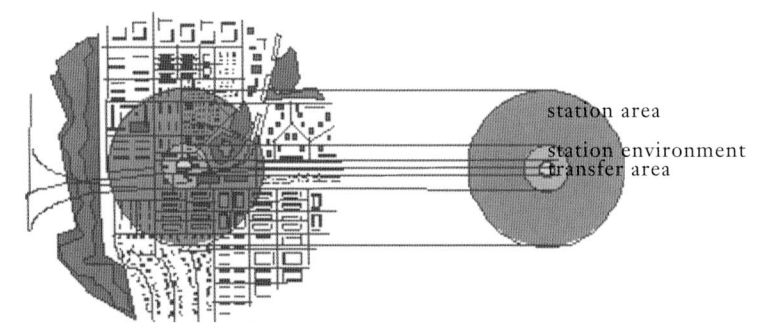

Spatial layout of station environment

Case study Amsterdam

The empirical part of the study examined the environment of seven stations in Amsterdam: Amsterdam CS, Sloterdijk, Amstel, Lelylaan, Zuid/WTC, Rai and Bijlmer, using the *distance decay method*. This method assumes that the impact of the presence of a station on the environment will diminish as the distance from the station increases.

The way a plot of land can be used is decided by the local authority. The revenue that the land can generate is determined by this. Station locations are designated for labour-intensive and visitor-intensive functions as part of national mobility policy. The case study in Amsterdam shows that as a result of this policy almost 50 per cent of the over 1.9 million square metres (gross) of office space built since 1981 is within 500 metres of a station.

The building use decision springs from the choice of location made by the office user as part of the process of finding business premises. Nearly every office user considers accessibility by car to be the most important factor. The importance attached to accessibility by public transport depends more on the individual company. In general this is not a decisive factor in choosing the location, although its importance is increasing.

The building use decision by users and owners of office buildings is laid down in a lease. The rent agreed in this contract provides the best indication of the user's rating of the location and building.

In the Netherlands the rents of offices are highest around intercity stations. At the same time building quality is higher than average.[4] If the weighted average rental transaction prices for Amsterdam in the period 1984-1996 are compared with the distance from the station, we find that closeness to the station has a positive effect on rental transaction prices in the vicinity of Sloterdijk, Amstel, Zuid-WTC and Bijlmer stations. The transaction rents in the area of Amstel, Zuid-WTC, Rai and Bijlmer stations are higher than the average transaction rent in this period.

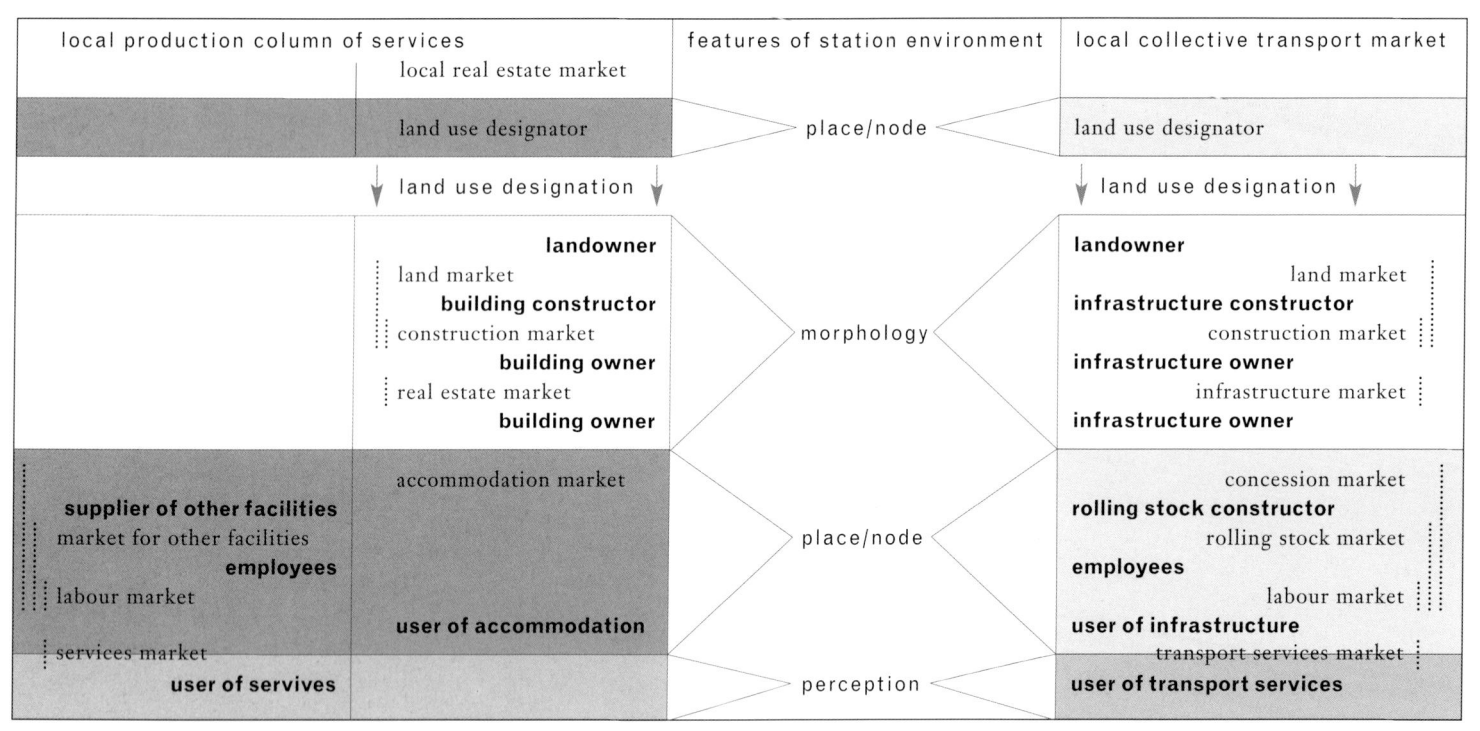

Interaction-model for concern and location synergy in the station environment

local production column of services		features of station environment	local collective transport market
	local real estate market		
	land use designator	place/node	land use designator
	↓ land use designation ↓		↓ land use designation ↓
	landowner		**landowner**
	land market		land market
	building constructor	morphology	**infrastructure constructor**
	construction market		construction market
	building owner		**infrastructure owner**
	real estate market		infrastructure market
	building owner		**infrastructure owner**
	accommodation market		concession market
supplier of other facilities			**rolling stock constructor**
market for other facilities		place/node	rolling stock market
employees			**employees**
labour market			labour market
	user of accommodation		**user of infrastructure**
services market			transport services market
user of servives		perception	**user of transport services**

Influence of the features place and node on the land use designation and accommodation decision

Conclusion

The Amsterdam situation shows that closeness to a station can clearly be instrumental in upgrading the value of offices. The main conditions for this are good accessibility by car and sufficient parking space. When the station area is not easily accessible by car, as in the case of Central Station, closeness to the station does not lead to increasing rents.

The study also shows that in the office development market, providers have a far greater influence on office locations than one would expect in such a demand-driven market. Local authorities' spatial planning policy has a tremendous influence on office locations. In addition there is a growing tendency for property developers to decide on the location. The preference of investors and property developers for a certain location has just as much to do with both sides acquiring confidence in a location as with the actual characteristics of the location.[5]

This analysis has concentrated on the synergy between the features *place* and *node*, describing its impact on the development of property values of offices near stations. However this is only a first step towards understanding the interaction of the four features of station environments. Research into this effect is urgently needed in view of the investment that is about to take place in connection with certain key projects (Amsterdam's southern axis, Utrecht Centre Project, Arnhem Central and Rotterdam Central Station). Research into integrated area development should not be restricted to station locations: the resulting information, methods and solutions are after all applicable to other city centre redevelopment projects too.

1
Bertolini, L., 'Nodes and places: complexities of railway station redevelopment', *European Planning Studies*, 3, 1996, p. 332

2
Zweedijk, A., *Knoop of plaats*: naar een operationalisering van het begrip stationslocatie (Node or place: making the concept of the station location work), Utrecht, Faculty of Town and Country Planning, University of Utrecht 1997, p. 2

3
Wijers, G.J., 'De onontkoombare vraag naar horizontale synergie' (The inescapable demand for horizontal synergy), *Holland Management Review*, 41, 1994, p. 14

4
Venema, P., en H.J.J. Kloosterman, 'De ideale kantoorlocatie' (The ideal office location), *Rooilijn*, 5, 1997, p. 243

5
Louw, E., *Kantoorgebouw en vestigingsplaats*: een geografisch onderzoek naar de rol van huisvesting bij locatiebeslissingen van kantoorhoudende organisaties (Office building and business location: a geographical study of the role of accommodation in location decisions by organizations using offices), Delft, Delft University Press, 1996, p. 107

Development in development
The creation of an ideal environment to use telematics in an expansion of Leeuwarden

Paulien Eisma
graduation project Urbanism

mentors
Prof. Henco Bekkering, Prof. Dr Paul Drewe, Rob Aben

Suppose that the office where you work is situated somewhere in the Randstad. You don't want to live there, however, but rather in Friesland. The province has always attracted you because of its spaciousness, the water, the space, the down-to-earth people who live there... Furthermore, the land prices there are much lower, so a slightly more luxurious lifestyle is also possible there. How can you do this?

By means of telematics it is in principle possible to maintain an office all over the world, so including Friesland. Teleworking is possible at home and outside the home. The home and the local environment become the centre for everyday activities. At home, a workplace is essential and should preferably not be in the living room. The home assumes a more public character, it must be larger and broader and it must be flexible. Outside the home, you can work in your car or in an office in the neighbourhood where several people work in the same way, with the necessary facilities. You cannot do without the requisite technologies, such as ISDN line, fax, telephone and computer.

By using telematics a location can occupy an important position in the national network. The entire country becomes the working area, so that a place of residence no longer needs to be close to the place of work. Leeuwarden can take advantage of this by creating an ideal environment to facilitate the use of telematics.

Because people live and work in a district, more people will spend more time in the local environment and the services will be used more intensively. Most functions acquire a more network-like structure and can therefore in principle be situated anywhere in the area. There is thus no standard model for a telematics expansion. Besides hierarchical development, a more distributed development is now also possible.

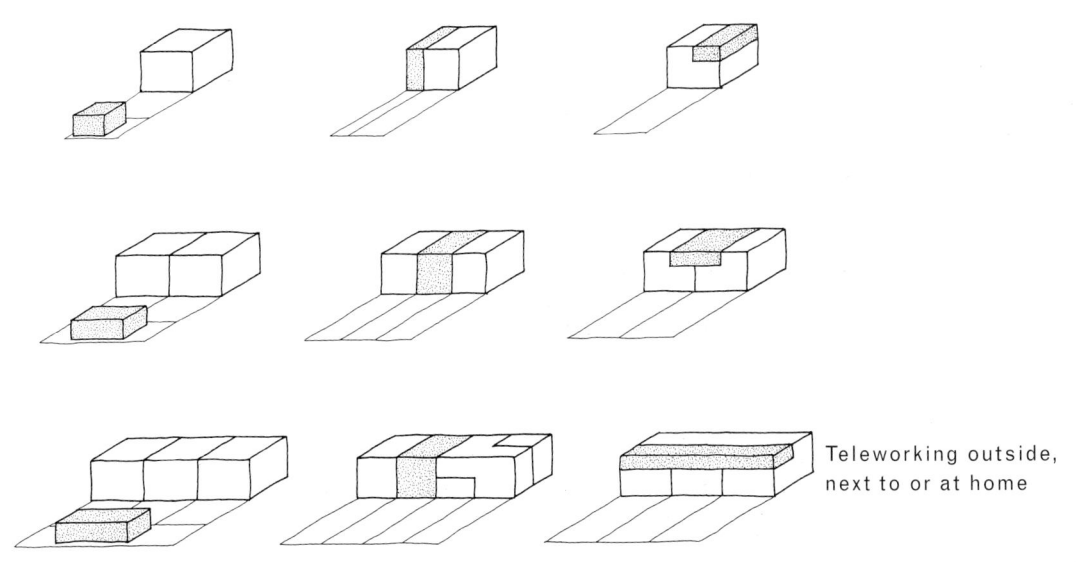

Teleworking outside, next to or at home

Development in development

dwelling and working places
small-scale facilities
large-scale facilities
virtual facilities
parks and green areas
business
schools

Functional layers

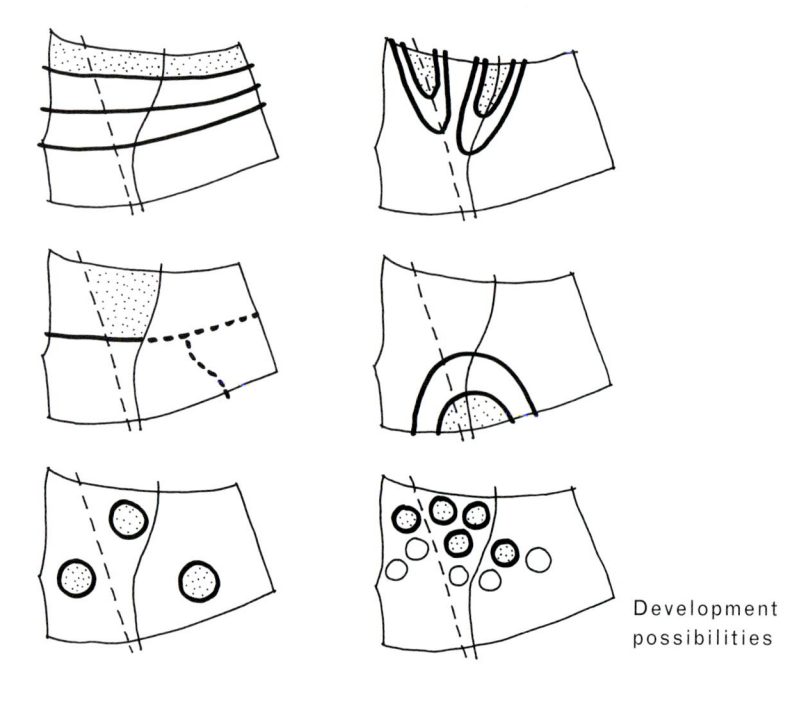

Development possibilities

The existing landscape and how it is perceived plays an important role in the design of a telematics development. There is more freedom in the choice of location. Homeworkers will choose their location on the basis of the quality of a house and the residential environment in attractive areas. Living *in* the landscape instead of *on* the landscape. The existing natural elements and the characteristics of the landscape must therefore play an important role in the design. The landscape can be experienced in many different ways.

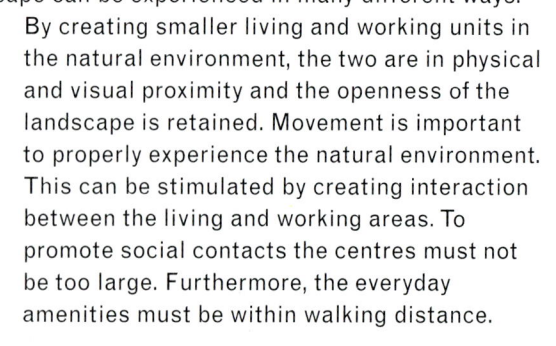

By creating smaller living and working units in the natural environment, the two are in physical and visual proximity and the openness of the landscape is retained. Movement is important to properly experience the natural environment. This can be stimulated by creating interaction between the living and working areas. To promote social contacts the centres must not be too large. Furthermore, the everyday amenities must be within walking distance.

Working in an attractive environment

I refer to the living and working units as *hubs* and each is a self-supporting unit where people can live and work and has its own amenities. The quality of a hub is partly determined by the structure and the location. The hubs can differ in time, programme, size, identity and density. They do not have to be simultaneously developed because they can function in isolation, thus not directly dependent upon other hubs.

Finally, the most important differences between an 'ordinary' expansion and this telematics expansion. No distinction between living spaces and working spaces is required. The expansion does not involve the transformation of the entire area into a living and working area, rather the creation of home-work nuclei in the green belt so that the natural environment continues up to the existing outskirts of the city.

This makes clear what influence the development of telematics has on the development of Leeuwarden. Hence the title "development in development".

Mobility

Utrecht coronary
A donor heart or body without organs?

Alex de Jong
graduation project Architectural Design

mentors
Bernard Leupen, Willem Hermans, Frans Boot

Urban railway station becomes conference centre and exhibition centre entrance

Mosque/market square between facade of exhibition halls

Exhibition square between exhibition halls and offices

According to the Utrecht ultra-right-winger Henk van Lingen, the city is suffering from a heart attack. In his opinion, the city is full and needs to be operated on. The council is completely in agreement with him. The fact that Mr Van Lingen talks about people while the council talks about programme and infrastructure doesn't really matter in the final analysis. Both solutions are prompted by an exaggerated obsession with identity and singularity.

Despite the city's substantial increase in surface area and population, the council continues to see the centre as the problem for its stagnating economic growth. The centre must be better and larger. In this way, the identity of the infrastructural hub of the Netherlands and thus Utrecht itself will not be lost.

If, however, the area around the Utrecht central railway station is analysed, it is clear than one of the best locations in the Netherlands is currently occupied by the exhibition centre, a 'B-function'. If this were to be moved, Utrecht would gain a 27-hectare high-quality location on which to develop offices and urban housing without much difficulty.

Exhibition halls as passive building block without perspective

Oscar Niemeyer's arches and vaults as technique for the *Kantian big*

The Cartesian triangle in the west of Utrecht will shortly be released for a new use. In this respect, the exhibition centre can be deployed as a 'tool', a first step towards a multi-dimensional Utrecht with a collection of centres instead of one centre and periphery. The exhibition centre can be employed as a new (sub)centre which improves adjoining areas. The overloaded area in the west of Utrecht must have an organization that opens up rather than excludes existing qualities for development. This organization is found in the infrastructure. Not only will the area around the station and the Leidsche Rijn benefit from good connections, but at least one third of the exhibition programme will also consist of the organization of infrastructure.

Two new approach roads connect independent urban elements. Specific moments are created from empirical data about the city. The exhibition centre lies passively alongside the infrastructure and the specific moments. The various elements, such as mosque, market square, conference centre and workshops shape the roof of the exhibition centre.

The diversity which exists between the urban elements can only remain understandable if there is not too much 'noise' around them. To achieve this, a design technique must be used which turns the halls into a single entity.

Inspired by clouds, mountains and buxom, perfumed women, Oscar Niemeyer discovered the technique of the large gesture in arches and basins. The building is not seen as a collection of architectural elements, rather the entire building as image. This technique can be used to make a construction with hollows and bulges, adapting its appearance to its surroundings, in this case the urban programme.

Mobility

Relief of residential district by connecting access roads

Separate urban programme between exhibition centre as basic principle for open organization

A construction must be found which endorses the above-mentioned properties. This construction must not disintegrate into a collection of elements or become a meta-structure of which the urban moments are a result.

The construction is seen as a space frame. Space frames can accommodate push and pull and do not transfer a moment onto their supports, thus facilitating economic building. Space frame supports do not have to be placed at regular intervals so that it is possible to optimally deal with the difficult location. With the emergence of CAD-CAM techniques in the design process, space frames can be used differently. As a result, irregular deflections are possible.

The roof can be high and low as required. In between, it has the maximum number of hollows and bulges permitted by the space frame construction. The specific urban elements push the roof downwards, the need for height under the roof pushes it upwards. The roof is a great gesture clarifying the individual parts of the programme. The manifestations of the roof clarify the position or the appearance of the independent elements.

Rotterdam Grand Prix

Rico Zweers
graduation project Architectural Design

mentors
Fridjof van den Berg, Prof. Jan Brouwer, Willem Hermans

A Formula One race through the streets of a Dutch city would produce a fantastic combination of stillness and speed, of man and machine. The only city in the Netherlands where such a race could be organized is Rotterdam, a city which has wide roads, a metro system, an airport, a ring road, and the sophistication and experience needed for the organization of major events. The layout of the circuit and the integration of the programme into a busy city were very important for the elaboration of this project. The resulting circuit is over five kilometres long, linking together the north and south districts of Rotterdam. The presence of the Nieuwe Maas means that much of the event's logistics can take place by water.

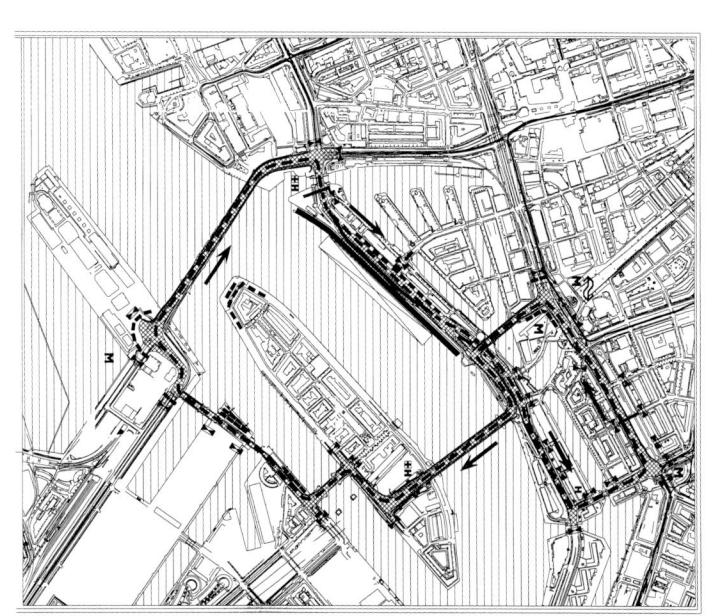

Rotterdam is a city where many events are organized, including the marathon, the summer carnival and the film festival. The largest event Rotterdam could have would be an annual Formula One race. A *Dutch Grand Prix* of this kind would bring together so many journalists, organizers and members of the public that it raises the issue of whether the special surface that would need to be made for the circuit could also be used for other purposes. This is what happens in the detailed proposal, which involves a special *event strip* that can be used throughout the year as the base for various events, with the maximum configuration for the *Rotterdam Grand Prix*.

The main constituents of the race are grouped around the start/finish, the *paddock*. This is the area for the mechanics, drivers, press, VIPs, organizers and sponsors. The minimum length of the starting area is about 800 metres. The start/finish is located on the Boompjes boulevard, halfway between the two bridges, the Erasmusbridge and the Willemsbridge. The Boompjes area was redesigned only a few years ago, but without meeting the requirements for a successful waterfront location. The lower level is now used as a car park, while the rest is a main road. The port and transhipment activities that used to take place on the Boompjes have been moved to a larger location nearer the Maas estuary, cutting off the Boompjes from its industrial heritage. When the derricks along the Boompjes also had to be removed during the construction of the Erasmusbridge, the result was a place in great need of improvement.

View of the eight towers at the Boompjes

Eight towers have been placed on the lower level of the Boompjes, identical in their main construction but each with a different set-up and purpose. Between the towers are large platforms that can be moved up and down. The main supporting framework of the towers bears the platforms. The towers contain stairs and lifts providing access to the platforms. There are three platforms between each two towers. During the Formula One race, the bottom level is used for the racing team, the next platform up is arranged as a press area and the top level is a VIP platform. When there is no Formula One race going on, the platforms are on the ground, creating a large public space. Not all the platforms need to be used when the marathon or other events are taking place.

The two outer towers contain stairs going up to the top level, so that they can also be used as observation towers. The two towers next to the start/finish line are arranged as offices. The outside of the other four towers can be used for a billboard and moving screen. In the future, when the Boompjes is financially attractive as a strip, offices can be placed in each tower as a separate element.

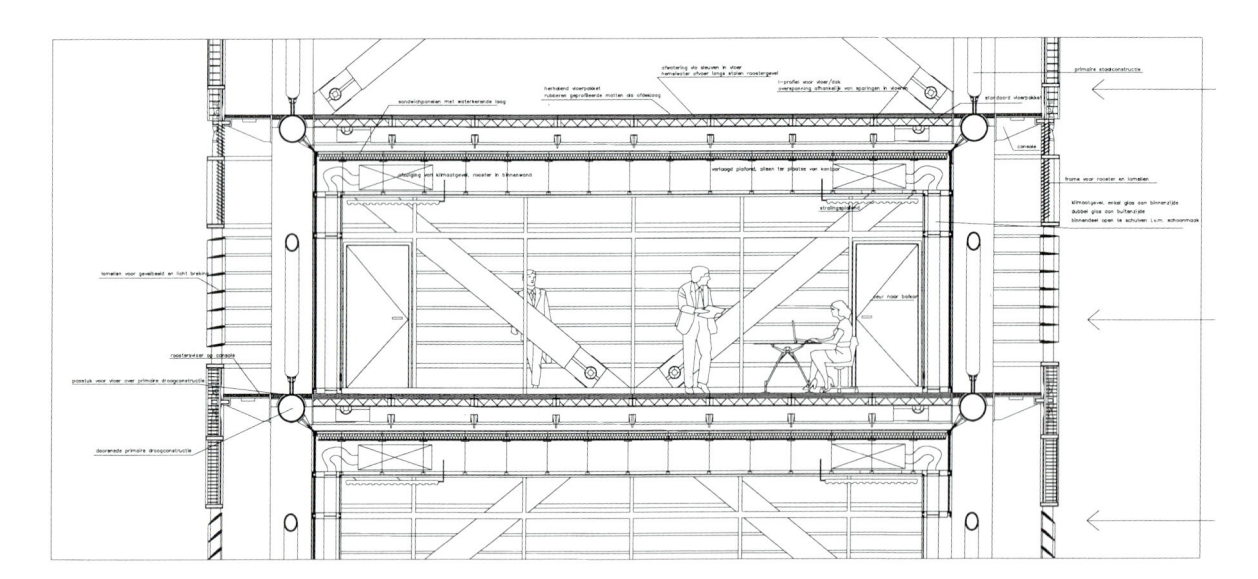

Mobility

Transformations

Optimization of land use on the Lelylaan in Amsterdam

John Westrik, Thijs van Heusden, Sandra Rozemeijer

The increasing scarcity of building land in the Netherlands necessitates urban development research into the optimization of land use within existing urban areas. Space for realizing new programmes is particularly to be found in post-war residential areas. There are various reasons why an intensification of the existing area is desirable. By improving the utilization of land that has already been developed, the green belt can be spared. By adding new types of housing, a more differentiated population structure is created. Furthermore, an increase in population guarantees greater support for services, including public transport.

It appears from earlier research that particularly the areas around urban trunk roads (the long lines) are suitable for an intensification of land use, because space is often 'wasted' here. There are various ways to optimize land use within the city. Three important questions play a role in this process: which programme can be realized, how can this new programme best be realized in the existing area and in which way can this intensification be facilitated?

These questions are the focus of the study by the Urban Design section: *Optimalisering Grondgebruik, case Amsterdam Lelylaan* (Optimization of Land Use on the Amsterdam Lelylaan). The study, which was completed in the spring of 1998, was commissioned by the *Team Optimalisering Grondgebruik* (Optimization of Land Use Co-ordination Team) in Amsterdam. Following on from two previous studies into the optimization possibilities of areas around stations, a number of relevant aspects with respect to the optimization of land use along urban trunk roads were investigated. The Lelylaan in Amsterdam, one of the long radials in the western suburbs, served as a test case for this.

The optimization of land use has both quantitative (how many square metres can be realized for housing, employment and services?) and qualitative aspects (which qualities does the new programme add?). Based on three spatial models for the Lelylaan, the study examines how many square metres of gross floor area can be added and new qualities are named. In the development of the models it was consciously decided not to create an urban design, but to make use of prototypes for reference purposes so that generally applicable conclusions could also be drawn from the study.

Quantity

In order to quantitatively measure densities, use was made in this study of the FSI (Floor Space Index) quotient. FSI indicates the ratio between the gross floor area of one or more buildings and the surface area of the location on which the building or buildings stand. This variable depends upon the location and thus upon the scale. An example: the calculation of the density of a house with a gross floor area of 100 m^2 on a plot of 50 m^2 produces an FSI of 2.0. A district with 2,000 of these houses on the same plots produces an FSI of < 2.0 because after all, a district can never function by simply pushing 2,000 plots together. At the very least, roads are needed to access these plots. In a word, the surface area of a district is always larger than the sum of the surface area of the plots and the FSI ratio is thus always smaller. To overcome this, the definition of FSI is linked to various scales. In this study, most use is made of the term FSI block. FSI block = gross floor area/surface area of the building block up to the centre of the street.

Another reason for measuring in FSI and not in houses per hectare for instance, is the fact that it is then also possible to measure functions other than housing. After all, the gross floor area of a building is not tied to function.

The programmatic management of the intensification possibilities of the Lelylaan is based on various programmes that are elaborated in three spatial models. The models vary from a green, suburban setting to a metropolitan, urban setting. The associated programmes differ in scale and FSI. Particularly the latter appears to be of essential importance. By clearly establishing in advance which level of ambition (which FSI) had to be achieved per model, the spatial image and the programme to be added were determined. The three models are defined as follows:

model	average FSI block	programme	reference examples
green axis	1.0	- homes for present residents - neighbourhood functions	*Wilhelminaplein*, R'dam *Borneo Eiland*, A'dam *Stadstuinen*, R'dam *Afrikaanderplein*, R'dam *Zenderpark*, IJsselstein
urban axis	2.0	- homes for both present residents and additional population - services at the urban (district) level	*Heinekenterrein*, A'dam *Afrikaanderplein*, R'dam *Osdorperplein*, A'dam *Van Noordtkade*, A'dam *Churchilllaan*, A'dam
metropolitan axis	3.0	- homes for both present and additional residents - services and employment at the city and Randstad level	*Weenatoren*, R'dam *Slachthuisterrein*, The Hague *Boompjes*, R'dam *Java Eiland*, A'dam

During the optimization process use is made of three urban design options. Firstly, the surface area for development is increased by partially reallocating the functions that are not built on, such as roads and parks. Like many access roads in post-war residential districts the Lelylaan is also well dimensioned. By narrowing the existing road profile, a larger surface area is utilized for development. It appears from the study that 25% of the optimization gain can be realized by means of this reprofiling.

A second option is to increase the floor area. By means of a more compact development than the original, the total floor area increases. This can be achieved by deploying new parcellation and housing types with a high FSI. It is also possible to transform the existing development into a more compact setting. From the study it appears, however, that for a quantitative optimization of the land use, demolishing existing buildings and replacing them with more compact types produces a lot more extra floor area than does a transformation. It appears from the investigated transformation variant for the Lelylaan that the maximum optimization gain is only one third that of the demolition/new development variant.

Finally, multiple land use is deployed in order to optimize land use. Space can be gained by combining functions. By situating parking spaces in or under buildings, more surface area can be used for other functions.

Quality

Amsterdam has developed over the years as a lobed city. The post-war suburbs form a lobe to the west of the city centre and these are connected to Amsterdam's city centre by means of a radial structure of roads. The Lelylaan is one of these radials and thus occupies an important position in the main infrastructure of the city. The road also plays a role at the regional level, both for the car (connection to the A10 motorway) and public transport (Lelylaan railway station). On account of its elevated situation, the traffic function of the Lelylaan on the lower scale level is almost insignificant. This contrasts with the road's immediate surroundings. This functions at the neighbourhood level and consists of a suburban residential area with extensive use of space (FSI *environment* = 0.5). In comparison: the central area of Amsterdam Zuid-Oost (south-east) has an FSI *environment* of 2.0, while the index for the VaRa strip in the city centre is 1.5 (source: *Oostlijn*, Delft, 1996).

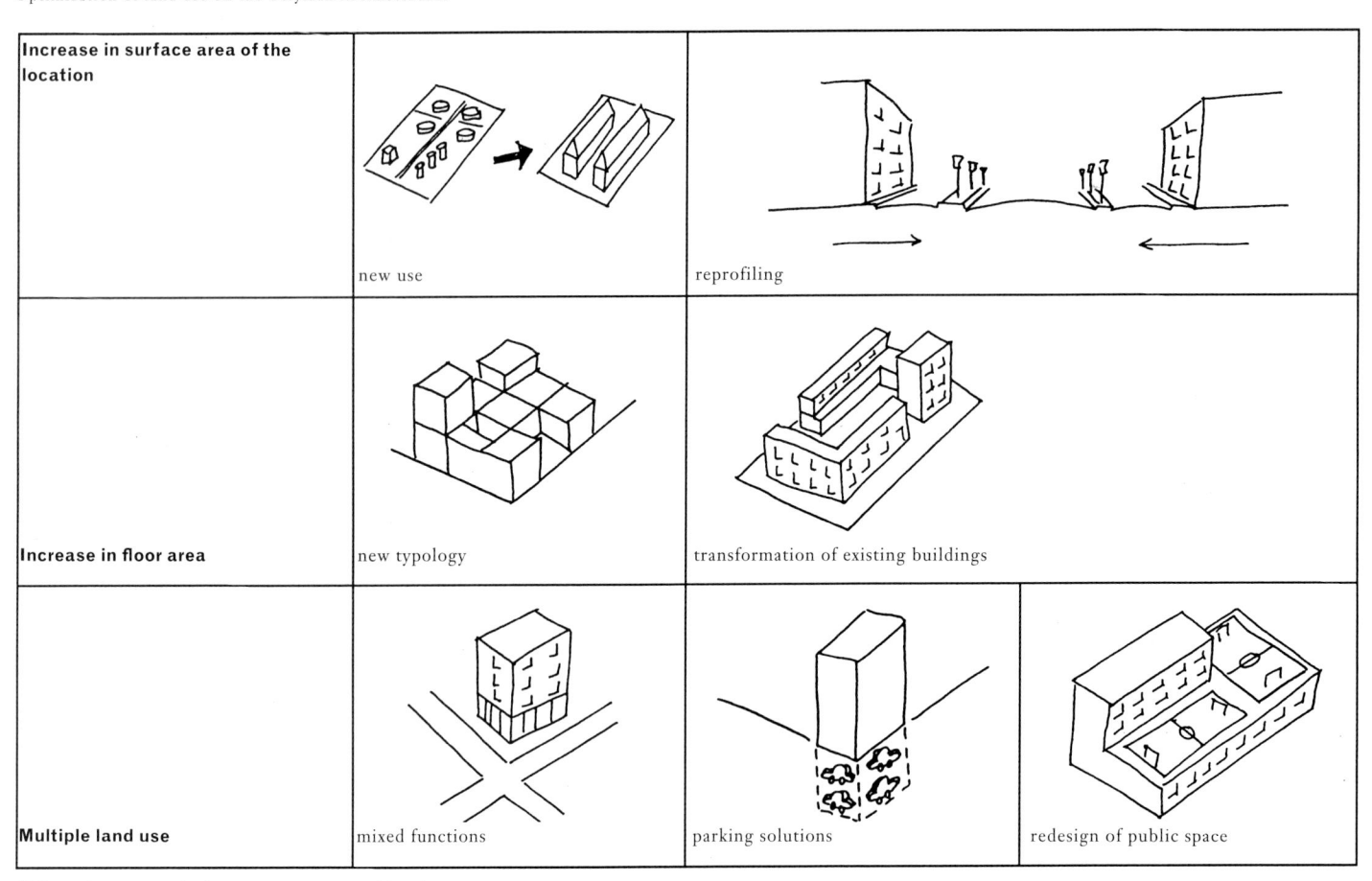

Increase in surface area of the location		
	new use	reprofiling
Increase in floor area	new typology	transformation of existing buildings
Multiple land use	mixed functions	parking solutions / redesign of public space

Urban design tools for optimization of land use

The different scale levels are taken advantage of when elaborating the three models. In this way, problems such as noise nuisance and barrier effect can be solved by adding a new programme and qualities such as a good access system can be better utilized.

In order to designate the new qualities for the Lelylaan, the following quality categories are distinguished. These categories, which can incidentally be used for other locations, are as follows:
– Integration of infrastructure; removing physical and mental barrier effect, improving the crossing possibilities for slow traffic, reducing noise nuisance and utilizing good accessibility for car and high-quality public transport.
– Identity of the axis and its surroundings; more recognition sites by mixing functions, respecting the existing suburban environment and maintaining cultural and historical development.
– Quality of public and private open space; clear segregation between public and private domain, improving possibilities for controlling public space, integration of parking solutions, increasing surface area for private outdoor space.

When comparing the three models with the current situation, all models score better than the current situation on many points. Particularly for the solution of noise problems and the barrier effect, it appears that the strategic deployment of new development is successful in the case of all models. The models also score well with the qualities for public and private outdoor space: the new building types are deployed in such a way that there is a clear segregation between public and private and the integration of parking solutions is realized. This improves the manageability of the public open space. Where the identity criterion is concerned, however, it is clear that the identity of the Lelylaan changes in all models. The cause of this is the increase in scale made by the road and its surroundings with the urban axis and metropolitan axis models and the reference examples applied with these models. It appears to be difficult to combine an optimization of land use in a quantitative sense with the suburban character of the long line.

Situation green axis

Situation urban axis

Situation metropolitan axis

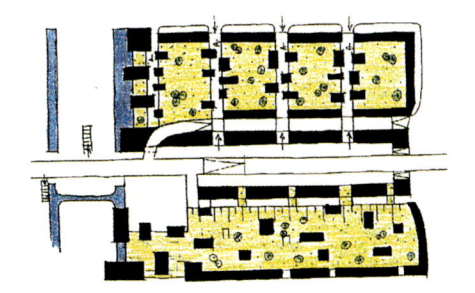

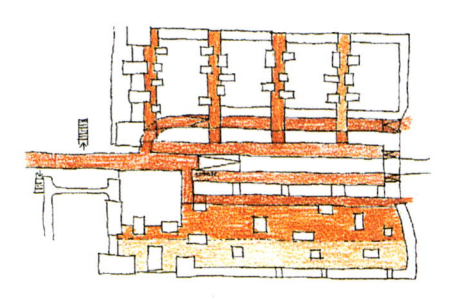

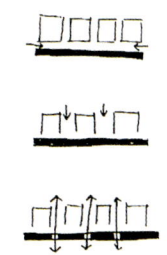

Impression of metropolitan axis

- businesses
- housing
- parking and storage
- offices

Conclusions

In summary, four factors play an important role in the optimization of the land use. First of all, it must be clearly established in advance which level of ambition is desirable. The level of ambition determines the use of the type of development with associated FSI. In this way it is possible to determine early on in the development process which spatial image will be created and what amount of new floor space can be built. Secondly, it is important whether the existing development will be completely demolished or otherwise retained and transformed. After all, transformation of an existing situation produces considerably less floor area than demolition/new development. Thirdly, it is important whether it is decided to reprofile or retain the existing road profile. It appears that reprofiling of the existing road profile to create a smaller profile produces a significant gain in space. Finally, it is important whether the undeveloped area is available for building.

If a high level of ambition is chosen, an FSI *block* greater than 2, i.e. total demolition/new development, reprofiling of the existing road profile and development of the wasted space, is essential. A low level of ambition (FSI *block* less than 1), i.e. no reprofiling and no development of the residual space, is not interesting from the point of view of the quantitative optimization of land use. It can, however, make a contribution to the increase in quality of the living environment around a long line.

Advice regarding the ancient harbour of Byblos in Lebanon
Harbour improvement in relation to the historic city and archaeological site

Prof. Frits van Voorden, Ron van Oers

Few places in the world convey such a sense of remote history as Byblos. Tradition dates its origins back to the dawn of time. There the god El made his home and enclosed it with a wall. Thus, beyond the reach of man's earliest memories, the ancients traced their origins back to the gods.[1]

Introduction

Besides education and research, the Restoration Section of the Faculty also works in the field of consultancy, giving advice to governmental organizations (Ministry of Education, Culture and Science, Dutch Department for Conservation) and non-governmental organizations (UNESCO, ICOMOS) on design and management plans for inner cities and urban areas. Over the past few years it has advised on projects in Willemstad (Curaçao), Paramaribo (Surinam) and Negombo (Sri Lanka) and is currently working on inner city renewal plans for Jakarta (Indonesia) and Cape Town (South Africa). The focus and range of these projects have always been on areas of *mutual heritage*, areas in former Dutch colonies where Dutch culture has blended with local cultural traditions creating mixed forms of urban planning and architectural design and construction.

Experience gained in these projects has now been successfully implemented in other inner cities and urban regions in the world and recently DUT advised the World Heritage Centre of UNESCO on projects in Lebanon (city of Byblos), Egypt (inner city of Cairo) and Morocco (city of Essaouira). DUT is internationally recognised as a specialist in the field of urban renewal and management processes in which cultural and historical values are interlinked with urban design and restoration. Apart from creating new projects for students and research trainees, these experiences and insights are used in the curriculum of the two-year international MSc course *Renewal and redesign of city areas*, which started in September 1998.

The case study of Byblos in Lebanon is presented here to highlight the different scope of problems and difficulties existing in various regions of the world.

Identification of Byblos World Heritage Site

Byblos is a small Phoenician port city located on a short promontory jutting out into the Mediterranean Sea. It claims to be the world's oldest continually inhabited city: archaeologists believe that the site has been occupied for at least 7000 years, and probably more. Undoubtedly, Byblos' greatest asset is the superposition, in one site approximately ten hectares (25 acres) in size, of ruins covering this timespan of 7000 years of uninterrupted human settlement and revealing at least 16 different civilizations.

In the second half of the 19th century Ernest Renas started excavation work at Byblos, followed by the Egyptologist Pierre Montet who undertook systematic excavations between 1920 and 1924. Later the Lebanese government took over the work and it continues to this very day. Now that the excavations have been completed in depth within the ramparts, they are being extended laterally further and further afield. Almost the whole of the Phoenician town has been cleared, and the Roman and Crusader towns have benefited equally from this work. The oldest settlement in Byblos dates back to approximately 5000 B.C. The different civilizations unearthed are:
1. Neolithic Period (before 3800 B.C.)
2. Chalcolithic Period (3800-3200 B.C.)
3. First Urban Settlements (3200-2150 B.C.)
4. The Amorite Period (2150-1725 B.C.)
5. The Hyksos Period (1725-1580 B.C.)

1
Dunand, M., *Byblos*: its history, ruins and legends, Beirut, 1973, p.1

Legend
1. Mediaeval city
2. Ancient harbour
3. Archaeological site
4. Arabic souk
5. Contemporary Byblos
6. New harbour extension
7. Public beach
8. Roman street

Preliminary plan for the extension of the ancient harbour of Byblos

6. Period of Egyptian Domination (1580-1200 B.C.)
7. Hegemony of Tyre and Aradus (1200-725 B.C.)
8. Assyro-Babylonian Rule (725-539 B.C.)
9. Persian Period (539-332 B.C.)
10. Hellenistic Period (332-63 B.C.)
11. Roman Period (63 B.C.-330 A.D.)
12. Byzantine Period (330-636 A.D.)
13. Omayyad and Abbasid Period (636-1098 A.D.)
14. Frankish Period (1098-1291 A.D.)
15. Period of the Mameluks (1291-1516 A.D.)
16. Ottoman Period (1516-1918 A.D.)

The unbelievable treasure-trove of ruins and artefacts uncovered forms the basis for Byblos' place on UNESCO's World Heritage List. The site registered at UNESCO covers the area of the archaeological excavations and the mediaeval city, including the ancient harbour. The paragraph on Identification in the nomination dossier explicitly states that Byblos is "the most ancient continuously inhabited city in the world. (...) About 7,000 years ago a small community of fishermen settled there."

The criteria which form the foundation for registration in the World Heritage Register are as follows[2]:
– Byblos bears an exceptional testimony to the beginnings of Phoenician civilization (criterion III),
– from the Bronze Age, Byblos has provided one of the primary examples of urban organization in the Mediterranean world (criterion IV),
– Byblos is directly and tangibly associated with the history of the diffusion of the Phoenician alphabet (on which humanity is largely dependent today) with the inscriptions of Ahiram, Yehimilk, Elibaal and Shaphatbaatl (criterion VI).

In 1984 ICOMOS (International Council on Monuments and Sites) also recommended "a wide area of protection, encompassing, besides the ancient habitat, the mediaeval city within the walls and the areas of the necropolis." The Lebanese authorities have taken a number of measures over the past few decades to protect the World Heritage Site and its immediate surroundings. The most important of these are:
– *"Classement de toute la plage au dessous du champ des fouilles avec une zone de protection de 300 mètres dans la mer sur la Liste officielle libanaise des monuments classés et inscrits monuments historiques et sites"*,
– determination of a *"Plan d'urbanisation générale de la ville de Byblos et ses environs"* (based on Decree no. 8645 of 1962),
– active implementation policy in the area of archaeology, documentation, tourism and supervision of building permits.

Outline of problems – general and local

In 1975 fighting broke out between the Lebanese Muslims and the Maronite-dominated Phalangist militias and Lebanon was plunged into a 17-year civil war, which only ended with a cease-fire in 1992. During this time Lebanon was effectively in a state of anarchy. Understandably, government control on issues such as the environment, private investment and building regulations was minimal. When the civil war ended the war-torn country had dramatically changed, especially in the coastal strip surrounding Beirut to the north and the south. Families that fled the city built their new homes on just about every site available, including on the doorstep of former more or less isolated archeological sites. The open countryside around Beirut has been transformed into a huge sprawling metropolis of close to 1.5 million people, virtually linking the capital to Byblos – approximately 40 km to the north. Besides neglect and significant damage to cultural sites during the war, the end of the war brings new threats: large investments, mainly by Lebanese businessmen living abroad, in infrastructure and construction, while the government is still rebuilding its management capacity, proper legislation and planning instruments.

For Byblos the most urgent problems are:
– uncontrolled construction encroaching on the World Heritage Site;
– public space being illegally privatized by entrepreneurs;
– construction in the protected site being poorly controlled, due to illegal building permits;
– poor site management;
– new harbour constructions threatening the historic city.

In cooperation with UNESCO's World Heritage Centre in Paris and the Lebanese authorities Delft University of Technology was asked to study a preliminary design for the harbour extension of Byblos, and to advise on possible alternatives and on the relationship between the development of the harbour and the historic city centre, and the archaeological site. The conclusions and recommendations were to be translated into a follow-up programme of strategic projects.

[2] Quoted from the ICOMOS recommendation, May 1984

Summary of the findings and recommendations

The preliminary plan put forward by the Lebanese authorities for the extension of the mediaeval harbour of Byblos is primarily aimed at safeguarding the existing harbour from ocean swell and high seas. At the same time, the plan aims to extend the harbour capacity and the facilities for fishing and tourist boats. Some aspects of the project began to be implemented from 1982 onwards.

We established that the new breakwater has brought about some improvement with regard to protecting the harbour entrance. Video footage made available to us by Byblos fishermen showed that – notwithstanding the improved harbour mouth protection – high waves still penetrate into the old harbour under extreme weather conditions. The boats are loosened from the quay, which itself is submerged under water. The waves even crash over the remains of the mediaeval wall to the north of the harbour mouth. During consultation with the Director of Transport, the point was raised that coastal defence, in this case protection of the harbour mouth, has the highest priority and that the construction of a marina is not part of the hydraulic engineering construction, although the plan put forward seems to indicate such a facility. In practice we found that not only the hydraulic engineering conditions of the harbour and harbour mouth require improvement, but that the coast directly to the south of the new dam is being damaged as a result of ocean swell and high seas. We noted that the steep edge of the 'table mountain' on which the archaeological site is situated is being damaged from underneath. If technological measures are not taken, parts of the ground level with the archaeological remains on top will end up in the sea.

The problems of the harbour and the harbour mouth must be judged as independent entities as well as being components of the coastal defence of the whole of historic Byblos. Both issues require a careful analysis of the current situation and of the developments expected in the future. Such an analysis must be based on systematic measurements of the movements of the sea in relation to the state of the seabed and coast and the wind direction. With the help of models, if necessary tested in a hydrodynamic laboratory for reliability and degree of reality, solutions can be studied. In addition to the purely hydraulic criteria, the functions and capacity of the harbour and the future use of the coastal strip is important. Should the construction of a pedestrian connection be considered at the bottom of the steep edge of the archaeological site, it will definitely influence the technical design. Until now, most of the activity has concerned solutions in and at the harbour entrance. In theory, solutions at a distance from the coast, by means of constructions and/or adaptations under water are conceivable.

The jetty, which represents the first phase of the preliminary plan for the harbour extension, and on which construction work began in 1982, fulfils a social function in addition to its protective, damming function. Local inhabitants and tourists enjoy the use of this exceptional 'esplanade' in the sea. There is, however, a risk that commerce will gain the upper hand and that structures and furnishings will be placed on the pier. The illegal parking area behind the cutting, at the beginning of the pier, is already being used as if it were an obvious amenity. It is of the greatest importance that the pier and the area behind the cutting do not become part of the commercial function of the city; they are strictly civil engineering constructions outside the dam.

Up to now no research has been done into the cultural-historical significance of the seabed to the west of Byblos. In view of the age of the site, which represents more than 7000 years of uninterrupted habitation, and the importance of the successive harbours, one can expect that underwater archaeology will retrieve a

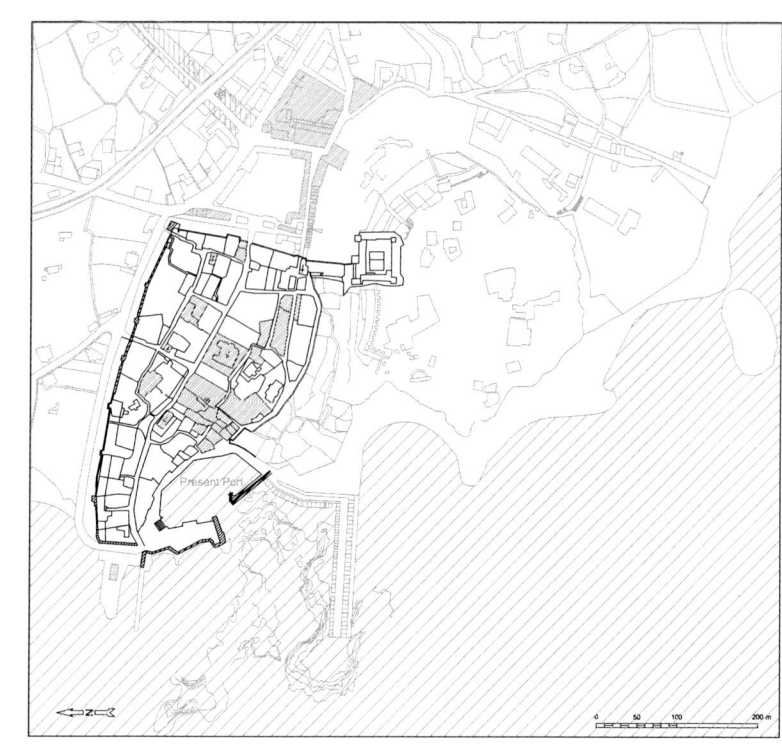

The archaeological site

The mediaeval city and harbour

wealth of new information on the culture of Byblos and Lebanon. It is self-evident that the archaeological investigation in the sea has high priority, because it must be implemented before decisions are taken regarding hydraulic constructions in the sea.

A variety of opinions and points of view regarding a possible marina, or harbour for yachts are circulating in Byblos itself. But the overall conclusion has to be that it is highly undesirable to combine the functions of a marina with those of the existing fishing and tourist harbour. The following reasons should be taken into consideration:
– a marina will hinder the systematic survey of the cultural heritage of the seabed and will irreparably damage this treasure-trove;
– a marina requires access for cars and trailers, wharf facilities, work areas, storage area for boats and accommodation for transients as well as permanent berths;
– a marina a priori determines the design of the damming provided at the harbour mouth and in the sea.

The final conclusion with regard to the preliminary design for the Byblos harbour extension is that carrying through the project will bring about undesired and irreversible changes to the vulnerable coast and harbour zones of the World Heritage Site, and that immense damage will be done to the underwater archive; at the same time, there is no evidence that the original aim, namely the protection of the fishing harbour and the harbour mouth, will be achieved.

In conjunction with research into the seabed archive, specialised hydraulic research is required to produce a sophisticated design. This design should cover both improvements/adaptations to the historic damming constructions (fortification and quay) as well as new constructions at a distance from the harbour mouth and coastal strip.

The souk (proposed addition)

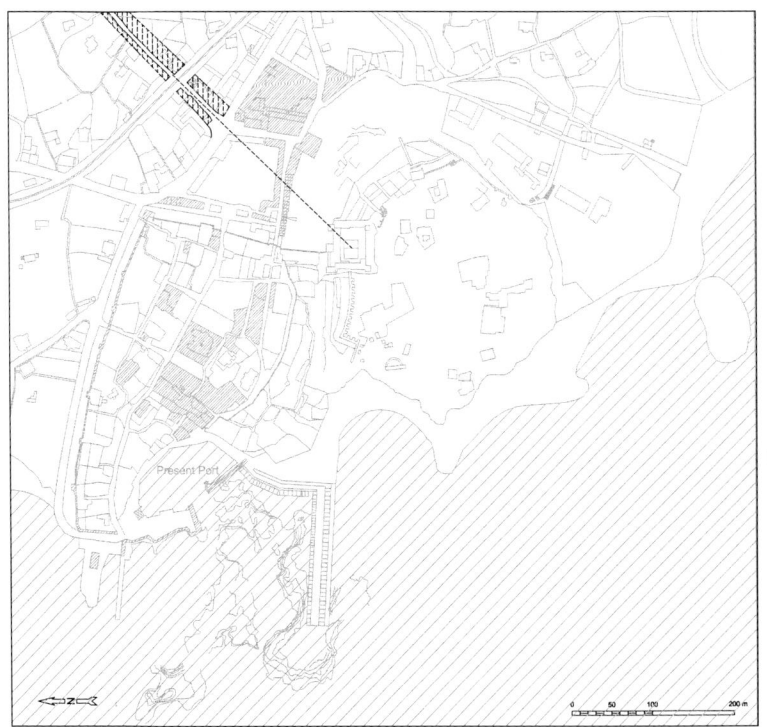

The Roman street (proposed addition)

Alternatives for harbour extensions

There is little scope for quantitative growth in the historic harbour. The small fishing boats (all of the same type) and the relatively small tourist boats (also all of one type) use about half of the harbour capacity. The aim should be to consolidate the fishing fleet, whereby facilities for repair, storage in bad weather, and the fishing trade should be improved. The expectation is that the type of boat used for tourists – also for reasons of safety – will gradually change. The result will be an increase in the space taken up in the harbour. Regulations with regard to the number of permitted fishing boats and tourist boats must therefore be drawn up to protect the interests of the fishing fleet, and to maintain the character of the fishing harbour. Arrangements should be made in conjunction with the fishermen (they are currently also involved in running the tourist boats). Consideration should be given to mooring some of the tourist boats at another location in future, outside the historic city and the historic harbour front. One possibility is to develop a shuttle service – when the seas are calm – to nearby marinas and to the parking facilities outside the historic city.

A brief survey of the fishing harbours and marinas to the north and south of Byblos was conducted. The result shows that there are six harbours in a coastal strip approximately 30 km in length. Those to the north are traditional small fishing harbours; those to the south are partly new marinas, partly traditional fishing harbours which are being developed into marinas. There is another conspicuous difference. The harbours to the south form part of the conurbation of greater Beirut; they are integrated into large-scale apartment complexes. The harbours to the north are still situated in open countryside; they are striking structural elements in the – as yet – partially undeveloped landscape.

If the municipality of Byblos wishes to build a marina near the city centre, it should choose a project on the northern coastal strip, preferably located at an existing harbour, or at a location that provides the geographic characteristics required (for example at a river mouth). The character of such a marina would have to be substantially different from the large-scale apartment harbours on the southern strip. It is an attractive thought to present Byblos as a location where the city area of Beirut stops and the open countryside begins. This theme should be further developed by the environmental planners in the region.

Transformations

Advice regarding the ancient harbour of Byblos in Lebanon

Legend
1. Underwater archaeological park as future addition to WHSite
2. Landscaping for redesign and technical upgrading of intermediate zone
3. Preparing guidelines for intermediate zone in contemporary city
4. Design & management plan for main entrance of WHSite
5. Landscape design for clear visual bordering of WHSite
6. Management plan for archaeological site
7. Management plan for mediaeval city
8. Harbour protection and small-scale improvements for local fishermen

Items for land-use scheme of Byblos World Heritage Site

Strategic projects

1. Research
Commissioning of two major research projects:
– study of coastal and harbour defence,
– study of the underwater archaeological archive.
In light of the pioneering nature of both studies, we recommend the formation of international teams under the patronage of UNESCO. Financing could be a combination of Lebanese and international funds.

2. World Heritage Dossier
To bring the World Heritage Dossier up to date and extend it. In view of the increasing pressure on the areas surrounding the World Heritage Site, it is, in our opinion, vital to adapt the identification of the World Heritage Site according to new insights, and to clearly delineate the location of the components and the whole.

In the first place, this does justice to the conservation policy of the Lebanese authorities, in the second place it provides a better link between internationally applied methods and local issues.

The following subjects and aspects should be added to the existing dossier:
– the mosque, the souk and the Roman street must be added as "evident monuments";
– to include the sea as an essential part of the Cultural Property and to designate it as an area for underwater archaeology;
– to secure the visual relationship between the archaeological site and the Crusader Castle and the landscape;
– to identify intermediate zones and to indicate morphological characteristics and individual monuments present.

The expertise of the Lebanese *Direction Générale des Antiquités* is qualitatively more than sufficient to prepare and edit the dossier. As regards methodology and implementation of the environmental planning, international support could play a stimulating role. Article 4 of the World Heritage Convention could form the foundation for this project:

"Each State Party to this Convention recognises that the duty of ensuring the identification, protection, conservation, presentation and transmission to future generations of the cultural and natural heritage (…) and situated on its territory, belongs primarily to that State. It will do all it can to this end, to the utmost of its own resources and, where appropriate, with any international assistance and co-operation, in particular, financial, artistic, scientific and technical, which it may be able to obtain."

3. Environmental planning
– Preparatory decision on a zoning plan for the area of the actual World Heritage Property (core area and intermediate zones);
– Determination of the strategic public works and infrastructure facilities, prioritization and budgeting;

and on a regional scale:
– An outline description of the most desired development and, as far as is necessary, of the phases in which the development should or could take place;
– Development of a regional plan to guide private projects and bind public projects. The regional plan is valid for ten years.

4. Land-use scheme – site management
Besides a detailed Design & Management Plan for the World Heritage Site and its immediate surroundings, the most important features are:
– Improvement of documentation and information at the archaeological site by means of an information desk, routing and information panels with outline maps and maps of objects;
– Improvement of the recognition of the site by landscaping;
– Addition of modest tourist facilities.

The advice has been adopted by UNESCO's World Heritage Centre and send to the Lebanese authorities in charge. Further co-operation in the near future between DUT, UNESCO and the Lebanese authorities in the follow-up programme, especially where it involves design plans, is expected.

Reflections on housing experts

Kees van der Flier

Introduction

During their studies students with a specialization in Housing – future 'housing experts' – regularly investigate the strengths and weaknesses of housing estates and regions, or of a landlord's housing stock, to reach conclusions about the opportunities for and threats to this housing using what is known as an analysis of S(trengths) W(eaknesses) O(pportunities) and T(hreats). The objective of such an analysis is to obtain the information needed to formulate and weigh strategies for the management of this housing. Twenty-five years of Housing as a specialization offers us an ideal opportunity to carry out this analysis in a slightly different manner: this time not on housing, but on the housing experts themselves. We shall use the analysis to come to some conclusions about the future of the houser and about the specialization at Delft. We shall carry out the analysis on the basis of the following characteristics of the housing experts educated at the Faculty:
- they are graduate engineers,
- they are architectural engineers,
- they are professionals,
- they have a target group.

Strong and weak points

Graduate engineers

Housing experts are graduate engineers. They are characterized by their results-oriented approach to reality; they can redefine a social problem in terms of a problem in their discipline, make an analysis, and provide a solution. Their effectiveness in terms of their ability to rapidly provide solution proposals for social problems is a strong point of graduate engineers. Housing experts are also results-oriented; the history of housing can be seen as a succession of programmes and plans to solve social problems: large-scale construction programmes in the nineteen-fifties and sixties to combat the numerical housing shortage, urban renewal plans in the nineteen-seventies and eighties in the fight against dilapidation and decay in the older urban neighbourhoods, and nowadays restructuring plans to counter the tendency towards segregation in the post-war neighbourhoods.

Graduate engineers' orientation towards results also has a drawback. Graduate engineers have the tendency to continue until all the problems have been solved. For example, De Kleijn pointed out that many urban renewers/housing experts are of the opinion that urban renewal is only 'finished' once all dwellings have been upgraded. He disputes the necessity of this, and makes a plea for the retention of a 'frayed edge', i.e. to leave some of the housing stock in urban renewal areas as it is, or otherwise to make only minimal improvements. This housing is destined for those groups in the population that prefer a lower quality at a lower price (De Kleijn, 1985).

Architectural engineers

Housing specialists are architectural engineers. Architectural engineers have an understanding of interventions in and management of the built environment. This is an important skill, since many social problems are related to this environment. For example a topical field of policy such as the Grote-Stedenbeleid (policy with respect to the large urban areas) makes a distinction between five themes in which it states the problems confronting the larger cities and endeavours to find suitable answers: work, education, safety, the quality of life, and care. The last three are certainly closely related to the built environment. Moreover interventions in the built environment have the advantage that they are clearly visible and (consequently) can have a motivational effect on people. Improvements in the built environment often constitute a stimulus to search for answers to other aspects of social problems.

Literature

The Municipal Executive of the Municipality of Rotterdam, *Vernieuwing van de stadsvernieuwing*, Rotterdam, 1988
Geus, J. de, T. Geurts, "Het volkshuisvestingsbeleid in Nederland: veroorzaker van inefficiëntie en onrechtvaardigheid", *Nieuw Tijdschrift voor de Volkshuisvesting*, Vol. 2, no. 5, 1996
Klijn, E., *Regels en sturing in netwerken: de invloed van netwerkregels op de herstructurering van naoorlogse wijken*, Rotterdam, Eburon 1996
Kleijn, G. de, *De staat van de stadsvernieuwing*, Amsterdam, 1985
Köbben, A.J.F., "De zaakwaarnemers", *Intermediair*, no. 16, 1984
Ministry of Housing, Spatial Planning and the Environment, *Woonverkenningen MMXXX*, Basisverkenningen, 's-Gravenhage, 1997
National Housing Council, *Marktperspectieven voor woningcorporaties: de klant in beeld*, Almere, 1997 (research conducted by the OTB Research Institute)
Noordanus, P.G.A., "Naar een herstructurering van stadswijken in regionaal perspectief", H. Priemus en E. Philipsen (ed.), *Postmodern lokaal volkshuisvestingsbeleid: balanceren tussen doelgroep, kernvoorraad en herdifferentiatie*, Delft, DUP 1996
Parlementaire Enquête Bouwsubsidies, *Rapport van de Commissie en Verhoren*, 's-Gravenhage, Staatsuitgeverij 1985
Priemus, H., B. van Rosmalen, F. Wassenberg, *Regionaal volkshuisvestingsplan Haaglanden: balans tussen herstructurering en behoud kernvoorraad*, Delft, DUP 1996
Priemus, H., E. Kalle, R. Teule, *De stedelijke investeringsopgave: naar vitale, ongedeelde en duurzame steden in Nederland*, Delft, DUP 1997

Reijndorp, A., "Social scientists looking for trouble: de vergeten factor van het verval", *Bouw*, vol. 40, no. 1, 1985
Rouwendaal, J., "Volkshuisvestingsbeleid: een kwestie van kosten en baten", *Nieuw Tijdschrift voor de Volkshuisvesting*, Vol. 2, no. 7, 1996
Wiel, C. van der, *Typisch Oude Noorden*: een onderzoek naar de effectiviteit van het grote-stedenbeleid bij de verbetering van de woonsituatie in een 19e eeuwse Rotterdamse wijk, Delft, 1997

Housing experts distinguish themselves from other architectural engineers in that they also have some understanding of the social processes that take place in and with respect to the built environment. They are able to place physical interventions in a broader context. This can be beneficial to the effectiveness of these interventions.

Nevertheless housing experts, like other architectural engineers, are cursed with a generous dose of physical determinism. In his classic article *"Social scientist looking for trouble, de vergeten factor van het verval"* Reijndorp demonstrates that many reflections about the problems of post-war housing are meticulous in their inclusion of a list of the social problems. However on reading further it transpires that these problems are not taken into account in the proposed solutions; they are comprised solely of interventions in architectural or urban planning (Reijndorp, 1985). But physical determinism is not a problem from the past. Nowadays many housing associations draw up plans to improve the quality of life in the regions in which they have a stock of housing. Some of these plans also indicate the social problems in these regions, but it transpires that in the details of the improvements the emphasis is placed on interventions in the dwellings and in the immediate surroundings. It would seem that the tailor makes the man. A form of physical determinism is also to be seen in the recent restructuring regulations issued by the central government. These regulations have been introduced in response to the concern about the tendency towards segregation and the concomitant social problems. This concern is expressed in regulations to make the restructuring, or rather the redifferentiation, of the cheaper housing stock possible. The implicit assumption is that the redifferentiation of housing stocks will make a contribution towards countering segregation and the concomitant problems (Priemus et.al.,1997).

Professionals

Housing experts are professionals with a range of professional standards. They work for institutions such as housing associations or municipal services, where these standards are shared with other housing experts. Examples of well-known standards are 'sober and practical', 'affordable and attainable' and a 'balanced cross-section of the population'. This basic uniform orientation means that when housing experts address a given problem they are able to move on relatively quickly to the 'what and how' question. The 'why' question requires little discussion. In his thesis Klijn shows how such a common disposition, which is given shape in the form of certain behavioural rules, was one of the success factors in Rotterdam's urban renewal (Klijn, 1996). The report of the Parliamentary Committee of Inquiry into Building Grants reveals how the standards and the rules within the housing sector have led to a very efficient production machine to combat the housing shortage. But this report also shows that these standards and rules have resulted in other standards being ignored, such as a meticulous compliance with the regulations for grants (PEB, 1985).

The disadvantage of shared standards within a professional group is that certain questions are not raised, such as the question: why does the government have to stimulate the construction of dwellings by means of subsidies? In the nineteen-eighties this resulted in the housing experts coming empty-handed to what were known as the reconsideration discussions held with economists. They had become so accustomed to these government subsidies that they were scarcely able to cite arguments for the present use of subsidies in housing. (De Geus and Geurts, 1996 and Rouwendaal, 1996).

Target group

Housing experts have a target group. They do not work for an anonymous market, but for clearly-identifiable groups of residents. They have a number of different forms of contact with this target group. Organizations representing the target group play a role in the institutional framework of housing; this takes place at a national level (including the De Nederlandse Woonbond, the Netherlands Residents' Association), at a local level (urban umbrella organizations), at a housing association level (tenants' councils) and at a neighbourhood level (neighbourhood groups). Housing experts also encounter the target group in projects and in day-to-day management. As a result they receive reactions to their work from a wide variety of sources, and there is a relatively large amount of feedback. This is beneficial to the quality of the work, and to housing experts' motivation. An (active) target group also contributes to society's support for housing, and consequently to the work of housing experts.

The fact that there is a target group sometimes leads to a fixation on that group, in particular on the housing that is intended for that target group. However the definition of that target group is the result of a political process that is subject to change, and consequently to a certain extent may be regarded as arbitrary: in the nineteen-sixties and seventies the target group included 'broad sections of the population'; following the Policy Note on Housing in the nineties the target group became relatively small, being defined in financial terms. An additional factor is that the target group is searching for housing in a market in which other groups are also active; this has an influence on the position and the opportunities available to the target group. The history of urban renewal reveals that in the long term a fixation on the target group, in this instance the 'present residents', can lead to unfavourable results. Many neighbourhoods that have undergone an urban renewal process now have an overdose of social-sector rented accommodation, which is one of the reasons that they are now the subject of restructuring plans (Noordanus, 1996 and Van der Wiel, 1997). The presence of a target group sometimes results in housing experts thinking for the target group. As such there is nothing against housing experts anticipating the wishes of the target group, but such an attitude may result to consumerism within the target group and the adoption of 'residents standpoints' that are difficult to control, cf. the discussion with residents' experts about the management of the affairs of others. (Köbben, 1984).

Opportunities and threats

Graduate engineers

It is not to be expected that the number of social problems will decrease in the near future. The same is true for the complexity of these problems. This complexity requires a coherent, or in other words integral, approach: in various areas, between various parties and various levels of scale. This integral requirement is also the Achilles' heel; an integral approach needs co-operation between parties with divergent points of view and methods of working, and such a co-operation is often difficult to achieve. For this reason, and perhaps paradoxically, there continues to be a need for graduate engineers who ignore the complexity and produce proposals for solutions to a part of the problem. The reason is that there is a risk that this complexity will lead to stagnation in dealing with the problems. One example is the establishment of a new management organization in the field of housing in response to the processes of increases and decreases in scale: the region.

Graduate engineers' reductive view of reality also poses a threat to their position. Should it transpire that an excessively narrow analytical framework results in the solutions that they have provided either not working or becoming contra-productive within a few years then the belief in the possibility that social problems can actually be solved will suffer a severe blow. This may be detrimental to the credibility of graduate engineers and to their approach to reality. An illustration of this is the discussion about the disappointing results achieved by urban renewal (The Municipal Executive of Rotterdam 1988).

Architectural engineers

Substantial architectural engineering tasks are awaiting housing experts; a large number of dwellings have to be built, subject to difficult preconditions, to accommodate the growing demand (the Supplement to the Fourth Policy Document on Spatial Planning, VINEX); the existing neighbourhoods need to be restructured to enable them to compete with the new neighbourhoods and to offer adequate housing to the groups that are not provided with a home in the VINEX locations. And this in addition to the normal technical management of 2.5 million rented dwellings. So there are opportunities enough.

In spite of these substantial building tasks housing is increasingly becoming a management task; it is largely a question of the management of existing housing stock and regions. Technical management is only part of the story, and it will continually need to be brought into relationship with other aspects involved in management. This is revealed by the reorganizations within housing associations, in which a wide range of variants of the housing service model are being implemented. This will result in a relative decrease in architectural engineers' contribution to housing. This is not necessarily applicable to housing experts, provided that they are able to link other disciplines to technical disciplines in their contribution.

Professionals

The housing sector is characterized by the presence of qualified professionals who work for institutions that possess a great deal of know-how. As such housing experts are in an excellent position to respond to new questions. One such question, for example, is: how are we to manage a housing stock or a region that almost exclusively houses households with a low to very low income, i.e. the target group? In the past the majority of these households were housed in the private rented sector. Urban renewal is one reason for the drastic decrease in the cheaper housing available in this sector, which is why the housing of the lowest-income groups has become a task of the housing associations. They will need to change their methods of working, and are in fact already doing so. The changes vary from an increase in the intensity of technical management: no longer painting the dwelling every seven years, but every four years, and of social management: more services and more supervision of the immediate residential surroundings to changes in the basis of their operation: no longer cost-neutral operations, but partly unprofitable investments covered by sales of their property. Some will say that it is undesirable to allow the creation of regions housing only the target group, but it remains a valid question; when 40 or 30% of all Dutch households belong to the target group then the correct management of a stock or a region housing only the target groups must be possible. In any case it should be a challenge for housing experts.

There are also threats for housing experts as a professional group. There is a great demand for owner-occupied homes. According to some scenarios the target group will decrease to less than 15% of the total number of households by 2020 (National Housing

Council 1997), and it is expected housing associations will sell a large number of their homes. This may result in a decrease in the magnitude of the rented sector and to a reduction in the demand for architectural engineers in the service of professional clients and housing managers. Possibly even more of a threat is a development in which renting a dwelling becomes a 'second best' form of housing, resulting in the rental sector becoming a sector of social 'losers'. Many of the standards of professional housing experts, and consequently their self-esteem, are linked to the rental form of housing and the appreciation of this form by society.

Target group

The objective of housing experts is formulated in terms of the housing of certain groups. This offers opportunities to give consideration to new activities that can contribute to the wishes of this group. This no longer primarily concerns the possession and management of dwellings with a standard level of quality and rent, but the development, construction, management and sale or purchase of dwellings of a wide range of quality, and the supply of services associated with the dwelling for, and sometimes with, the target group. For example this could be housing associations that supply only management services and which leave the question of ownership to investors or residents. However they will need to be able to compete with other companies that (will) supply these kinds of services.

No matter which Central Planning Bureau scenario may be used, it is expected that the target group will become smaller, and more specific (Ministry of Housing, Spatial Planning and the Environment 1997). This means that it will become more difficult for housing experts to maintain the relationship with the target group. After all, it is easier to maintain contacts with indigenous residents who organize themselves neatly into residents' committees than it is with immigrants with other organizational cultures or with first-time tenants who have absolutely no motivation whatsoever to participate in housing organizations. The distance between housing experts and their target group may increase. In the longer term this may undermine the foundations of housing as a separate sector.

Conclusions

The first conclusion is that the houser must remain an architectural engineer. There are still a large number of social problems that have a relation to the built environment. Results-oriented architectural engineers will continue to be necessary in order to tackle these problems. Housing experts educated in Delft have an advantage in comparison with housing experts receiving their education elsewhere as a result of their more general approach and their knowledge of the market (the target groups), the product (the dwelling and the immediate surroundings) and the financing (the rents, and the operations). Two aspects will continue to require attention. They must possess sufficient knowledge in the disciplines in which they distinguish themselves from other housing experts. This is the case, for example, in the area of building technology. They must also be able to place problems and answers in a broader context. A contribution could be made by a greater emphasis on theory and a theoretical approach in the educational programme.

The second conclusion is that a discussion is required about the professional standards and objectives of housing experts. This discussion is not merely a question for the professional housing experts, but is also of concern to the target groups and their organizations. A discussion about the description of the target group is required; for whom are we doing this, and why? Are we going to adhere to the fairly arbitrary delineation of the target group, or do housing experts also have a duty at the lower *and* the upper end of the housing market? This discussion is also necessary with respect to rental as a form of housing: is purchasing a dwelling indeed preferable to renting a dwelling, as many claim nowadays, or does renting a dwelling have specific advantages that should be retained in new forms of management?

A platform is needed for this discussion. Consequently there is a task for organizations such as FORUM for housing and the housing section of the NIROV (Netherlands Institute of Land Use Planning and Housing). An aspect that will need attention is the contact with the world outside housing that is required to provide a benchmark for the housing experts' standards and views. Another aspect requiring attention is the strengthening of the relationship between the specialization and the professional world to ensure that future housing experts will also be able to participate in the discussions.

Finally, and probably inevitably; the education of housing experts who are engaged in questions concerning housing and the stimulation of discussions about housing are possible without a separate specialization in housing. However the existence of such a specialization does greatly facilitate these tasks.

An unsentimental journey

Prof. Pi de Bruijn

"Everything's fine with architecture, I thought. The amount of public interest is tremendous, the presses are churning out more books and magazines than ever before. There's intensive architecture tourism – to Paris, Barcelona, Tokyo and the retail bank in the Bijlmer – while the number of competitions and multiple commissions is growing by the day. The prizes, awards and honourable mentions are pouring in like gentle rain. A very small group have actually achieved stardom in the international flying circus... We're enjoying all this to the full but... there's still a gnawing feeling of unease. Something reminds one of the previous fin de siècle with its tendency towards romanticism and narcissism, architecture automatically written with a capital A and preferably immediately accepted as art. It's not something I like the sound of. In my view this overly one-sided focus on the artistic or form side of architecture is sentimental and eventually leads to formalism, i.e. rigidity and sterility. This is architecture as an empty shell, with no substance. It leads to architects who are like clowns, showing their tricks to the highly honoured public. That's why I want to focus attention in this lecture on the other two fundamental components of architecture: societal orientation and technology."[1]

With these words in 1995 I began my four-year appointment as professor in the Faculty of Architecture in Delft. Now this period has come to an end, it is time to look back and see whether the issues which then seemed to demand attention are still important today. Everything is still fine with architecture. And architecture tourism is just as popular, although the destinations have changed or, as in the Bijlmer, other developments are now attracting the visitors. However, the narcissism and craving for romanticism have abated slightly and the above quotation is clearly recognizable as a picture at a given moment in what feels like a different age. The architect as clown is hardly a valid description in these business-like times, but the desire to focus attention on societal orientation and technology is just as appropriate today.

The appointment of three visiting professors at the same time was then not only based on the usual ideological and practical considerations but was certainly a logistics issue too. There was a real build-up of final year students requiring supervision and attention. With so much demand and not knowing the students, I had no opportunity for selection and had to supervise a whole stream of the most diverse projects, displaying equally diverse qualities. This, combined with the time being limited to one day a week, led to considerable emphasis on supervising final year students at the expense of other educational tasks. During the many supervision sessions, it became clear to me that the field of tension that exists in day-to-day practice between the client's fairly practical requirements and the limited scope of the location – with the architect somewhere in the middle – provides a quality that does not exist in most graduation projects. This is largely the fault of the fuzziness with which students formulate their own assignments.

[1] Quotation from *Bouwstenen*, inaugural speech Pi de Bruijn, 2 July 1995

A fairly substantial part of the supervision process was therefore devoted to firming up the terms of reference and defining the precise area where the architectural intervention would show up to best advantage. Romantics who wanted to set the whole world to rights and almost foundered on their own ambition had to be brought down to earth, while others turned up with proposals that were too limited. Finding the right balance between utopia, reality and architectural challenge was the most difficult task.

This dilemma applies to almost every graduation project and is, I believe, connected with two issues: firstly, the pure knowledge relating to the possibilities and limitations of the field of study and secondly, whether or not there is a societal orientation. I was struck by the fact that there is not much relationship between what appears in the papers every day and the graduation topics. This is due to lack of training during the course in handling societal themes in relation to the opportunities that this field provides for tackling such themes. The ground that the two have in common is often only fully appreciated by the final year. Many graduation projects fall behind for this reason; few took less than a year. Up to a point this is not a problem because the period leading up to graduation is also a form of emancipation, in which students have an opportunity to develop their talents. And so the signs of panic and haste shown by this four-year generation with a graduation deadline sometimes raised questions about the academic content of the course. With more practice in seeing the links between opportunities and limitations on the one hand and the societal domain on the other, it would be possible to examine more fundamental issues with greater regularity during the graduation projects. A broad orientation is indispensable, particularly for an architect. The work often calls for far more than professional knowledge in the narrow sense. It involves problems that reach way beyond that and have to do with political relations as well as psychological and general human relationships. This includes considerations concerning the cultural value of buildings or the townscape and the preservation or demolition of these. An architect needs to have a certain amount of intellectual substance to be able to join in discussions with a knowledge of his/her own possibilities and limitations.

The faculty can play an important role, particularly in this area. The research studios are an example of how this has been done in a structured way in recent years. The *OVerstapMachine* research studio, in which I have been closely involved, is an organization of this kind, where the focus is on studying a theme with a clear societal orientation – mobility and accessibility in relation to urban planning and architectural design. This is an exceptionally important area that urgently requires consideration and design work, both against the background of accessibility as a condition for urban life and in the light of the physical position that infrastructure holds in the urban fabric. The areas around the urban interchanges present real problems; they are often disadvantaged neighbourhoods for which we need to find architectural and urban planning solutions. In the long run the thematic approach to problems produces a collection of different solutions to the same or similar problems. This makes comparisons possible and scrutiny of the findings may highlight certain trends. Apart from mobility, there are of course numerous examples of socially relevant dilemmas that are worth the effort of research and design.

Ecology is another example of a field that presents a great challenge to architecture in all its many facets. During my work in Germany I was struck by the fact – as I still am every day – that the Germans are far more advanced in the various applications involving ecology in the building industry. Whereas in the Netherlands the concept often seems to be viewed as part of the counterculture – in a way that, incidentally, is way behind the times as regards the possibilities and techniques – in Germany ecology is simply one of the preconditions for the construction of a building and there is no further discussion. The reason for this difference may lie in the way that ecology was first introduced. It is typical of the architectural profession that certain heroics are expected of it, both by those within the profession and outsiders, and if a new approach is not promoted in this way, there may be considerable delay in acceptance. In this connection it is of course striking that Foster, one of the world's leading architects, has been working on energy conservation in buildings and the building as an organism for the last ten to fifteen years – in fact, very much in the tradition of his equally legendary predecessor, Buckminster Fuller.

The heroics I have just referred to as part of the architectural profession form the core of a two-sided nature. On the one hand this is indispensable as the basis for a certain drive to excel and the continual search for new ways of approaching a design, on the other hand it can also be dangerous and actually prevent the development of new concepts. Research into societal trends may reveal things that diminish the role of architecture. This kind of trend is evident in the *OVerstapMachine* studio. Many participants in the studio joined out of a kind of sentimental fascination with station buildings and large station roofs. On closer consideration and after studying mobility and accessibility in relation to the town, including various means of transport, it is becoming clear that the train is losing ground and will have to adopt a more modest approach. The initial idea of creating a nice large, heroic station specially to house the trains may, following research, end in something more modest: the integration of a number of access roads into an underground transport system in an existing row of shops. The New York subway entrances are a good example of this. This is often a great disappointment to the student, because there is no scope for the grand gesture. The theme of building underground produces similar disappointment, also failing to appeal to the desire to place something in the world. However, we need to examine this on its architectural merits too, because it may conceal unexpected new programmes and tasks, which only become evident if one goes beyond the existing situation. And that, in my view, is where the challenge lies for this faculty, both in technical design and research terms. A number of final year students have taken up the challenge of "designing away" what once had heroic pretensions. I would like to mention two of these. Both projects present proposals for an underground solution for Central Station in Delft. The first is the project *Change at Delft* by Ada Beuling, which leaves nothing at ground level except a bridge marking the site. The other solution is *Station Delft 2000* by Nivard Hol, who also leaves the surface free for other developments. Apart from the fact that these projects broach the subject of "designing away", the opportunity to compare two solutions to the same problem is also interesting here. The big challenge is to extend the thinking along these lines and extrapolate from the possibilities highlighted by interventions of this kind.

One consequence of many assignments of this kind is that the architectural task is often little more than the design of a civil engineering structure. Knowledge of one's own profession and related fields is vitally important when it comes to this common ground. To take another example from Germany, in many cases the situation is examined by various disciplines, from both a modern and historical perspective, before designing anything at a particular location. This helps to clarify groups of considerations that may be helpful in connection with design decisions. The workshop Amsterdam CityPort was held in June '97 as a mental exercise for everyone involved in the Overstapmachine studio. It consisted of presenting a large number of options for the south axis area of Amsterdam in terms of national and local transport links, both public and private. This workshop brought together expertise from various disciplines in the form of lectures and writings by a range of professionals, thus forming the basis for an integrated approach to the area[2]. Early recognition of the possibilities and restrictions of the various fields involved ensures that integrated thinking has a head start in the design process. In a similar way a symposium called *The synergy of form & structure* was organized in partnership with *DBSG Stylos* around the same time. Here too the emphasis was on the positive and mutually inspiring collaboration between different fields.[3] The subject of debate at this symposium was a new way of thinking that blurs the dividing lines between the civil engineer and the architect.

Returning to my quotation at the beginning, I believe it is fair to say that although the text is slightly dated and the developments and activities in the intervening years have shown a closer relationship between societal orientation and technology in the Faculty of Architecture, the call for further orientation in that direction is just as relevant today. The societal orientation should provide the skill to identify developments and recognize them as the issue, while the study and practice of technology should provide the resources to solve these issues.

2
E.g. M. Zwarts, Prof. J. Busquets, H. van Hoogdalem, J. Bach, C. van Ees and A. Staalenhoef. A publication on this workshop has appeared under the title *Amsterdam CityPort '97*, S. van der Spek (ed.).

3
Speakers included Harry Seidler, Christopher Wise (Ove Arup), Antoine Predock, Katherine Hill and Meinhard von Gerkan. J.N.J.A. Vambersky (Faculty of Civil Engineering) led the forum discussion.

D12 International renovation

Leo Verhoef

D12 is an international module. Dutch students, participants in the Erasmus study programme (who already study in Delft) and students from abroad can take part in the project. Other universities are also involved, among them the E.T.H. Zürich, TU Frankfurt, PT Cracow and FH Münster. In 1998, the universities of Delft, Cracow and Münster participated.

The project

The students were required to create a design for the former *Werkplaatsengebouw* of the Holland-America Line (HAL) designed by the late Professor J. Bakema. The project involved both technical and architectural problems.

The building is situated on a peninsula in the old port of Rotterdam, from which passenger and cargo vessels used to sail for America. The entire peninsula was used by the HAL. Other buildings on the complex included a hotel, arrival and departure halls, and warehouses. The *Werkplaatsengebouw* was one of these warehouses. It was where people emigrating to or returning from America stored their luggage. Furniture belonging to the Holland-America Line was also repaired in this building. Nowadays, the peninsula is no longer used by the HAL. However, it is located in the middle of Rotterdam's biggest developing area, the *Kop van Zuid*. This area is being transformed into an office and business district and is linked with the old commercial centre of Rotterdam by the Erasmus bridge.

The assignment

The assignment was to create a high-quality office building with related facilities. Technically speaking, the facade is very interesting, because it is a minimum facade intended solely to keep out the wind, rain and burglars. To adapt this building for new functions it was necessary to solve both architectural and technical problems. One of the main questions was how to renovate such a recently built listed building.

Why international?

Architecture has ceased to be strongly nationalistic. We no longer speak of typically Flemish or Spanish architecture. Moreover, big assignments are often awarded in prize contests in which architects with an international reputation take part. The influence of architects who are operating on an international scale on the current architectural scene is very clear. This applies both to new buildings and to existing buildings that need renovation to fit them for their future purpose. The interested public is well-informed about buildings designed for tomorrow, and can read about them in international publications today.

In many ways, the borders of countries have almost ceased to exist. Regulations specifically designed for one country are now viewed on a European scale. Students who are studying in Germany or Poland today may find themselves working in the Netherlands tomorrow. This means that universities must take a European view, while also being aware of the worldwide opportunities for employment of their skills.

The Mast *was chosen as the best plan. The* Mast *divides and regulates the light entering the building, creating an extraordinary atmosphere.*

In the Netherlands, the trend in building is more towards re-using existing buildings rather than opting for new construction. On a global scale, however, economic development in SouthEast Asia in recent years has led to an enormous demand for new buildings. Local architects alone are unable to fulfil the sudden demand for architectural design immediately, which means that architects are designing wherever they are needed.

Since the trend in Europe is moving more and more in the direction of the re-use of existing buildings rather than building new ones, renovation has become topical. At the moment, renovation, re-use and maintenance form the major portion of the work of the building industry. So in countries like these more attention will need to be devoted to renovation in university education programmes. Later, when there is an increase in commissions for this type of work in other countries, we can expect architects with experience in this field to go where the commissions are.

All in all, it is necessary for students to learn from each other at an international level. They can learn a great deal by trying to design for specific buildings in other countries which use building materials in a manner that for the students is unusual. One of the first basic requirements is to learn how to cope with existing buildings in an aesthetic, architectural and economical manner. In doing so they will appreciate that many buildings were designed for a specific purpose.

Nowadays, requirements change very quickly and buildings have to be flexible enough to accommodate these requirements. A challenge for renovators is to adapt buildings to serve new purposes in such a way that if there are further changes in the future they remain potentially strong enough to cope with the new requirements. This is another international aspect that needs to be understood as quickly as possible.

The best way to learn is to listen to architects who have proved capable of extending the life of buildings by using good methods for altering them. That is why the international module D12 attracts well-known architects, who are willing to show students what can be achieved, while at the same time implicitly teaching them about the philosophy behind the renovation of buildings.

The international lecture evenings featured:
– Herbert Bühler, Munich, Germany
– Günther Domenig, Graz, Austria
– Arnoud Fougerasse, Paris, France
– Joop van Stigt, Amsterdam, The Netherlands
– Aldo van Eyck, Loenen aan de Vecht, The Netherlands

In June an exhibition was organized at the Faculty, at which the results of this international cooperation were exhibited.

Transformations

Dwelling(s)

Supporting structures for density increase
A residential building on Binnenrotte Square

Julie-Anne van Gemert
graduation project Architectural Design

mentors
Bernhard Leupen, Willem Hermans, Rogier Verbeek

Binnenrotte Square in the centre of Rotterdam has the potential to function as a link between the shopping centre (Lijnbaan, Beursplein) and Waterstad (the areas by the river – Leuvehaven, Oude Haven). The link is not clear at present, partly due to the lack of diversity in functions around the square. The residential density is also very low for an urban area, at 25 dwellings per ha. Hence the point of departure in planning the situation between Steigersgracht and Binnenrotte Square is to increase the residential density to 200 dwellings per ha. and add shops, commercial space and working areas on the ground floor and two large multi-functional areas underground.

It is my belief that one cannot increase the density without having open space, as a square or river provide room to breathe in an old city centre. The design for Binnenrotte Square therefore includes open zones as recognizable large and small-scale elements providing the plan with structure. The zones have a connecting function and are the supporting structures of my plan.

Each level has its own supporting structure, from the urban level, the existing Binnenrotte Square, to the district level, the route in the urban ensemble to the level of the building, the street inside the building to the apartment with the corridor. Together they provide clear routing within the densely populated fabric of the city.

The existing Binnenrotte Square, without any changes, can be seen as the support for the urban level. The support for the urban ensemble, the route, provides a link from the large scale of Binnenrotte Square to the smaller scale of the area around Steigersgracht, making this area more accessible. The route itself also has a vertical link with the underground car park.

maximum slice for building on:
20-25 m

open space at site of former marketplace

high volumes for relationship with surrounding area

separating these to form an ensemble of elements

Analysis of urban planning implementation

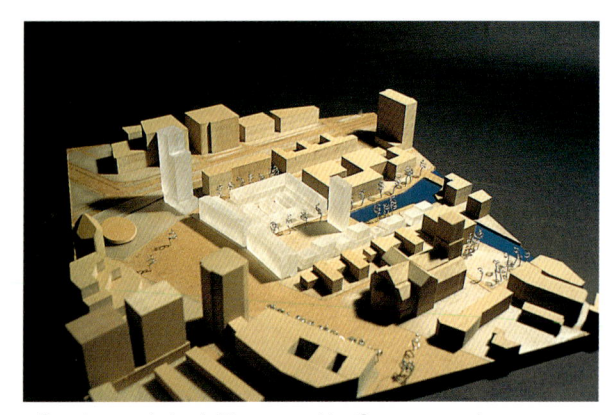

Scale model of Binnenrotte Square and surroundings

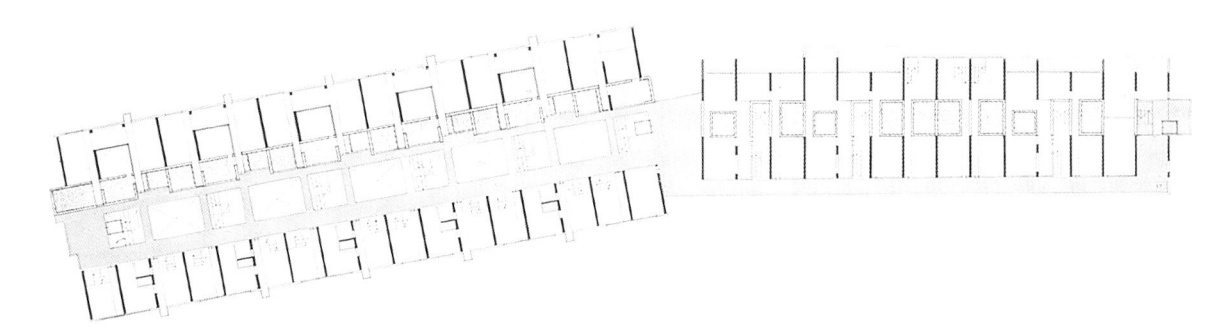

Plan of fourth floor

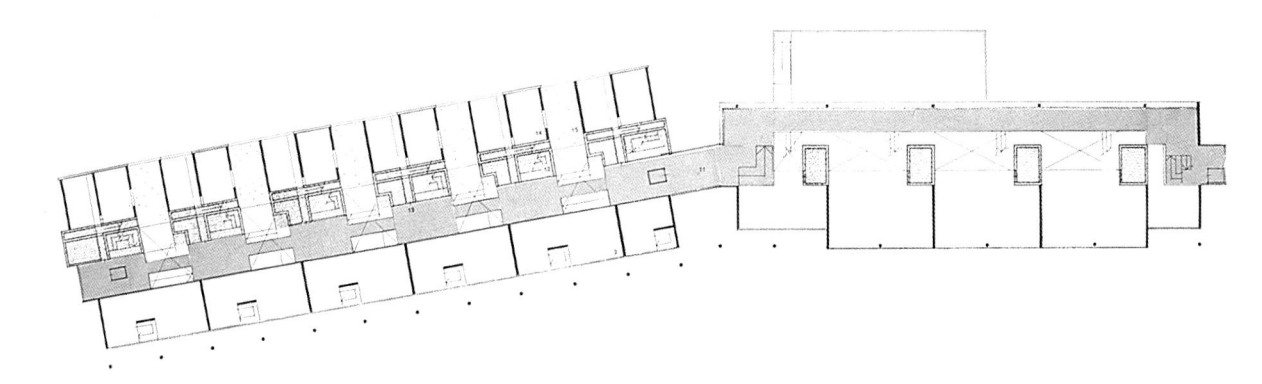

Plan of first floor (with indoor street)

1. Indoor street
2. Shop
3. Entrance to staircase
4. Staircase
5. Atrium
6. Entrance to apartment
7. Corridor
8. Toilet
9. Bathroom
10. Kitchen
11. Stairs
12. Living area
13. Storage area
14. Balcony
15. Underground car park
16. Underground room
17. Working area

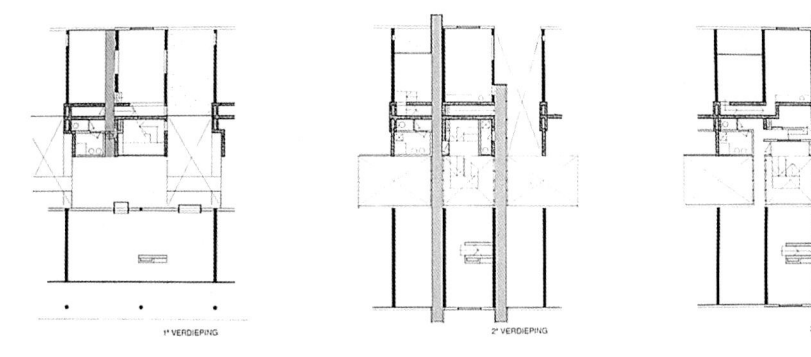

Example of connection of apartments by means of the corridor

Dwelling(s)

The indoor street inside the residential building consists of a central zone, providing access to all the flats. The building itself is based on the 17th century canal house in Amsterdam. The depth of the lots provides this type of house with a degree of privacy. There are rooms that have direct contact with the outside world and rooms facing a private inner courtyard, where the residents can enjoy the kind of privacy that is particularly important in a densely populated area. The danger of providing as much privacy as possible is that the property may turn inwards and no longer have a relationship with the communal outdoor space.

The canal house with entrance hall, back of house and inner courtyard has therefore been transformed into a residential building. This results in a building with three zones: the entrance hall, the rear section and an open zone, the atrium. A fourth, enclosed zone has been added to the 23-metre-deep building, containing all the toilets, bathrooms and kitchens, so that all the pipes and wiring are combined in this spot. This zone also provides stability.

At first floor level the atrium runs along the length of the building, forming an indoor street, and along the breadth, connecting the entrance hall with the rear section. The vertical atrium and openings in the rear section ensure that the apartments receive sufficient light despite their depth.

The result of the transformation is an apartment consisting of rooms that are adjacent to various outdoor spaces: Binnenrotte Square, the atrium and a balcony facing west. The residential building contains nine different types of apartments, divided over three corridors. The rooms inside the apartments are situated on several levels and fit together like a Chinese puzzle. The final support, the corridor, is a long, narrow, connecting element running through the apartment and continuing through the outside wall as a bay window.

Cross-section (from left to right) of back of house, enclosed zone, atrium/indoor street, entrance hall

Scale model of four bays, east facade facing Binnenrotte Square

Instant housing

Annemieke Punter
graduation project Architectural Design

mentors
Susanna Komossa, Willem Hermans, Jan van de Voort

The number of flexible workers in the Netherlands is growing. The term "flexible workers" refers to people who have a contract of employment with flexible hours and people with a temporary contract of employment. This group is a sizeable proportion of the labour market. Looking at the current housing market, it is noticeable that there is no form of housing that properly matches this social phenomenon, in which flexibility and hence mobility are important factors. What is needed is a form of housing somewhere between a home and a hotel, cheap, independent and available on a flexible lease (e.g. per day or per week), in short, by analogy with the instant meal, *the instant home*.

In the area of the study, Rotterdam, the gateway district of Katendrecht, just behind the Kop van Zuid, emerged as a suitable and interesting location. The programme benefits from the neighbourhood here, with its central location, good connections with the public transport network and a range of amenities, such as cheap places to eat, a supermarket and a launderette. In addition, the district itself can make its own contribution as an amenity in urban planning terms, both on the city level as a new link in the developing city axis, and on the neighbourhood level as the first step in the transformation and upgrading of the gateway district and the edge of the Afrikaander neighbourhood.

It is important for the building to be *cheap*, as we envisage low rents for the housing units. The addition of other programmes makes it possible to share building and management costs, as well as connect the building with the location. The additional programme consists of a supermarket and a filling station, which are already present at the location but would benefit from a better setting and image in the context of the restructuring project. On top of this, another public programme has been added as an attraction for the future residents of the building as well as the existing residents of the surrounding neighbourhoods, with features such as a fitness club, a pub and/or Internet café and a day-care centre.

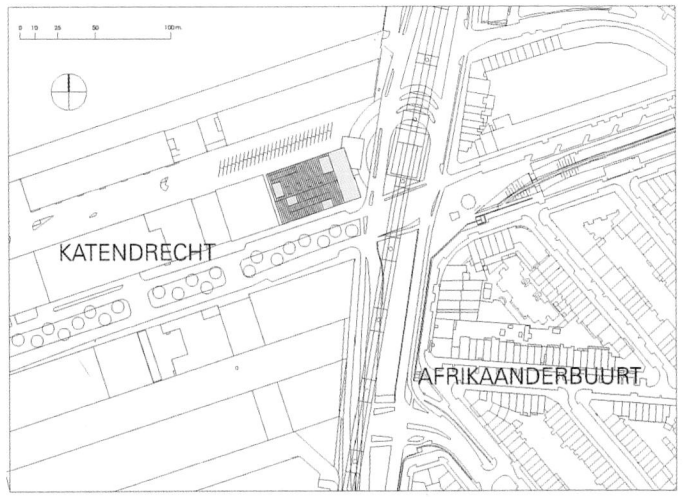

Situation

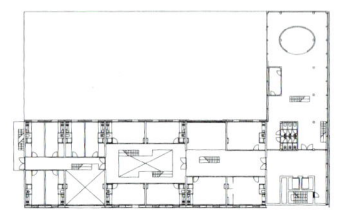

Instant housing

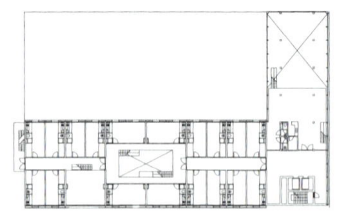

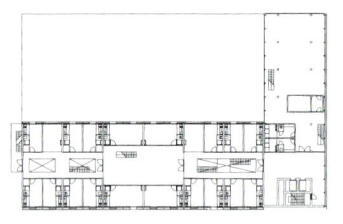

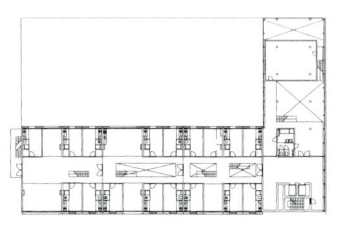

Floor plans of levels 1-6

Cross-section of corridor with the clusters and internal access points

The underlying principle for the housing part is a corridor typology. The use of various types of housing which are partly interchangeable makes it possible to achieve high occupancy. The various types have rooms of varying depths, based on certain module sizes. By grouping similar types in clusters it is possible to create an exploded corridor, which can vary from a passageway to an atrium. In this way the corridor is a collective addition to the basic home. As well as their spatial impact, the clusters also provide scope for potential large tenants, such as Shell, Dijkzicht Hospital or Erasmus University, to rent a section on a permanent basis, making it easier to let the units and guarantee low rents. The central communal entrance to the homes and the public programme

Effect of the transparent screen combined with the facade of the homes

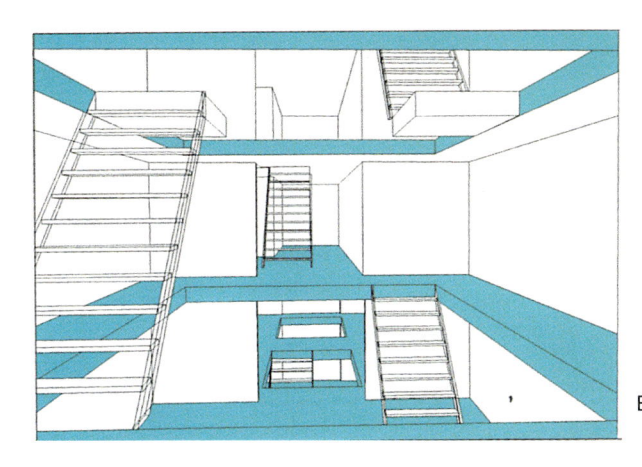

Exploded corridor

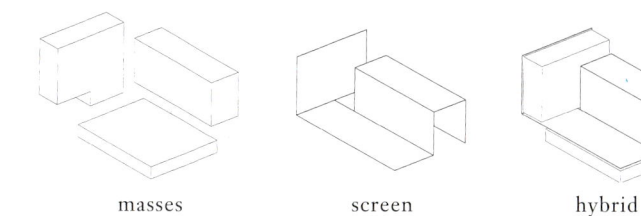

masses   screen   hybrid

is linked to the filling station shop, which is open 24 hours a day and can therefore serve as the lobby and check-in desk for the homes. Access to the homes themselves is provided initially through the corridors. In addition each cluster has an internal access point. In the wider context these internal access points provide a secondary access route, which is less formal and enhances the spatial quality and convenience of the exploded corridor.

The various programmes give the building as a whole a hybrid character. These programmes appear as individual masses, each with their own facade. A screen of transparent corrugated sheets folded around the building provides cohesion and emphasizes the programmes' *interdependence*. However, the various facades behind provide a constantly changing effect, so that like a chameleon the building fits into the city in a different way on each side.

Building on the urban axis

Dwelling(s)

Lake Shore Drive-in Apartments

Simon van Amerongen
graduation project Architectural Design

mentors
Bernard Leupen, Prof. Henco Bekkering, Rogier Verbeek

The overlap concept

Lack of space seems to be an ever-recurring problem in the Netherlands. Owing to the huge demand for housing, the city of Amsterdam has decided to expand into the IJmeer, a large lake to the east of the city. IJburg will consist of five artificial islands, providing enough space for about 18.000 homes. In a sense, the islands will form a "tabula rasa", which can be planned almost freely; an ideal situation for "re-inventing" urban design.

The aim of this design was to create an urban scheme with the simplest set of rules possible. This should result in a large amount of freedom. Freedom to build "whatever the consumer wants". Freedom that allows individuality within living. Freedom that creates diversity and complexity, qualities appreciated in historical city centres.

Re-examining the given program, which mainly consists of housing, a new subdivision of nine different types of program arises: 1. housing above the water, 2. on the water, 3. high-rise/high-density, 4. low-rise/high-density, 5. high-rise/low-density, 6. low-rise/low-density, 7. shops, 8. offices and 9. public services.

Now each type is fitted onto the site individually, in the most logical way possible, using only the island contours, the main infrastructure and different contextual factors (wind, water, sun, noise pollution, etc.) as guidelines.

In this way, "overlaps" between the different types occur, creating a kind of urban patchwork. Almost each of the newly created patches contains a mix of types especially suited to that particular patch. As in cross-breeding, there is potential for new types with an intermediate form, containing a proportionate mixture of all the characteristics of the various types involved.

Adding an extra set of quality rules ensures that every patch has its own unique formula, with which architects now can start realization. The result will be a town with a rich diversity, yet with a logical layout.

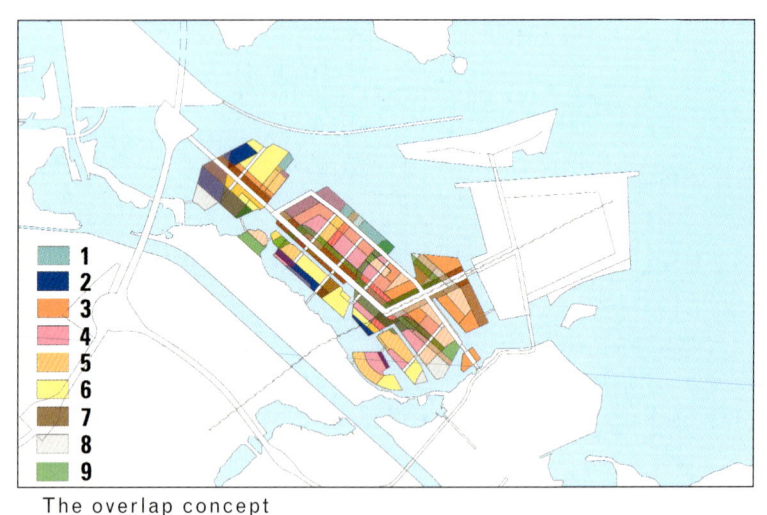

The overlap concept

The complex

Car access

Lofts · Lofts · Cores · Street

Building concept

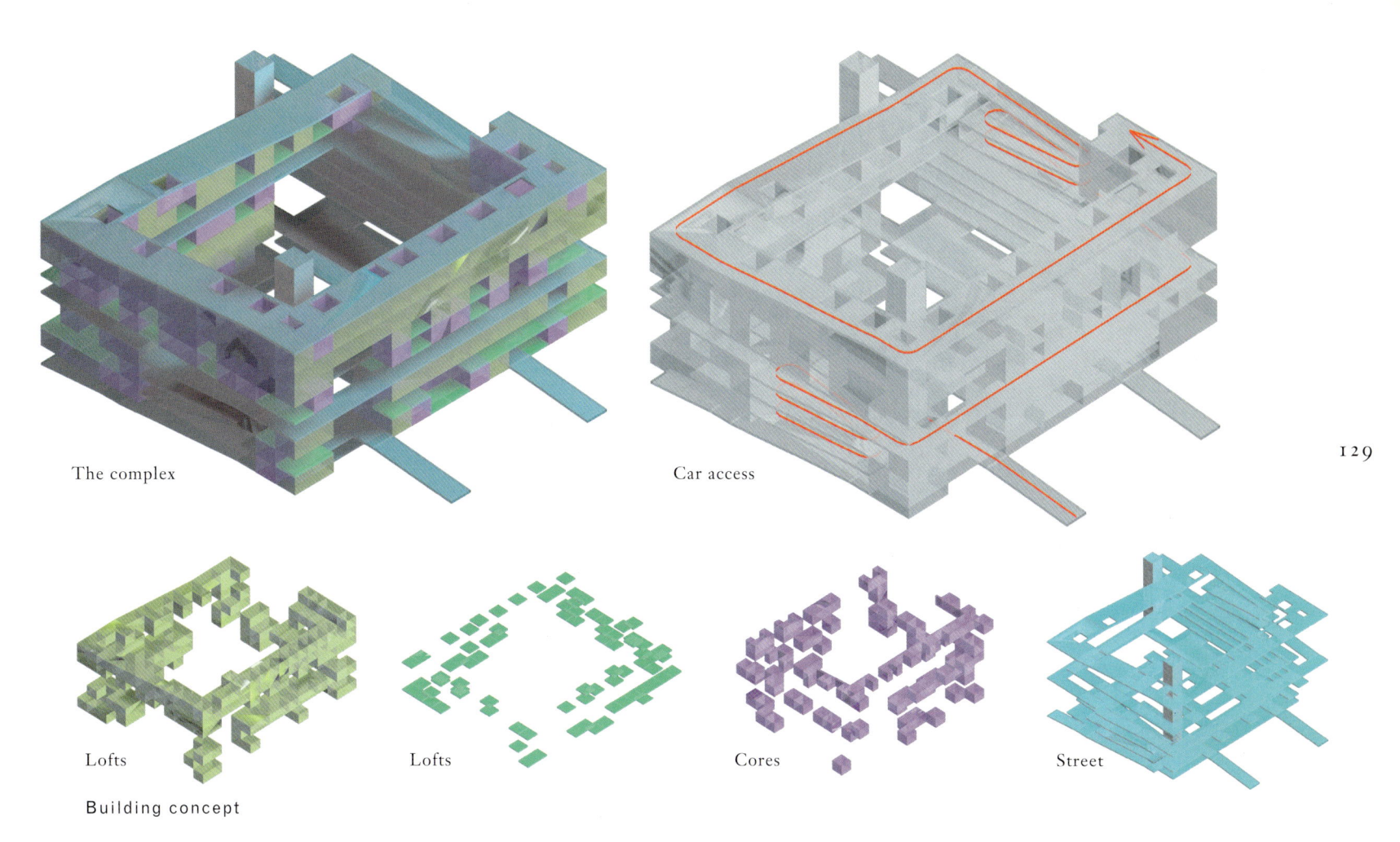

The building complex
In view of the costs involved in constructing the islands, the housing density of IJburg will be twice as high as the density of an average suburb. With the increasing emphasis on consumer-oriented markets and a rising popularity of low-density private housing, solutions for higher-density housing now need to be based on quality rather than quantity.

One of the patches described above resulted in a study for a new kind of building. In the design for "Lake Shore *Drive-in* Apartments", the qualities of popular low-rise/low-density housing are incorporated in a building seven storeys high.

The building contains 98 apartments. It is situated above the water, alongside IJburg's main boulevard. The concept of the building can best be described as "two low-rise suburbs stacked on top of each other".

Access galleries, seven metres wide, function as a three-dimensional street, taking cars, bicycles and pedestrians right up to the front door. Combining these different groups of users will provide a much better social climate than traditional gallery high-rises.

Dwelling(s)

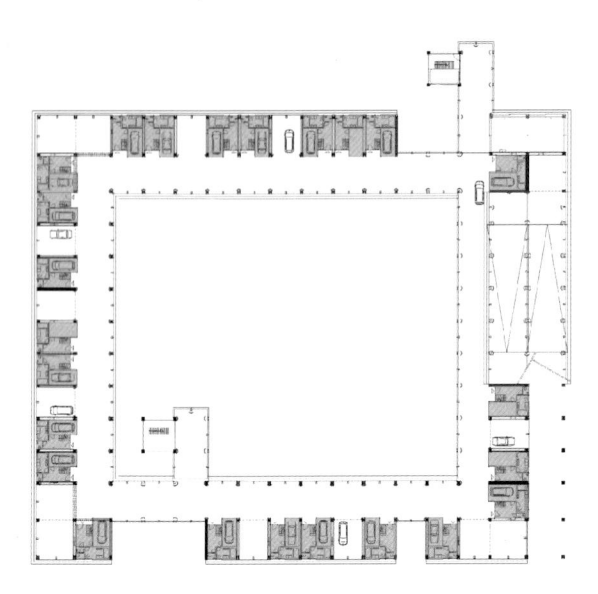

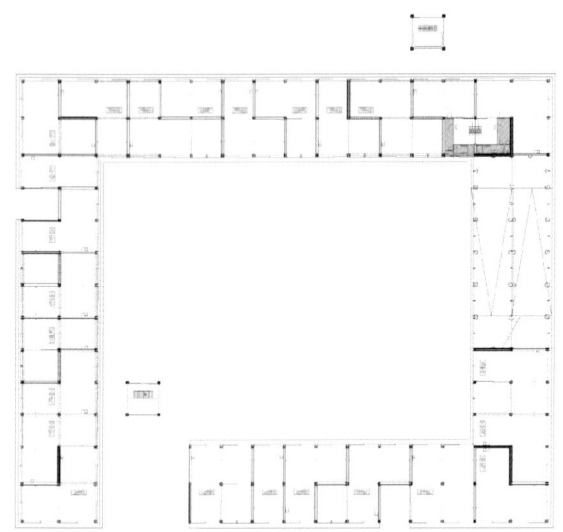

Two typical floorplans

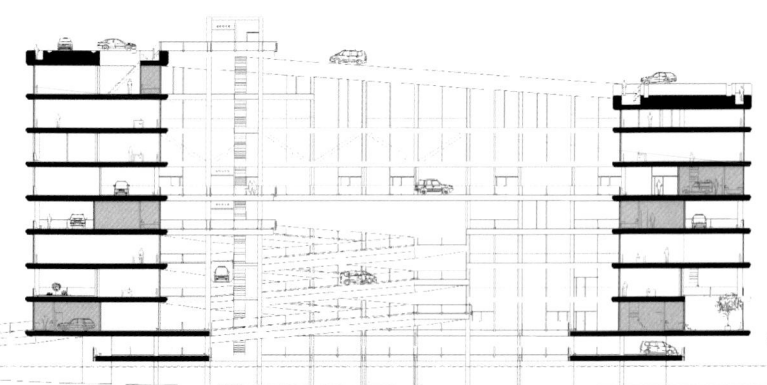

Section

Every single apartment has a drive-in garage or a parking space in front of the door, as well as a private outdoor space measuring at least 40 m². The apartments measure a non-traditional 3.35 metres between floor and ceiling to create flexibility within the interior. Walls and floors have a soundproof construction to ensure total privacy. The floor plans are kept as free as possible, specifying only front door, garage and bathroom, the core. The large space that remains, the loft, can be adapted to different lifestyles and creates the possibility to give each apartment its own character. There are four different sizes of lofts, but in combination with the different cores and different outdoor spaces, the lay-out of every single apartment is unique.

The main theme of "Lake Shore Drive-in Apartments", consistent throughout all scales, appears to be freedom of choice and individuality.

STAM + P: living in the suburbs

Densification through the introduction of new programmes in the existing parking areas, respecting Lotte Stam-Beese's 1967 design for the district of Ommoord in Rotterdam

Nynke Jutten
graduation project Architectural Design

mentors
Susanna Komossa, Jan van de Voort, Dr Han Meyer

STAM + P is a project dealing with the problems of Dutch suburbs built in the 1960s and more specifically with Ommoord, which is part of Alexanderpolder, Rotterdam. Studies of the area by the Dutch CIAM Group *De Opbouw* have had a major influence on ideas of urban design. Alexanderpolder was regarded as an independent town adjacent to Rotterdam and high-rise buildings were introduced to create a vertical residential area. For Lotte Stam-Beese the main advantage of the high-rise concept was the fact that the ground level remained free for collective use.

The central part of Ommoord is an area of high-rise flats in a green public space. The residents' perception of the area is reasonably positive; many people who moved there in the post-war reconstruction period still live there today. However, there is a strong increase in the ageing population and the place makes a drab impression. From close up, the blocks of flats fail to make the powerful impact you expect from a distance. The neighbourhood is disorientating, with all the flats looking alike and the same green spaces everywhere, while the ground-floor storage rooms are dark and the facilities back onto the public areas. Later housing developments between the flats have further encroached on the green area, which is also fragmented by private fencing and access roads.

In order to make Ommoord attractive for new residents, there needs to be differentiation in the types of housing and facilities. How can these new features be incorporated into Lotte Stam-Beese's original plan, while at the same time reinforcing the qualities of the area?

The green public spaces can be a quality amenity for the neighbourhood, provided they are kept free of private fencing, residual greenery and dark walls at ground level. This has resulted in STAM + P, a project in which new programmes are situated on the existing parking spaces near the flats. The project is designed to ensure that each block has an individual character, the ground level by the building is under semi-public management and the public green spaces remain free for collective use.

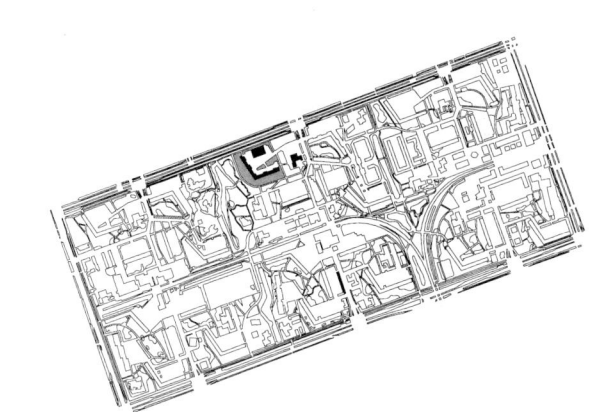

Transformation of Ommoord

Integration of parking spaces into the building

1967
green area - building

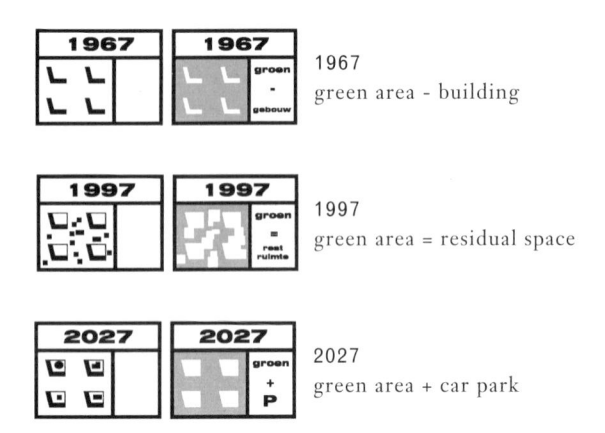

1997
green area = residual space

2027
green area + car park

Ommoord, being situated just outside Rotterdam, is attractive for young people who want to live in a setting that is both urban and green. This target population can initiate a process of greater mobility among local residents and their presence will result in more differentiated facilities. A collective housing and commercial building has been completed on one of the parking areas, containing units where people can live for a short period or start their own business. The units have their own entrances at ground level. These units and the collective facilities, such as sports and office functions, are available for rent. The facilities can also be used by residents of the block.

The building needs to make a strong gesture towards the flats, but it must not be an obstacle. The ground level goes up inside the building, ending on the second floor in a collective deck with sun terraces. The deck is accessible by bike and provides access to the units on the third floor. As the building is in a parking area, the parking spaces are integrated into the building. The units on the ground floor and first floor can also be accessed from this car park. The building is a monolith, which makes a powerful impression in relation to the block of flats, while at the same time remaining subdued in appearance. The outside walls are constructed in materials that catch the light, such as frosted glass and anodized aluminium.

The residential/commercial building is an example of the STAM + P strategy. It shows how use of the ground level can be intensified in an acceptable way. The blocks of flats are retained in their present state but the surroundings are enriched. Now let the other parking spaces follow!

Transverse sections

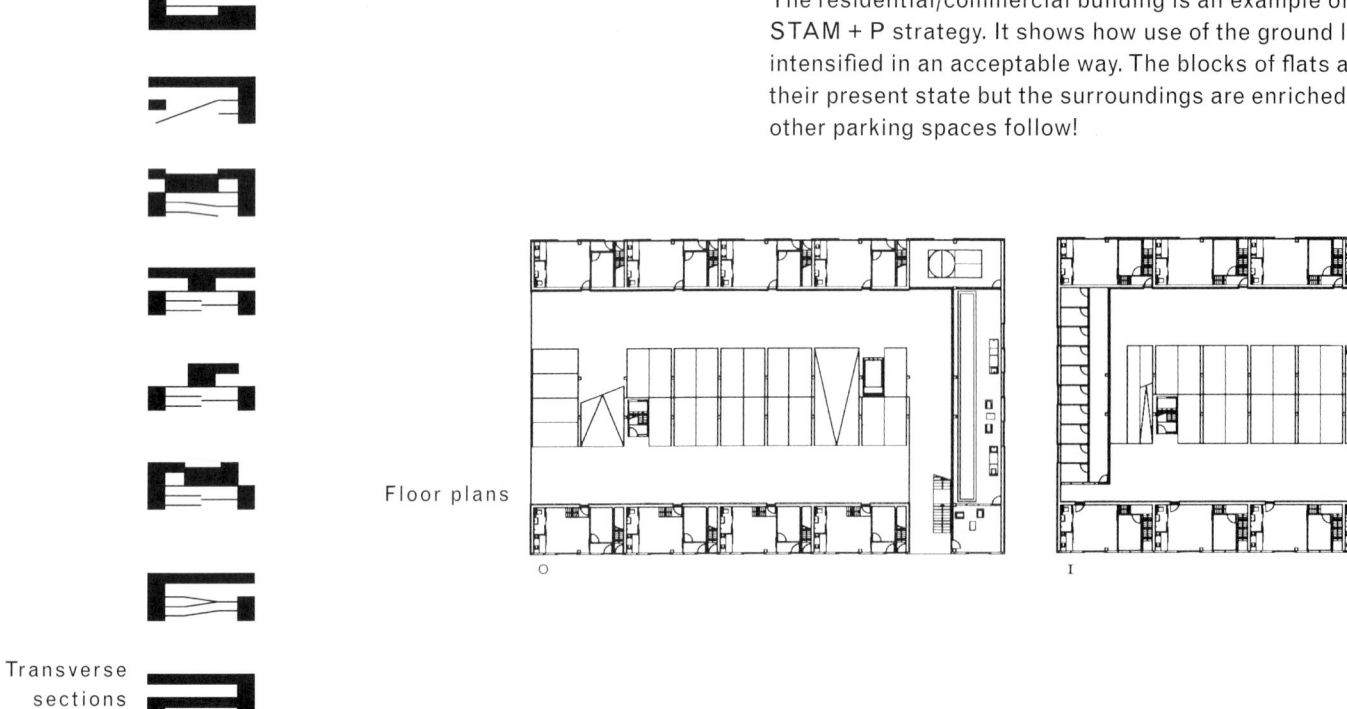

Floor plans

Pinhole photograph of residential/commercial building on the site

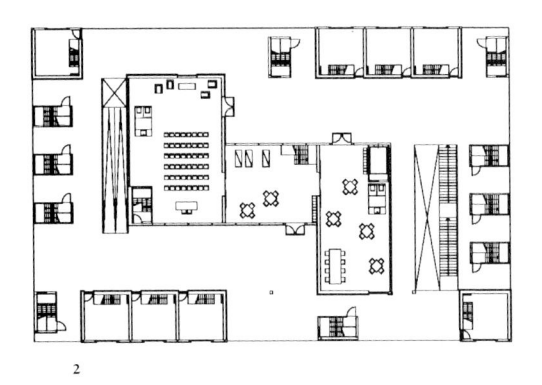

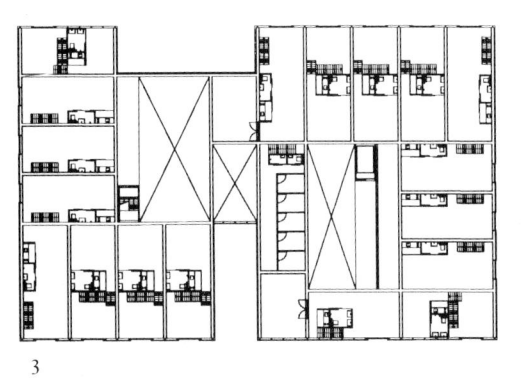

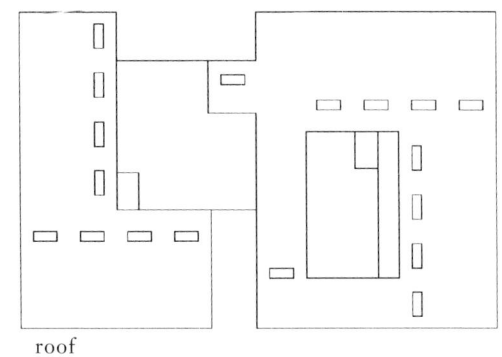

133

2   3   roof

Dwelling(s)

Viewmaster by the Maas
Density and urban space

Greetje van den Nouweland
graduation project Architectural Design

mentors
Bernard Leupen, Rogier Verbeek, Eric van der Kooij

On the south bank in Rotterdam, near the Kuip stadium, are two buildings with a distinctive shape, the *Viewmaster by the Maas*. These buildings draw attention to the variety of the view and the immense curve in the river. My fascination with this site was inspired by the current transformation processes in the city of Rotterdam: the westward shift of the port followed by the development of the Kop van Zuid. The river Maas is the geographical centre of Rotterdam, providing a unique guarantee of open space on an exceptional scale in the middle of the city. The riverside locations that are becoming available as a result of this transformation process also provide the opportunity to make the Maas the psychological centre of the city.

If we want the Maas to function as the city's psychological centre, and to accentuate the space of the Maas, two questions arise: what urban planning criteria does a riverside location in Rotterdam have to meet and what conditions does the building have to fulfil in order to create an awareness of the space of the Maas. *Viewmaster by the Maas* provides the answer to these two leading questions.

For the Maas to function as the city's psychological centre, its banks need to be easily accessible and the riverside location needs to show spatial and programmatic cohesion at every level. The first six transformations of the site define large public spaces, visibility lines and access routes. The result is a solid foundation, the plinth, preserving the unity of the plan on a large scale. The urban planning regulations lay down more specific conditions for the development of the site. The regulations define the shape and function of the plinths more precisely, as well as the use of different density levels and corresponding programme combinations of the buildings on it. Thereby spatial and programmatic cohesion are guaranteed, while at the same time achieving a certain freedom in shapes and typologies. The various density levels ensure concentration and dispersion on a large scale, giving the location significance as corridors between the Maas and the Kuip. The accompanying programme combinations provide the programme with a logical division, enabling it to contribute to the area's accessibility.

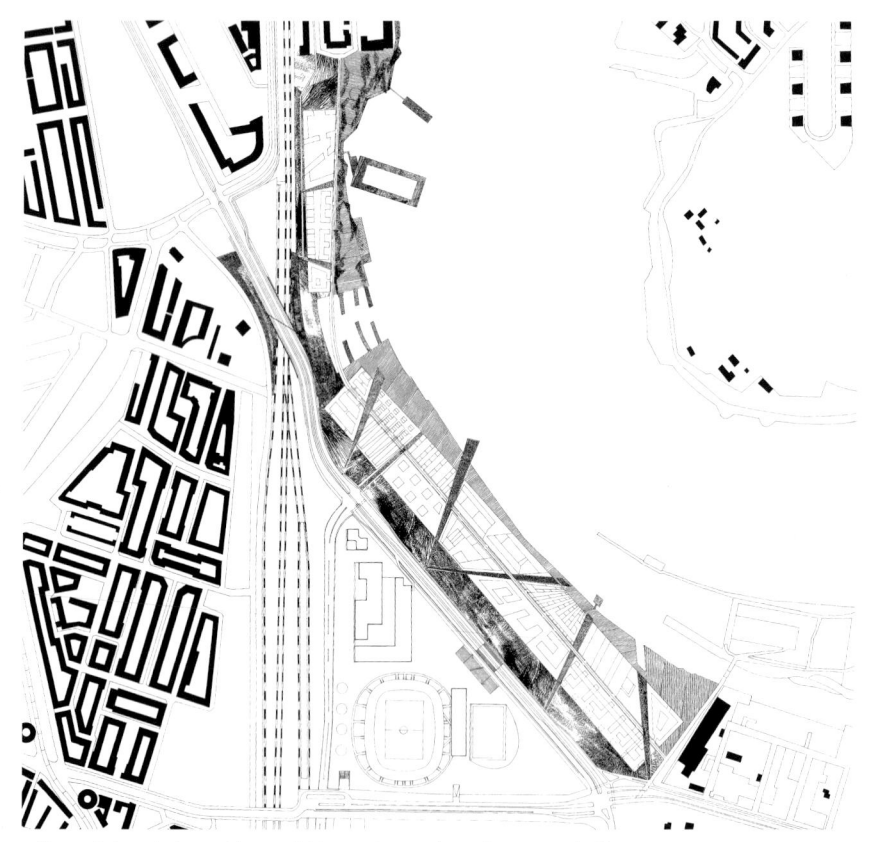

Possible elaboration of the urban planning regulations

public programme

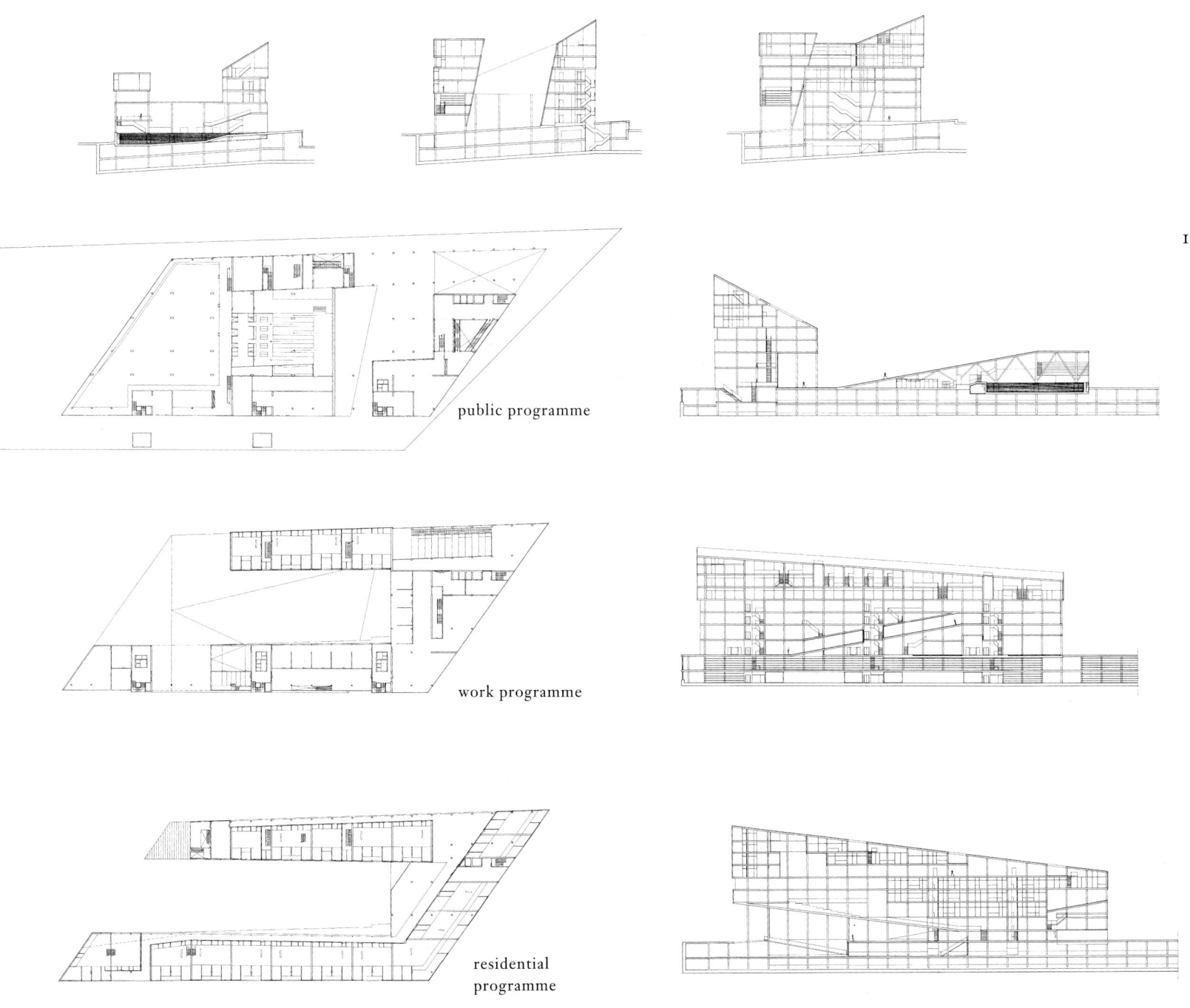

work programme

residential programme

Shape of the building in horizontal and vertical cross-sections

Dwelling(s)

Viewmaster by the Maas

Elaboration of the Viewmaster by the Maas

The *Viewmaster* is the product of both my fascination with the location and the more objective urban planning regulations. The need to answer the second question has resulted in two large monoliths, together shaped like a pair of glasses, each focusing on a specific view and capable of grasping the scale of space provided by the Maas. Together the buildings need to provide 29,000 m² of programme space. One building focuses on the Rotterdam skyline, which is emphasized by having the public inner square sloping upwards in that direction. A confrontation between this principal shape with the programme combination and the necessary provision of sunlight results in a distortion of the shape of the inner court, which smoothly accompanies the movement towards the magnificent view. The programme is incorporated efficiently into this unusual shape, emphasizing the Maas even from the apartments in the building. The view from the apartments is framed by the organization of a number of fixed residential functions in a zone bordering the outer wall. The apartments need a great deal of glass in the outside walls. In order to give the building the solid character appropriate to a monolith, the facades have been built in relief. As one approaches the building, the wall structure and wall zone help the building assume human proportions.

My objectives – to make the Maas not only the geographical but also the psychological centre of Rotterdam, while emphasizing the spatial character of the location, combined with the urban planning regulations – resulted in the *Viewmaster by the Maas*. The Viewmaster functions like a pair of glasses, enabling one to see the Maas in a new perspective.

Stacked villas in Middendelfland

Margreet van der Woude
graduation project Architectural Design

mentors
Prof. Herman Hertzberger, Meynardt Scheers, Willem Hermans

This housing development scheme is an urban planning and typological study of housing. It is a reaction to the traditional growth centre, always situated on the outskirts of a town or urban area. Placing the housing programme some distance away from the existing suburban area makes it possible to skip the stage of suburbia which has neither urban nor rural features. This urban planning principle can also be found in heroic projects such as Van den Broek and Bakema's Plan Pampus (1965) and Kenzo Tange's Tokyo Bay Project (1960). Both plans contain a dominant main artery embedded in the landscape and reshaping that landscape. This artery gives rise in an artificial way to further incorporation of the landscape into the housing and overall programme. The autonomous nature of these plans has been adopted in this project, even though the scale discussed in the plans belongs to an outmoded set of ideas.

The basic principle of a home in the largest, most open space possible leads to stacked housing in the last remaining open area in Middendelfland, the belt running from The Hague-Delft-Rotterdam, an area with views of Delft, the centre of Rotterdam and the spectacular skyline of the port and petrochemical industry. This idea of an exclusive home above the Randstad conurbation has been realized in the plan by means of a sharp contrast between the private and public domain. The route via the car park, entrance hall and vertical traffic to the house is very plainly designed. The lift stops *inside* the property and from that point on, the spaciousness of the house unfolds along horizontal and vertical diagonals.

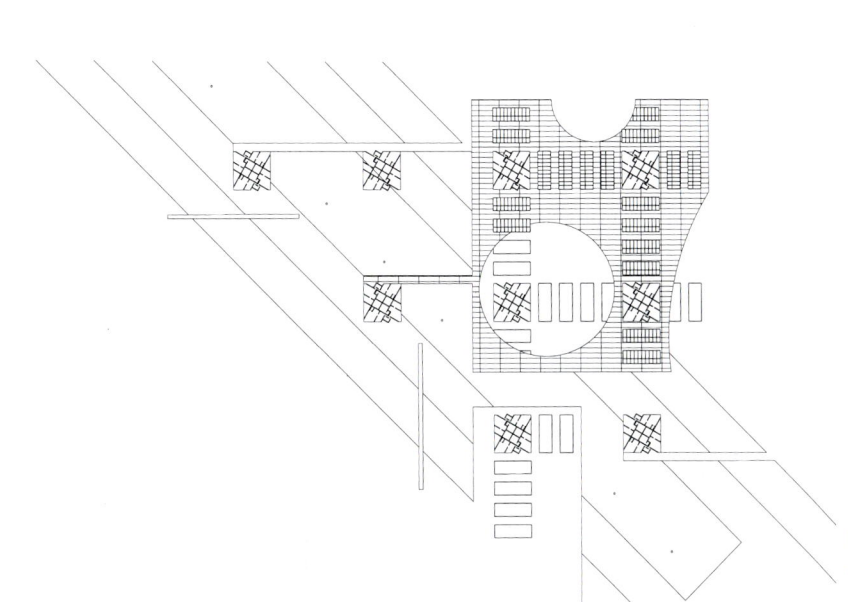

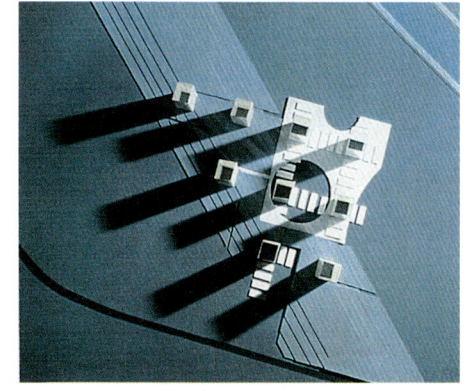

Site of the nine towers

Deck level with store rooms and entrances

Stacked villas in Middendelfland

Floor plan +35.00

Floor plan +37.70

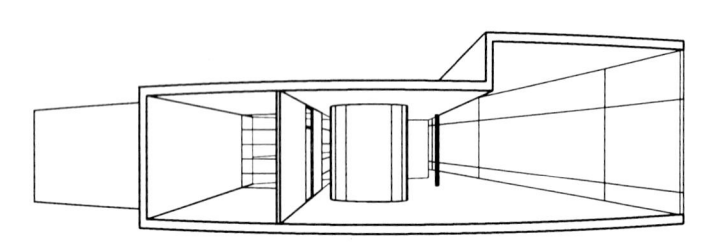

View from centre house

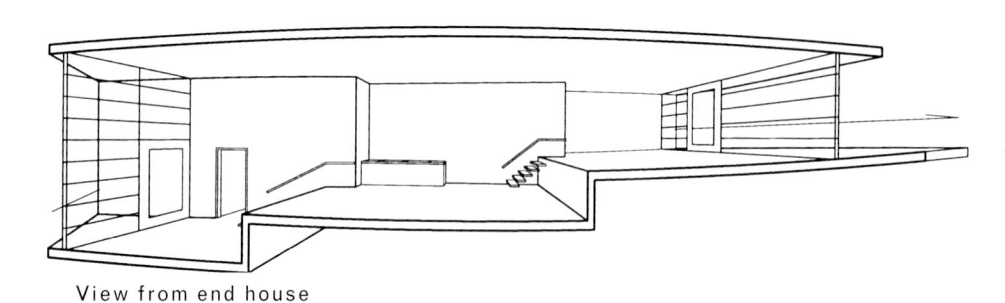

View from end house

The typology of the towers is the solution to a three-dimensional puzzle. Roughly speaking, one can distinguish two typologies in tower construction. One type includes the Lake Shore Drive towers by Mies van der Rohe (1951), with access from the centre and apartments as cells around this core. In this way a good relationship between the necessary lift and the number of apartments per floor is created. The disadvantage is the one-sided orientation of the apartments. Whereas some apartments are well situated, others are left facing either north or south. In the other type of tower, the apartments are organized in the same way as in a slab. This solves the question of orientation. However, here the apartments are no longer accessed from the centre but via a gallery (Plaslaan apartment block by Van Tijen and Maaskant, 1938), unless you have no more than two apartments per level, as in Charles Correa's Kanchanjunga tower block (1983).

Floor plan +40.40

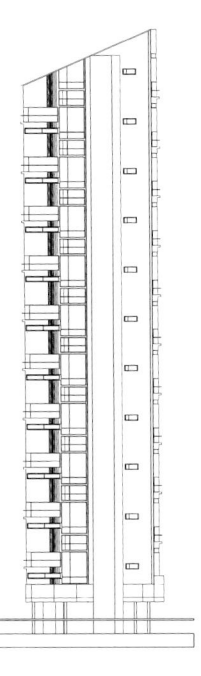

Floor plan +43.10

A cell structure is avoided by designing the floor plans diagonally through the mass of the tower. By rotating the homes on each level 90 degrees, views in all directions are provided. Finally, by placing the lifts in the angle of the cross shape, it becomes possible in this design to provide individual access to four homes per floor of 23 m by 23 m.

This internal labyrinthine complexity means that the tower could now stand in any urban space. But 80 homes per tower would not be sufficient to justify a number of practical aspects, such as the construction of a road, sewers, etc. This makes it necessary to concentrate the housing programme, resulting in three centres, based on the recreational programme. There is one location near the railway line, one at the point where water, a new motorway and a recreational programme meet, and finally one on the bank of the River Maas.

Dwelling(s)

Interpretations

Sustainable housing in Europe

Anke van Hal

There is considerable variation in the extent to which environmental measures are adopted in housing construction in various European countries. Whereas sustainable housing is clearly part of day-to-day building practice in some countries, in others the topic seldom receives serious attention. None of the environmental measures which are considered as such in the Netherlands are adopted frequently in all countries. On the other hand, several measures are adopted regularly everywhere. An overall comparison of 24 countries shows that Denmark is currently the country where the greatest number of sustainable housing measures are actually adopted, followed (some way behind) by Austria and Sweden.

In September 1997 the Second European Ministerial Conference on Sustainable Housing Policies was held in the Netherlands. One of the surveys conducted in preparation for this conference was carried out to determine the extent to which environmental measures are adopted in housing construction in the 24 countries attending the conference. This survey forms the first part of my PhD research, for which Kees Duijvestein, Faculty of Architecture, and Han Brezet, Faculty of Industrial Design Engineering, are the supervisors.

The aim of sustainable housing is to minimize damage to the environment and, where possible, to improve environmental quality. The term covers the topics energy, traffic, water, materials, waste, health, and flora and fauna, and relates to planning, design, construction and dwelling/use as well as to demolition.

Environmental measures are design and/or technical measures which contribute to the sustainability of housing. The measures relate to both the dwelling and the dwelling place (the concept of "domicile"). In this sense, housing construction can thus be seen in terms of different levels, on an ascending scale: detailed level, dwelling/workplace level, building level, neighbourhood level, district level, and urban level. The environmental measures in the research are measures which are considered as such in the Netherlands.

It was not possible to carry out extensive country-by-country research, and it should therefore be emphasized that the results simply give an approximate picture of the current situation regarding sustainable housing in the various countries. The data for Spain, Hungary and the Czech Republic were unreliable.

Sustainable housing in general

There is considerable variation in the extent to which environmental measures are adopted in housing construction in the various countries. Whereas sustainable housing is clearly part of day-to-day building practice in some countries, in others, the topic seldom receives serious attention. None of the measures listed are adopted frequently or (almost) always in all 24 countries. On the other hand, several measures are adopted regularly everywhere. In particular, these include measures designed to reduce the use of CFCs and HCFCs and products containing formaldehyde, and to limit the use of asbestos.

The scores in figure 1 can only be interpreted properly with reference to the country analyses. This is because in some countries (such as Estonia) new building only takes place on a very small scale. Environmental measures are usually very common in such cases. Yet the situation there can hardly be compared to the situation in a country such as the Netherlands, where large numbers of new dwellings are currently being built and where extensive sustainable housing measures are adopted in 5% – and in the case of the "national package of sustainable housing measures" in about 15% – of all new housing. Irrespective of such background information,

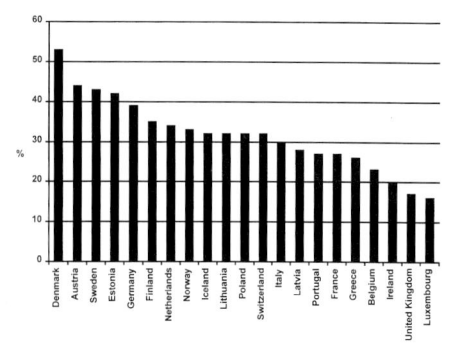

Figure 1 Measures adopted in the 24 countries: all measures listed in the questionnaire

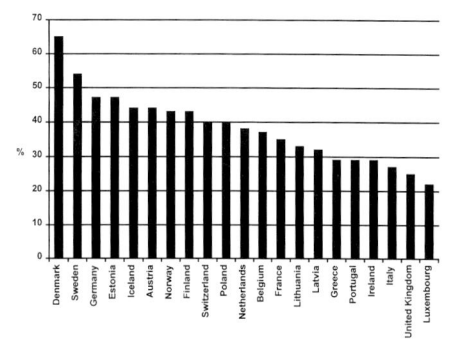

Figure 2 Measures adopted in the 24 countries: energy

however, this comparison indicates that Denmark is currently the European leader in sustainable housing.

The various countries were also compared topic by topic.

Energy

Energy is the topic which receives the most attention almost everywhere. Here again, Denmark is the leader, followed (at some distance) by Sweden. As expected, energy-saving measures are only adopted to a limited extent in southern European countries. The scores in this chart thus make reasonable sense in climatic terms. Iceland adopts fewer energy-saving measures than might be expected in view of its geographical location; however, this is explained by the fact that the main local source of heating is geothermal energy, which is available in such abundance that energy-saving measures have relatively low priority.

There are large differences between countries when it comes to thermal insulation values. Climatic factors obviously play an important part here. The Scandinavian countries pay a great deal of attention to thermal insulation of dwellings. Various Danish and Swedish respondents quote an Rc value of 6.50 m² K/W for roof insulation, which is a high value compared with other countries. In Belgium, on the other hand, surprisingly little attention is paid to this topic. Belgian respondents indicate that an Rc value of 1.50 m² K/W is usual for facades, ground floors and roofs. A number of countries do not lay down requirements for individual parts of buildings; instead, a sort of overall energy coefficient is calculated for the entire building.

Traffic

There are more significant differences between countries in the case of traffic than in the case of energy. In Luxembourg, for example, average incomes are relatively high and petrol is cheap, so cars are used a great deal and there is little interest in measures to limit motor traffic. In many countries, however, such measures are common, either for environmental reasons (CO_2 emissions) or for practical reasons (time lost through traffic jams). The popularity or otherwise of cycling also helps to account for the differences. In Poland, for example, cycling is a popular sport, but one respondent says it is 'not done' to cycle to work (unlike in Finland and the Netherlands, where cycling is very common).

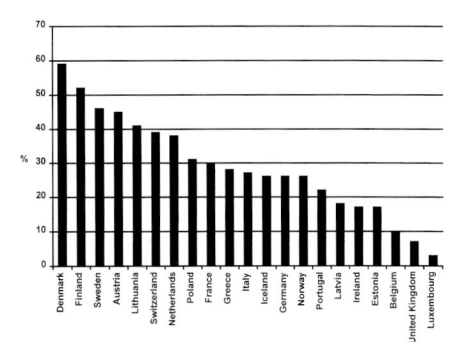

Figure 3 Measures adopted in the 24 countries: traffic

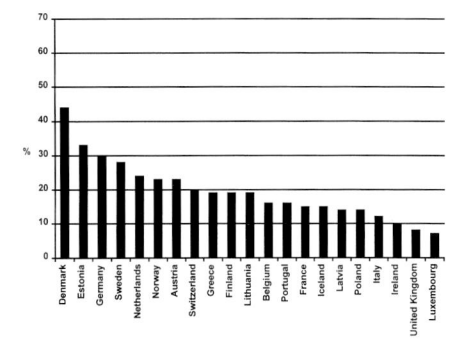

Figure 4 Measures adopted in the 24 countries: water

Water

Water is a topic that appears to be receiving increasing attention. Dehydration is currently a problem in many countries. Since the survey is based on the situation in the Netherlands, the scores in this chart do not always reflect the true picture. The water-saving measures listed in the questionnaire (such as water-saving toilets, taps and showers) are too advanced for many countries. In some countries, installing water meters in all dwellings and/or increasing the price of water are the main measures used to reduce water consumption. These measures, which all greatly reduce water consumption, were not listed in the questionnaire.

In some countries, certain measures listed in the questionnaire are quite simply prohibited. In France, for example, recycling of rainwater – and, according to one respondent, even the use of rainwater barrels – is against the law.

Materials

All 24 countries show at least some interest in the environmental impact of materials, and the differences between countries are not very great with regard to this topic. The use of asbestos, red lead, products that damage the ozone layer and products with high levels of formaldehyde has been reduced to a minimum or completely banned almost everywhere. Another striking detail is that many countries have replaced PVC with the less harmful PP and PE for use in internal drains. Some countries still have many traditional measures which were not originally adopted on environmental grounds but now turn out to be environmentally sound. A good example is the use of European wood. Other countries which switched over to tropical hardwood in the past are now switching back to traditional types of wood for environmental reasons. Another material which has traditionally been used almost everywhere is brick; one Danish respondent, however, says that brick should not be considered environmentally sound, because of the large amount of energy used in producing it.

Waste

Domestic waste is separated in most countries, but the number of fractions varies considerably. Paper and glass are separated almost everywhere. There is also a great deal of variation in the extent to which building-site waste is separated (ranging from no separation to seven different fractions).

Several countries take specific measures to ensure that dwellings are accessible to disabled people (so that less waste is generated when the dwellings are adapted), but few measures have been adopted as yet to limit the use of foams, sealants, etc. so that materials can be separated more easily at the demolition stage.

Health

The questions on the topic of health mainly concern sound insulation. There is also an occasional question on radon and emissions of harmful gases from open fireplaces. Austria appears to adopt the most measures in this area. Denmark and Germany also pay a great deal of attention to this topic. Only seven of the 24 countries frequently take measures to deal with radon. Dwellings in a number of countries never have open fireplaces, but this is usually for reasons of cost rather than environmental reasons. In Portugal, in fact, open fireplaces are very popular at the moment.

The respondents' replies indicate that sound insulation measures are adopted to some extent everywhere. At least one such measure is said to be adopted frequently or (almost) always in every country except Latvia, Italy, Poland and Portugal.

Flora & fauna

The chart shows that Austria adopts the most measures relating to flora and fauna. The measures listed in the questionnaire can be subdivided into those adopted at urban development/dwelling environment level and those adopted at dwelling level. Few extensive measures are adopted at dwelling level, but far more are taken at urban development and dwelling environment level. The most common measures are inventories of archaeological and historical features and soil quality investigation. In principle, all 24 countries take account of existing flora and fauna, but the extent to which they do so varies considerably. Specific features such as ponds for frogs and tunnels or viaducts for fauna are not common anywhere.

Conclusion

Sustainable housing practice varies considerably from one country to another. Sometimes there are good reasons for these differences. But there are also differences that cannot be easily explained. Why, for example, is water saving so common in countries with no shortage of fresh water, like Sweden? And why is water saving not common at all in a country like Italy which has a lot of water problems? Why does Belgium 'score' worse than the Netherlands, and Denmark so much better? And why do countries with a comparable climate not take the same energy-saving measures? These questions require further research. For the moment the conclusion is that the various countries can learn a great deal from one another, and that it is definitely worthwhile to look at what other countries are doing.

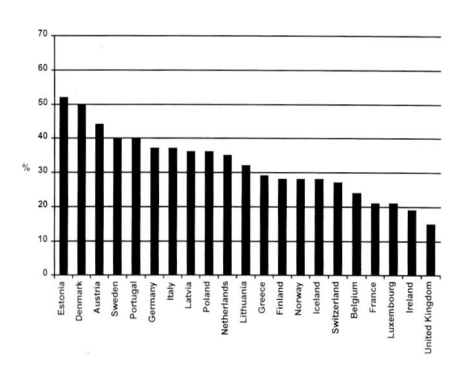

Figure 5 Measures adopted in the
24 countries: materials

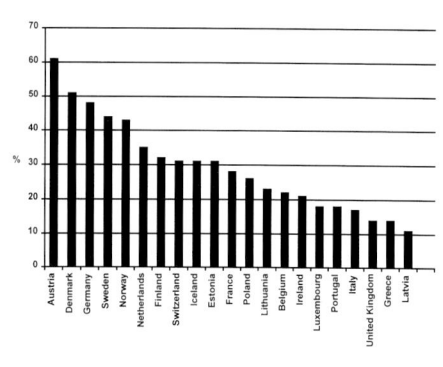

Figure 7 Measures adopted in the
24 countries: health

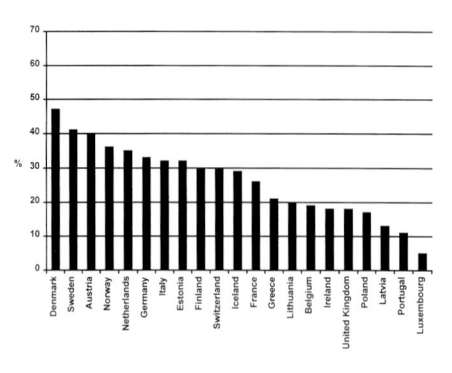

Figure 6 Measures adopted in the
24 countries: waste

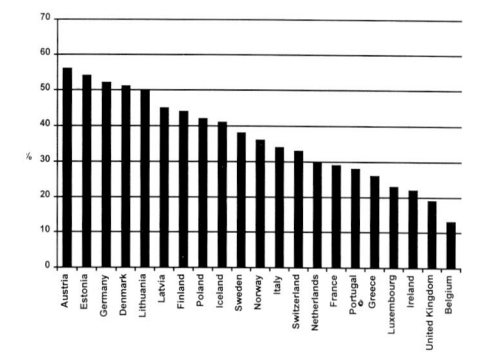

Figure 8 Measures adopted in the
24 countries: flora & fauna

IMPression
On the rules of 'The International Style' (1932)

Dr Rypke Sierksma

1
Gombrich, *Art and illusion*, 1962 ed., p. 78

2
Tafuri, *Theories of history and architecture*, 1980 ed., p. 153, states that one should not criticize buildings, but the theories behind them; compare Gombrich in his *Meditations on a hobby horse*, 1978 ed., p. 52: 'You cannot argue with shapes, but you can argue with painters and with those philosophies of art that have resulted in a situation that is as torturing to the artist, as it is stultifying to the critic'. In a somewhat obscure, but nevertheless relevant comment on Tafuri, Jameson in a conversation with Speaks, in *Assemblage 17*, says that 'all theories [including political, cultural theories, RS] now have to pass *through the code* [italics mine] of the spatial in order to match their object of analysis'.

3
In my title "IMPression" I have inserted a pun. As this article is on the relationship between art and rules – the 'modern' artist wanting to be free of them – I refer to one of Edgar Allan Poe's tales, "The Imp of the Perverse". The imp that is, which makes us nót do what we should, while making us do what we shouldn't.
Cf. Poe, *Tales*, New York, Random House, 1944, p. 440/1

4
Cf. Wittgenstein, *Philosophical investigations*, par. 19, 23, 100, 564. This also means that the same game can have various uses (see par. 21).

The rules of chaos

For argument's sake let's suppose that all figure and line in the history of architecture is projected upon it by the historian. This pure historicism still does not explain why architects themselves have always sought to bring order into their business by promulgating rules – much more so than in other arts. Only in architecture do writers of rules present themselves from the very beginning as bearers, not so much of an aesthetic code, as of aesthetic *truth*. Even in our days where the talk is of 'architectural views' with an implied free will, the debate still gives the impression of *armed pluralism*. Even though from the perspective of a chaos-oriented historian architecture seems to be scattered and accidental, architects still seem to crave for rules.

More generally the art historian Gombrich in his classic *Art and illusion* asserts that 'the form of a representation cannot be divorced from its purpose and from the requirements of the society in which the given visual language gains currency'.[1] What motivates this urge for architectural rules? How are they connected with these 'social requirements'? What character do these rules have? An analysis of documents in which rules are elaborated should not so much ask whether such codes *actually* got established, as why they were *formulated* in the specific way they were.[2] I shall adopt this approach to The International Style of Hitchcock and Johnson.[3]

Tools of analysis:

I. Types of rules

Instead of the one universal and purely rational language proposed in his *Tractatus* (1918) Wittgenstein developed in his *Philosophical investigations* (1945) the idea that there are many language games instead of only one, each with a different issue for which its language functions as a tool. *O*ne of these language games may consist 'purely' of scientific reports, but there are countless other language games as well, between which there is no demonstrable or provable hierarchy. Each game needs rules, but these rules need not necessarily be of the commanding or the reporting type, and they can be more or less vague. Games do not only have rules but also a 'point' – a purpose – and depending on that purpose, one might differentiate between types of rules.[4] The question is what the point of *The International Style* is.

Instead of *separating* commands on the one hand, and rules on the other, it is theoretically more productive to think in terms of both normative and commanding functions of one and the same rule. The *commanding function* establishes a relation of obedience between the one who commands and the one commanded; the *normative* or regulatory function of a rule implies regulation of interaction among subjects who are informed by that rule about the legitimate expectations they may have about each other's behaviour or about artefacts produced.[5] Such rules may be implicit or unconscious and may sometimes inform a document (for instance one about architectural theory) that explicitly propagates *other* rules. The hidden rule must be tracked down via the context of the document.[6] Some behaviour can also be called 'instructive', other behaviour 'regulative' – depending on the *dominance* of one of the two functions, but it would still involve rules having *both* functions at the same time.

It is well accepted that creative behaviour cannot be 'instructive' – ruled, that is, by command or instruction. Following rules, yes – obedience, no! No critical conclusion can be reached 'by application of a rule', as each work of art is in the end by nature unique. Scruton concludes that 'there is something truly absurd about the attempt to command obedience to a rule which can be formulated only when it is *already* obeyed'.[7]

This resembles the pragmatic position taken in Dewey's *Art as experience*, in which a clear distinction is made between using standards and using criteria in judging art, whereby standards are understood to mean benchmarks that are determined in advance, and criteria are yardsticks that are developed on the basis of the works themselves. Dewey also quotes 'special movements like Functionalism in architecture' as complicating and obscuring the issue of aesthetic judgement, because of notions of partisanship – in short, judgement in the juridical sense. When a rule is regarded as a law, its authority substitutes precedent and prestige for what is actually vital in art: direct experience.[8] Apart from 'direct experience', we do find rules galore in architectural theories, and they *do* provide both architects and the users of architecture with a frame of reference. The question I am posing now relates to the textual functioning of these rules.

II. The effects of rules

The 'requirements of society' mentioned can be conceived of as the sedimentation of society in a scheme of rules. Habermas argued consistently that the attempt of the Surrealists to fill the gap between art and life, by abandoning all rules for art and taking life in its ready-made diffuseness, ended with the end of Surrealism – with nothingness.[9] My conclusion is that only *because* there was some scheme present, did Surrealism have its day for a while. Purely for market reasons, that is for reasons of being able to produce *and* sell, socially shared frameworks of reference are needed.

Putnam argues against those who have a 'derogatory attitude towards rules' and against their notion that 'all rules have exceptions', because this leads to a 'completely empty situation ethics' where anything goes, as long as one is 'sensitive'. He claims that the very notion of 'an exception to a moral rule' is meaningless, unless the exception is carefully 'hedged', which means: specified as to its limits. And to think in terms of hedging exceptions, is to think in terms of rules.[10] As all aesthetic rules seem to have an ethical implication, Putnam's argument is also pertinent here.[11]

If such a hedged scheme of rules were not there, each act of aesthetic production would become an idiosyncratic expression, in other words completely personal and hence *not* communicable – something that is at best interesting to others for its shock value (and does not even 'shock' presuppose some preliminary scheme?) As far as the profession is concerned, it is interesting that architects, like other artists, not only need a scheme of rules; above all architects demand some long-term market value for their product. Not only is there a speedy erosion of architectural conversation pieces with which some cities try to find themselves a place on the map; Paine noticed a long time ago the very thin line between the sublime and the ridiculous. But the production of only shocking conversation pieces would definitely kill their conversation value. So architects especially, given how expensive their product is, have a vested interest in establishing rules, a style – a scheme without which they would be ephemeral mayflies, and without which clients would find it increasingly difficult to make a choice. In discussing *The International Style* it is evident that there is no shortage of political motives when it comes to establishing rules.

In Kant's view we should never manipulate others to achieve something we desire, and we should certainly not use dishonest means to do so.[12] This may be an honourable position in ethics, but it does seem to have only a relative descriptive value. *Normal* power differences make this position unrealistic. Norbert Elias analyzed social order in terms of configurations or *networks* of people who have become mutually dependent. De Vries posed the question as to their scope – who does, and who does not belong to such a social network? It is not that such a network has specific limits (x number of members). De Vries specifies the rules that members of such a network have to follow.

Once this scheme of rules has been established, the number of members may change; hence the scheme defines the network. When people have conflicts, they are part of a configuration with certain rules, and the conflict is not just about some specific goals but basically also about the rules. There are fundamentally two methods of putting an end to such conflict – either by manipulating the rules, or by manipulating the context in such a way that the other members are obstructed from applying the rules in a way that is favourable to them. With an acknowledgement to Nietsche, Schattschneider interprets both solutions as 'mobilizing a perspective'.[13]

De Vries concludes that by manipulating the context in such a way that only very specific rules may be followed, one actually diminishes the number of people that may participate in networks belonging to the context. This seems to be the strategy for an already

5
Glastra van Loon, *De eenheid van handelen*, 1980, p. 25/34. See also the first chapter of Siorksma's PhD, *Toezicht en taak*, 1991. For the difference between game and play see also Mead, *Mind, self and society*, (1934), 1962 ed., p. 151ff. Specifically p. 158ff where it is stressed that a game has a definite aim, which makes the organization of all action into a whole necessary. Hence it is a text about the varying intensity and scope of rules.

6
Cf. Foucault's notion of epistème in *Les mots et les choses*, 1963. Also Porphyrios, "Aantekeningen bij een methode", in *Oase*, transl. 1984, p. 366. One can also learn a language game, however, without explicitly learning the rules, a point that Wittgenstein makes in his *Investigations*, par. 31 and 54.

7
Scruton, *The aesthetics of architecture*, 1987, pp. 238, 227, 55ff

8
Dewey, *Art as experience*, 1934, pp. 298/309, 288. Also Rossi in *Architectural Design*, op. cit., pp. 26, 19, quoting the apolitical Mies in support of an anti-metaphysical experiential-data conception of architecture.

9
Habermas in: Tzonis ed., *Reader: moderne en antimoderne architectuur na 1945*, 1986, p. 78

10
Putnam, *Realism with a human face*, 1990, p. 193ff

11
This is a matter of debate. In his book Scruton wants to remove Kantian autonomy from aesthetic and ethical judgement, but reserves autonomy for a truth judgement. (op. cit. pp. 1 and 164ff). According to Peirce, ethics depends on aesthetics, cf. *Philosophical writings of Peirce*, ed. Buchler, 1940, p. 62. This, however, seems to be based upon a categorical opposition between the realms of ethics and aesthetics, cf. Reilly, *Peirce's theory of science*, 1970, p. 18. See also M. Frank, *Einführung in die frühromantische Ästhetik*, Frankfurt a. M., 1989, chapter 1. Lyotard goes even further than Scruton and sees both the truth judgement and the ethical judgement as being grounded in one's ability to make aesthetic judgements, which more or less reflects the view of Nietzsche, for whom every individual judgement was a question of 'power'. Cf. *Apathie in der Theorie*, transl. 1979, p. 27. I think that, although differentiation of the three

realms of science, art and ethics has marked the advent of modernity – cf. Habermas, *Der philosophische Diskurs der Moderne*, 1985, pp. 16ff, 64, 140, 367 – most aesthetic argument or criticism implies claims to both authenticity and aesthetical appropriateness, albeit often camouflaged as 'l'art pour l'art'. Cf. Wellmer, in *Adorno Konferenz* 1983, p. 164. Post-modernism shows the extremes; pseudo-autonomous art and kitschy environmental art, feminist art, etc.

12
Putnam, op. cit. pp. 195, 197

13
Cf. Elias, *Wat is sociologie*, transl. 1968. De Vries, *Sociale orde, regels en de sociologie*, 1977, pp. 125, 169ff, 214ff. This manipulation of others has various strategies and various intensities; compare, for instance, the difference between agitation and propaganda of the Agitprop Ministry of the former Soviet Union – here *propaganda* is the explanation of many ideas to one person, and agitation the explanation of one idea to a large public, cf. *Winkler Prinz Encyclopedie*, Part 1, p. 454. But power over rules can also be instrumental in the structuring of biographies, De Vries, op. cit., p. 214ff.

14
Cf. Tafuri and Dalco, *Modern Architecture*, 1976, p. 240. I doubt whether Colquhoun's 'paradox of reason' explains the complexities of the Hitchcock/Johnson text. This paradox only points out the contradictory value of, on the one hand, efficiency of means/ends and, on the other hand, aesthetic, philebic bodies like the cube, the sphere, etc. Cf. Von Moos, in: *Raumplan versus Plan Libre*, Delft 1987, p. 21ff. Also Frampton, *Moderne architectuur: een kritische geschiedenis*, transl. 1988, p. 309; Porphyrios, op. cit. in: *Architectural Design*, op. cit., p. 23; Scully, in: *Collaboration*, ed. Diamondstein, 1986, p. 53

15
Cf. for instance Tzonis, *Reader* op. cit., p. 13, with basically a market analysis on four points; cf. also Tafuri, *Theories* op. cit., p. 323ff

16
Tzonis, Berwick and Freeman, *Les systèmes conceptuels de l'architecture en France de 1650 à 1800*, 1975, p.1. Compare with my comments on Wittgenstein and the language games.

stronger party. The *weaker* party chooses the strategy of socializing the conflict – stressing more general rules which more people feel are applicable to their behaviour.

It seems to me that there is a link with the distinction drawn between imperative rules and regulatory rules or norms. A stronger party in any of the defined markets (intellectual market of architects, market of use-definitions of the users, market for appreciation schemes, etc.) would profit by being able to formulate rules that have an imperative or command dominant, which it might manage to impose on others, with the possible exception of exclusive loners who ignore such rules and may profit from the set-up – the young Koolhaas springs to mind. A weaker party, on the other hand, would seek to formulate more *normative rules*, functioning as a frame of reference that informs the productive and perceptive individuality of the participants – thus potentially broadening the scope of the network. What, in my view, is vital is the possibility of *more* conflicts being at issue in one and the same text of rule codification. This implies that one and the same proposed rule, with its dual aspects of command and regulation, addresses at the same time two different parties in two different conflicts with two different power positions (viz. weak/strong) – tension and contradiction will probably be the result. I shall prove my point.

Reading *The International Style* superficially

Quite a few critics[14] regard *The International Style* as a reduction of the phenomenon of architecture to the mere fact of style. They ascribe analytical and explanatory intentions to it, and because of this they accuse it of being short-sighted. Yet the book is in no way intended to be a full-scale analysis or explanation of architecture. Conversely, the critics, who claim to take a scientific standpoint, often put forward ideological arguments. *Both* sides, both critics and the authors of *The International Style*, are pursuing politico-ideological aims – Tafuri, Frampton and Tzonis, for example, the humanistic aim of a non-oppressive environment of human behaviour; Hitchcock and Johnson something like that, but in a far more restricted context.

Both sides cover up their ideological intentions – either by presenting it as a scientific or historical analysis[15], or by presenting their analysis as one that is restricted to pure principles of style. Barr, in his 1932 introduction to the book, explicitly underscores my reading by pointing out that the authors had earlier dedicated other texts to the technological and social aspects of architecture, which they see as 'extremely important factors', something that is confirmed in the text itself under the heading *History*. Hitchcock comments on this issue in 1966, stating that neither the text, nor the exhibition for which it served as the catalogue, was *intended* as a collection of recipes for architectural success, nor was it intended as a 'prognosis' or as a 'premature obituary' of *The International Style*. This self-assessment nicely covers my next interpretation, but contradicts Tafuri, Scully, and the others who interpreted the book as pure reduction of architecture to style. The original text may well be primarily a stylistic analysis of rules (subsequently mistakenly denied by Hitchcock), but closer analysis reveals that this is a manifestation of what it actually is: a *social treatise*. It is not, therefore, 'merely a description' as Hitchcock claims, nor is it a 'predictive' analysis of a set of *pure* aesthetic rules.

A hidden agenda

Tzonis gives us a nice summa of the statute of design 'discourses'. A design discourse does not always tell us the truth, sometimes deliberately not. In that case, discourse analysis must reveal the thinking that lies *behind* the discourse, 'We must look at the game that was played with it'.[16] There is a hidden agenda in *The International Style* – more games are played all at the same time under the apparent cover of a discussion on style. Both the text and the introduction by Barr suggest that the book is primarily 'proof of the existence of an original modern style', this point being stressed again in the appendix of 1951 (p. 11,255, page numbering in the cited edition)[17].

Barr, however, does not give an explanation for the fact that the two authors who both find the social and technical aspects of architecture of prime importance have, nevertheless, written a primarily 'aesthetic' and regulatory treatise. He does, however, give us an indication: 'The section on functionalism should be of special interest to *American* architects and critics' (p. 13). The text even directly addresses '*our* architects' (p. 43). It must have struck any reader of the book that there is virtually no section in which aspects of American and European architecture are not played off against each other.

My claim is that the book fundamentally addresses *only* American architects and not architects in general; it served as a catalogue for an exhibition in the MOMA, which seems to have been mainly of polemic interest. The same discourse served as a completely different document when read in the States, than when read in the Europe of the 1930s. Only by *mis*interpreting it as an 'analysis' that is aimed at providing a general explanation of modern architecture intended for a general public, does it make sense to accuse it of its peculiarities. The moment it is taken as a discourse with which a special game was played under the special circumstances prevailing in the USA in 1932, only then do these peculiarities become historically interesting. One might test this claim by comparing *The International Style* with Gropius' *Internationale Architektur* from 1925 – a discourse primarily addressed at Germany/Europe at that time. That synchronous comparison, however, is not the subject of this article – nor is the interesting diachronous comparison between this discourse and Jencks' *Emergent rules*.

The situational agenda in the Hitchcock/Johnson discourse is hidden by way of a Hegelian argument that had become popular again in the first decades of the century. 'The 19th century failed to create a new style *because* it was unable to achieve a *general* discipline of structure and design *in terms of the day*, while the revived styles were but a decorative garment to architecture, not the *interior principles* according to which it lived and grew' (p. 18).

Hegelian history can be conceived of as a time-tube, cut up into periodical slices each having a radically new principle, which, taken together, are seen as so many successive stages of the evolution of the Idea. Hitchcock and Johnson tend to think in terms of this principle as being primarily technological; for them, the modern style is deduced from, though not reduced to the effects of building with steel and concrete (p. 22ff, 40ff, 36). They also use Hegel's well-known formula that Reason or essence is real, and that Reality is reasonable or rational: 'Architecture is always a set of actual monuments, not a vague corpus of theory, the international style already *exists* in the present; it is not merely something the future may hold in store...The new style did not spring from a single source, but came

17
I have used the 1966 edition, with a new foreword by Hitchcock from 1965 and an Appendix compiled by him from 1951, under the title *The International Style, twenty years after*. An abridged version of the book leaves out many of the passages that I shall quote in support of my thesis of a hidden agenda. For the multilingual abridged edition see Benedikt Taschen, ed. 1990. As a matter of fact this abridgement is copyrighted not by the authors, but only by the publishers.

generally to life' (p. 21, 33, 93). 'Some architects *still* design in mass' (p. 42). This last remark suggests in typical Hegelian style that 'mass' architects are obviously backward, *survivals* from a bygone age.

Even in 1966 Hitchcock – who by then had to concede that not everything had turned out as he had hoped – still uses Hegelian formulae concerning survivals that have actually become *revivals* (p. xi). It all reminds the reader of Mondrian's view of history, in which some architects 'fall back into the past', into romanticism and classicism, as generally happens to 'modern' movements.[18] They deny the 'principles' of their own period, their *Zeitgeist*. Survivals and revivals 'complicate' the architectural scene according to Mondrian, Hitchcock, Johnson et al. As good Hegelians, they conclude that the purpose of their own text is to enlighten their fellow artists, to ensure the transition from the unconscious, half-modern development of the 19th century towards 'a directed evolution' (p. 20). The 1932 discourse accuses, for example, Wright of a 'refusal of the shackles of a fixed style' as well as what Hitchcock and Johnson see as an *illusion* of 'infinite possible styles' that complicates our *Zeitgeist* (p. 27).

Such Hegelianism claims universal validity and suggests to the reader that the discourse is intended as a conversation between world citizens. In actual fact in this discourse two quite *different* types of reader are addressed at the same time, and this only works because both are *assumed* to be *universal* world citizens: on the one hand American builders who, when acting as architects, refuse to be modern, and on the other hand European 'functionalists' who – although denying aesthetic choice its own autonomy – are nevertheless, according to Johnson and Hitchcock, *un*consciously working in the international style of architecture (p. 41ff). But the prime addressee of this discourse is the American architect, which is evident from the fact that the reader is assumed to be acquainted with 'Fifth Avenue' (not even the city is mentioned by name!) and with various 'superficial books and articles published in the United States'.

One interesting point for my analysis is Hitchcock's comment in 1966, that he finds 'the point in time' of the publication remarkable, because in 1932 the 'two finest houses in the new style' had just been built – Mies' Tugendhat house en Corbusier's Villa Savoye – while new developments in the style were not yet discernible. In an aside Hitchcock remarks: 'this, quite *aside* [italics mine] from the political proscription of modern design after 1933 in Germany' (p. ix), as if this were an issue that is irrelevant to their 1932 discourse as such. My thesis is quite the contrary, as we shall see.

18
Mondrian, *The new art – the new life*: the collected works of Piet Mondrian, eds. Holtzman and James, Thames and Hudson London, 1987, p. 237ff, talked about 'continuing evolution' and 'risk' in 1930. See also Pevsner's version, *An outline of European architecture*, 1966, 421: 'Although all healthy styles from the past essentially began internationally, they have all assumed decided national characteristics in the end'. Curiously enough we find here a replay of the Semper/Winckelmann match, now with a 20th-century rerun of the Winckelmann thesis 'from ordered style... to decadent confusion'.

Modernity

Modernity is defined by the hegemonic power of the bourgeois classes – a definition that implies the intended and eventually realized integration of the working class in the socio-cultural system of civil society. Comte, as one of the first analysts and ideologists of the epoch, described this in 1844 as 'the great problem of our time'.[19] This as yet unsolved 'problem' produced a tendency within the (petty) bourgeoisie to individualize and to distance oneself from the 'mass'.[20] The ideal is a social order in which all citizens are equal before the law, in which money, as universal equivalent, equalizes all social relations and in which no specific geographical locus has preference over any other, which amongst other consequences implies perfect transportation.[21] A classless, civil society, in short, in which class differences have disappeared into the generalized 'citizen'.

Modernism has interpreted this condition of Modernity in terms of the 'alienated subject'. Gropius understood *style* as an instrument that could be used to absorb this alienated person into the social unity through 'generalized surroundings'.[22] Style is *more* than just a symbol of such unity; according to the modernists, style is the only concrete experience of totality left to us in a world otherwise elementarized into moneyed monads. Gropius, Muthesius and Mondrian meant the organism-as-body to be organized into ordered behaviour, thus leaving the individual mind free to be a *personality*.[23] The lack of social connection between people – the result of an alienated, moneyed society – would thus be compensated by material and architectural living conditions. Modernity does not have to result in mass minds.

The mainly European avant-garde linked up body and mind into a Hegelian concept of history. It might be considered a Benthamite utilitarianism, softened by J.S. Mill's admonition on the preservation of the meditative quality of the human mind.[24] Bodily behaviour should be standardized so as to eliminate class differences, in order that a social unity results and also in order that the mind may find time and energy to meditate freely upon itself. We have here the typical European dialectic of heroic socialism – the notion that from the disorder of moneyed capitalism the masses of labour power cannot by themselves evolve into a 'people'. Only a heroic intervention by the artist, the philosopher or the architect would help these masses out of their alienated misery.[25]

The United States seemed in the eyes of its inhabitants – at least in the period between the two World Wars – to be a melting pot of races, classes and cultures, a classless society of producers and consumers in the making. There is no denying that there were serious conflicts between employers and unions, but very few Americans perceived these to be class struggles. The American trade unions actively sought collaboration with the bosses.[26] It is against this background that the discourse of *The International Style* coughs up its hidden agenda. The authors do not have any affinity with the crucial problem of the European avant-garde, so nicely summed up in Corbusier's dictum: 'Architecture *or* revolution'.

As far as American ideologists were concerned, their own revolution had already taken place a long time ago, i.e. the democratic revolution at the end of the 18th century that *preceded* the industrial revolution – a pattern that was reversed in Europe. 'America's Democratic Revolution occurred before her Industrial Revolution. European and other nations which have developed a measure of political democracy, have done so *after* experiencing their industrial revolutions. As a result, most of them produced men with a feeling of bitterness toward finance capitalism, and experienced a class conflict that

---

19
Comte, *Het positieve denken*, (1844), transl. 1979, p. 137ff. See also Gramsci on the concept of 'hegemonial power' in his *Selection from the prison notebooks* from between the two World Wars, transl. 1971, passim.

20
See my argumentation in *Massa en minoriteit*, Delft, 1992, Faculty of Architecture report, pp. 26-31.

21
It is this threatening problem of a totalitarian order, which at the same time runs the risk of entropy – simply because the equalization of all elements and all relations leads to despair, which in turn merely intensifies the totalitarian urge – that, in my view, was the actual theme on which Hegel was working in, for instance, his remarks on 'the collisions of love..in their highest grade of being incidental', see *Aesthetik*, par. II,3 chapter 2 a/e. The same applies, in my view, to Kierkegaard's *Either/Or*, with its exciting paradox of an aesthetical ethics via despair! Could it be that Howard Hughes – with his various houses that look exactly alike inside, and between which he transported himself in armoured vehicles in order to arrive at the same place he had just left – ideally exemplifies this modernity paradox? See Virilio, *L'esthetique de la disparition*, 1980, pp. 29-36. Civil society – conceived of as the split between public and private, see Jameson/Speaks, "Envelopes and Enclaves", in: *Assemblage 17*, p. 33 – is seen here in its extreme form, while at the same time being negated in that this transition is eliminated. I am increasingly convinced that such an *Aufhebung* of the split between public and private, which post-modernity seems to have witnessed, is *the* index of social and personal insanity.

22
Cf. Bernauer, *Die Aesthetik der Masse*, 1990, pp. 202ff, 214, 224

23
It seems to me that Corbusier also had this idea in mind; cf. Scruton's comment, op. cit. 30/1

24
For a more detailed analysis of Bentham en Mill in this context, see Sierksma, *Toezicht en taak*, SUA Amsterdam, 1991, chapters II and III, par. 4.

25
A reading of the writings of Mondrian is very instructive on this point. See, in particular, his struggle with the concepts of 'society' and 'tragic individuality', *The new art – the new life, the collected writings of Piet Mondrian*, 1987, pp. 205-219, 166ff. An interesting parallel text – which may turn out to be the ideological link between the European and the American avant-gardes – is Newman's "The Sublime is Now!", in *The tiger's eye*, 1947, p. 53, where he claims that 'in America, some of us are free from the weight of European culture..and answer by completely denying that art has any concern with the problem of beauty'. The issue then is 'absolute emotions'. We find this same theme in Mondrian's thought and work, op. cit., p. 17, but Mondrian, *as a European*, was somehow forced to accommodate an obvious class society with its 'wrong' form of massality. For Newman European culture could *only* be 'oppressive' – for Mondrian, on the other hand, it was a social phenomenon to be squared with aesthetics. The parallel between these comments and my analysis of the discourse of *The International Style* is obvious.

26
Cf. Guérin, *Die Amerikanische Arbeiterbewegung*, 1867-1967, transl. 1970, p. 52ff

27
Boyd and Worcester, *American civilization*, 1964, p. 177

28
Hyper irony in our discourse under study: 'So bad in every way have been the façades of most American commercial edifices that their rear elevations...seem by contrast to possess architectural qualities' (79). See also a quote from Scarlet in the same vein in Tzonis, *Reader*, op. cit., p. 62.

is almost completely absent in the United States'.27

As a result of this, nowhere in the history of American art do we find an avant-garde that is not exclusively aesthetical. If conflict is involved, it is cultural conflict about 'roots' and ethnicity. Thus Barr in his introduction: opposition to the international style, according to him, is to be expected from two main sources, the commercially successful modern architects who concern themselves with fine façades, and 'American nationalists' who oppose every 'European invasion' and perceive the new modern style to be primarily a European phenomenon (p. 14ff). The discourse itself explains 'the continuing existence of Romantic individualism' not in terms of 'architecture alone', but as a result of 'a dichotomy of the spirit more profound than any mere style can resolve'. This 'profound dichotomy of the spirit' turns, amongst other things, on the distinction between Europe and the United States (p. 27).

According to my reading of *The International Style* it is basically an attack on *American* architects who, under conditions where 'clients can still afford architecture in addition to building' (which applies to all countries except Russia (p. 80ff)), sell out to these clients by considering 'design as a commodity' (p. 37ff,14,79,65).28 In short, façades to order, an idea that is at odds with the anti-decorative principle of the international style.

Now we become aware of a subtle ideological move on the part of our writers. They present their 'international style' as consisting of three general principles – architecture as *volume* in contrast with the traditional architecture of mass, *regularity*, and thirdly the avoidance of applied *decoration*. This purely aesthetic style was officially negated by 'functionalists' – another word for constructivists and strict CIAM adherents who are not differentiated in the text, but who are shown in photographs. Hitchcock and Johnson have this to say about these functionalists: 'In their choices these European functionalists follow, rather than go against, the principles of the general contemporary style. Whether they admit it or not, is beside the point (p. 37,13). The idea that building is a science and not an art is an exaggeration of functionalism... (p. 35), but we must not [that is: we *Americans* must not, RS] be misled by the *idealism* of European functionalists' (p. 91).

Here we finally get to the crux of the ideological matter. Although the Soviet Union is only mentioned once as an aside, and likewise Hitler's Germany – as something 'regional' that does not pertain to the discourse of *The International Style* – it is in these phrases on 'the idealism of the European functionalists' that the hidden story of the text comes out into the open for just a moment. What the authors call 'European idealism' is of course a kind of socialist 'materialism', taking into account the fact that CIAM functionalism had its origins in European class society. The *only* way American architects might be conceived of as being *misled*, seems to be that they would begin to interpret their own society as *not* classless – that is, as a kapitalist system with classes that are covered up under the ideology of the American Dream – a dream which is, by the way, precisely the ideological position of Hitchcock and Johnson. The European functionalists in Germany and the Soviet Union had their ideological counterpoint in the rising fascism and national socialism of their time; like the Americans, they denied the existence of a class society. The rather silly illusion in the quoted remark on *The International Style* that, having been written *before* 1933, it consequently has *no* relation to this aspect of history, now becomes apparent.

Interpretations

'A broad sociological justification'

The authors point to the fact that in *industrial* building the traditional styles of the past were not so 'repressive' (p. 29), which implies that the real breakthrough of the modern style can best be witnessed in housing and public buildings. This, by the way, seems to be the complete opposite of the statements made by Hitler on the subject – he vetoed the application of modern style principles to housing and public buildings, while actually approving it for factories.[29] In this respect Hitchcock and Johnson are touching on a sensitive issue. Most of the pictorial examples in the book are in fact of the housing type. There then follows an interesting remark: 'American functionalists cannot claim for skyscrapers and apartment houses the broad sociological justification that exists for the workers' housing, the schools and hospitals in Europe' (p. 89ff).

Unfortunately, no reasons are presented in favour of this broad statement or in support of the unclear use of the word 'sociological', where surely 'social' would seem to be intended. It is not difficult to interpret, however. According to the American Dream, there *is* no 'sociological' or social class problem as in Europe, and the only vital issues at stake in the American design of housing for its citizens are aesthetics or the fulfilment of actual needs. Thus, the authors support their argument for a modern style for houses with the statement that 'excessive sentimentality about homes of the past does not become a modern classless society' (p. 93). They continue their discourse: 'The architect has a right to distinguish functions which are major and general from those which are minor and local. In 'sociological' (!) building he ought to stress the universal at the expense of the particular. He may even, for economic reasons and for the sake of general architectural style, disregard entirely the peculiarities of local tradition unless they are soundly based on local... weather conditions'. The only stricture then, as far as the USA is concerned, is that 'houses should not be lived in under protest' (p. 93ff). Setting this aside, every possible effort should be directed towards using a style that is *not* tied to location.

What Hitchcock and Johnson claim here is primacy of aesthetics over function... *unless* function has 'natural' primacy over aesthetics – a rather vague sort of primacy indeed! The crucial meaning of all this may be found in an earlier passage in the text. Europe has widely differing problems that can be solved by the *Siedlung*, a German word that is explicitly used to describe the CIAM solution to new urban expansion. Whereas the American architect is called on not to build contrary to the wishes of individual citizens, 'the *Siedlung* implies preparation not for a given family, but for a typical family, a statistical monster... Too often in European Siedlungen the functionalists build for some proletarian superman of the future' (p. 92ff).

At the same time our authors criticize the American traditionally styled garden suburbs for being 'excellent illustrations of sociological theory, but seldom examples of sound modern building' (p. 90). This very much reminds me of Dewey's statement in *Art as experience* (1934) in which he accuses 'extreme functionalists in architecture' of 'insincerity in art' because they claim that 'necessary elements should be evident in perception...; such contention confuses a rather

---

29
Quoted in Hochman, *Architects of fortune*, 1990, p. 236

30
Dewey, op. cit., p. 127
31
Bernauer, op. cit., p. 207
32
Jameson, *Postmodernism*, 1991, p. 318

33
Cf. Hochman, op. cit., pp. 94ff, 218ff

bald conception of morals with art'.30 The difference between this statement and that of Hitchcock and Johnson is purely terminological: 'moral' means the same as 'a social justification for buildings'. American architects are apparently in an ideal situation because they can design for the needs of *citizens*, and not for some 'proletarian superman', a fact that makes their devotion to traditional façades even more annoying.

European architects have to cope with historical problems in the form of different social classes; *nevertheless*, they have managed – however unconsciously – to find the right new aesthetic style. This explains why *The International Style* claims aesthetic principles for American architects, principles that are distilled from mainly European buildings by European architects who, according to our authors, have purely because of their 'privileged, real genius' (p. 63) *unconsciously* developed this new style, even though they have been *consciously* restricted by the typical 'functionalist' constraints on architecture in Europe's class society.

So contrary to Bernauer[31] whose analysis of the European avant-garde so brilliantly pointed out the paradox of style – being both expressive of social culture, and at the same time its determining origin – I do not agree with him that this paradox defines modernism as such, but more specifically *European* modernism. From the very core of their American Dream this option was not open to American modernist ideologues. When Jameson concludes that 'modernism, during its own life span, was not hegemonic and far from being a cultural dominant'[32], I think he also makes the mistake about 'modernism' being the same everywhere. *Being hegemonic* is first and foremost a matter of intent, so I even think he is wrong on this point. Modernism in *both* the European *and* the American version was hegemonic, but only in the USA did it achieve something like cultural hegemony, which might explain why post-modernism in architecture *did* explode over there and not here in Europe. What the discourse in *The International Style* achieved is a mystification of the word *international*. It did so by claiming no 'sociological' significance of architecture in the American case – implying that the USA had surpassed the class society; *and* it did so by neutralizing the definition of *style* – which in itself is not neutral but ideologically loaded – by reducing style to the mere expression of 'structure and the architects' provision for function', which is conceived of as 'the *true* character of a building' (p. 44).

Is it coincidence then that the heroes of Hitchcock and Johnson's discourse are the Europeans Oud, Corbusier, Gropius and Mies who gave up their socio-revolutionary intent for architecture at precisely the historical juncture when *The International Style* was written?[33] Style is being depoliticized and then projected upon American society, which is supposedly classless. It is also no coincidence that there is no ruling on the new style for public buildings – incidentally Hitler's second exception to the international style. The only thing that is mentioned is the fact that theatres, churches, cafés and schools 'stand out' in the design for a *Siedlung* – which is saying nothing at all in a text that is rather strict on other issues (p. 91). No coincidence, because this would have been a tricky subject in a country where all public buildings were built in a very symbolic classical style and even have classical names like The Capitol.

153

Interpretations

National internationalism: in conclusion

Hitchcock, in his review of his own text in 1951, states that there **'is always some sort of style in the arts of self-conscious periods'**, style being understood as **'implying restraint or discipline according to *a priori* rules of one sort or another'** (p. 240, 238). In another passage this is interpreted as **'condition of a true style, the price of an architecture generally of a high level...that aesthetic disciplines should be rigid'**, only **'genius'** having the privilege to **'interpret'** these disciplines (p. 62ff). The **'international style'** is described as being **'a single body of discipline, fixed enough to integrate contemporary style as a reality and yet elastic enough to permit individual interpretation'** (p. 20).

Setting aside the woolly language, this passage seems to point to a liberal undertone of the discourse. The three principles are characterized as *not* being **'formulas'**, but **'fundamental'** like, for instance, the principle of organic verticality of the Gothic style (p. 20). Another thing that strikes us as being liberal is the thesis that the disadvantage of **'rigid rules'** is that they are **'easily broken once and for all'**, not permitting **'growth of style'** (p. 21). Nevertheless, according to Hitchcock and Johnson, in a discourse like theirs **'the appearance of a certain dogmatism can hardly be avoided'** (p. 21), but the impression should be avoided that **'the critic determines *in advance* how far, or even in what direction the creative interpretation may go'** (p. 63, 90). But these ironic remarks do not alter the fact that in several passages the authors use distinctly authoritarian terms like **'conversion to the new style'** (p. 60), **'thoroughgoing aesthetic discipline'** (p. 43), **'submitting to the disciplines of the International Style'** (p. 27), **'requirements'** (p. 45) and the like. They also issue some rather strict, carefully defined proscriptions. Hence, they make harsh judgements on American architects who *continue* to work in Tudor and Georgian Style, *purely* because they do not want to conform to the three principles formulated (p. 90, e.p.).

This is to be expected from a discourse in Hegelian perspective, which conceives of itself not so much as *laying down* the law of a style, but as *expressing* the evolutionary *necessity* of that new style, in which everything that is different is regarded as backward. Discipline then becomes natural and authoritarian in the same move. What must strike any reader are the rather strict rules on things like the use of colour, decoration and materials, *precisely* the issues where criticism of the American architects is strongest (Ch.V,vii). Although Hitchcock and Johnson would appreciate variation *within* the style they propose, which would create **'interest'** in the viewer, they nevertheless **'prefer a boring building to a building by the easygoing modern architect who has failed even to apprehend the existence of a principle of regularity'** (p. 65).

In short, the discourse of *The International Style* is based on the idea of growth *within* a style in the USA, on the notion of *elimination* of the **'wrong'** kind of building from the USA, and on the hope of *multiplying* buildings in the **'right'** style. From the theoretical perspective of games, rules and power positions, the battle of Hitchcock and Johnson is waged against the American façadologists who use a tradition that is European, but... *a traditional* tradition that *cannot* be expressive of the classless society of the States, which in turn is based on a supposedly global technological progress of civilization. In this battle against the Americans the strict *command-type rule* is useful and necessary, and one that we come across in all kinds of carefully formulated proscriptions. On the other hand, the European functionalists are seen as *allies* – Europeans who are more or less unconsciously international, classless and primarily aesthetic, and who have to be *taken up* into this international network. Here, however, *prescriptive and normative* rules are needed, and these are primarily found in the three general principles that the book champions.

In their position as writers of the catalogue for the Museum of Modern Art exhibition in the USA, our authors are **'on top'** compared to their American colleagues; from the perspective of *inclusion* of the European architects in the network whom they also criticize for being short-sighted addicts of a class society – they are on the *defensive*. In its ideological structure *The International Style* is per se an ambivalent discourse in its use of the two types of rules – prescriptive and normative – alternatively and in relation to varying potential partners. Thus the irony of Hitchcock and Johnson's discourse is more or less insincere compared with Jencks' *New Rules* for **'post-modern classicism'**[34], because in the latter case the new style is deliberately conceived of as just *one* among many others. Hitchcock and Johnson did not display the same liberalism.

34
Cf. Jencks, *Postmodernism*, op. cit., p. 317ff. Incidentally, this does not imply that I am not equally critical of Jencks' approach; cf. my *Massa en minoriteit*, op. cit., pp. 9-12

Managing corporate real estate

Peter Krumm, Prof. Hans de Jonge

Introduction

A large proportion of the buildings constructed in the Netherlands are used to accommodate industrial and commercial activities. The appearance of these buildings is often the subject of criticism. The Dutch architect Maaskant even claimed that the lack of good architecture in the Netherlands was "not due to a lack of good architects but to a lack of good principals" (Staal, 1987, p. 94). Corporate architecture in the Netherlands is, however, not limited to the shiny, mirror-plated buildings that can be seen alongside Dutch motorways. Buildings like the Van Nelle factory in Rotterdam, the corporate headquarters of the former NMB in Amsterdam, and Royal Dutch Shell headquarters in The Hague are examples of corporate architecture that reflect a corporate interest in the architectural design of buildings. Although many architectural books and studies explore the changing design and usage of corporate and other types of buildings, the role, activities and interests of the owners or users of buildings are often ignored.

This article focuses on the changing role and position of those departments within Dutch multinationals involved in the construction and management of corporate buildings. Although real-estate departments often act as liaison between the various corporate stakeholders and the architect, constructors or developers, little is known about the arguments for establishing these departments or about the tensions that exist within them. The objective of this paper is to make the various parties involved in the construction and accommodation process more aware of the changes in the corporate setting and of the impact of these changes for real-estate departments. Corporate real-estate management (CREM) is the discipline which focuses not on maximizing wealth in real-estate investments, but on contributing to the performance of the business of a corporation by managing its real estate. The business of the corporation may be industrial activities, banking, retailing or any other, non-real-estate business. Activities relating to CREM include the acquisition, planning, management and disposal of real estate.

The issue of CREM is addressed in a PhD thesis "Corporate real-estate management in multinational corporations" which is currently under way in the cluster of real estate and project management. One of the objectives of the thesis is to gain insight into the evolution of the present role of real-estate management in Dutch corporations. The changing role of the departments representing the corporate principals in the construction process has an impact on the role of other parties involved in the process.

Following an overview of the evolution of both the corporation at large and the real-estate departments within those corporations, a case study is presented. The case study describes the story of the real-estate and architectural department within Philips Electronics. The paper concludes with a summary of the current issues facing corporate real-estate management departments, the impact of these issues on corporate architecture and the relationship with external service providers like architects and project managers.

Evolution of real estate from a corporate perspective

Although the history of buildings dates back well before the beginning of the modern age, the chronicle of buildings constructed to accommodate either commercial or industrial activities is relatively short. A glance through any book on architectural history reveals that up to the nineteenth century the vast majority of buildings were constructed for the glory of either the Church, the State, or the army. Town halls, palaces, churches, monasteries and barracks were, for a long time, used to accommodate administrative activities. One example of these so-called "cassia deli official" is the Uffizzi in Florence – built in 1560-1571 by Giorgi Vasari – which housed the city government, a number of guilds, and other official organizations (De Gunst & De Jong, 1989, p. 11). Walton (1988, p. 6) even considers the Uffizzi to be Europe's first corporate headquarters since it was the centre for the many business interests of the Medici family.

For a long time industrial activities did not require specialized accommodation due to their limited scope; activities were either accommodated in part of one's house or simply in the open air. The size and scale of the real-estate portfolio did not require any professional help with regard to construction, maintenance or management. Designing industrial structures tended to be in the hands of engineers; architects were employed if the owner wished to place emphasis on the appearance of the building (Bowley, 1966, p. 30). The question of cost was of no great importance since architects were not concerned with designing buildings for those who required small, inexpensive houses (Bowley, 1966, p. 31).

The industrial revolution and the subsequent expansion of the economy resulted in a growing need for new buildings that not only satisfied the increasing requirements in terms of space, but also enhanced the image of insurance firms as benefactors of society (Walton, 1988, p. 172). Expressive buildings were erected to glorify the company that built them or to hide the less pleasant industrial activities that took place behind the impressive facade.

Up until the industrial revolution the director of a firm both owned the company and controlled the business. As a result of expanding industrial and commercial activities, the simple structures of the early organizations were no longer capable of supporting continuous corporate growth. As a result, ownership of corporations fell more into the hands of shareholders while control of business processes became more the business of professional managers (De Gunst & De Jong, 1982). As a result of increasing cost-consciousness (Ferry and Brandon, 1984), at the beginning of the 20th century owners of industrial and commercial buildings became more concerned with the profit and loss associated with the use of the building, instead of merely focusing on the costs of erecting a building (Bowley, 1966, p. 330). The more capital there was tied up in a building, the less there was available for use in the direct productive activities of the business, or, if the building was financed on a mortgage, the larger the interest payments that would have to be deducted from income. This changing attitude to building costs is illustrated in the following quote from Henry Ford (Schulitz, 1990, p. 21), who is famous for his buildings, which were reduced to the bare minimum:

"We will not put up elaborate buildings as monuments to our success. The interest on the investment and the cost of their upkeep only serve to add uselessly to the costs of what is produced – so these monuments of success are apt to end as tombs... We... would prefer to be advertised by our product than by where we make our product."

The continuing increase in the size of industrial and commercial concerns resulted, however, in a growing demand for new head office premises and, possibly, in an increase in the importance attached to prestige buildings in this field (Bowley, 1966, p. 381). As Philip Johnson pointed out:

"the people with money to build today are corporations – they are our popes and Medicis" (Walton, 1988, p. 9). The rapid growth of business activities, and the consequent need for accommodation at the beginning of the 20th century resulted within many corporations in an urge to establish in-company departments dealing with real-estate matters. The lack of knowledge and time to manage the growing need for accommodation led to specialized real-estate departments being set up. Examples include the construction department of the Netherlands Trading Society in 1919 and the technical department of the Philips light bulb factories in 1924. The objectives underlying the creation of these departments were primarily to supervise and control construction activities – functionally, technically, and financially. In addition, establishing a staff department provided a guaranteed supply of skilled employees and enabled corporations to maintain a corporate image with regard to the architecture of their buildings. These first real-estate departments incorporated all disciplines relating to construction and management activities, ranging from in-house architects, engineers, cost engineers through to gardeners.

Until well after World War II most real-estate activities were restricted to the home country, and were mainly concerned with monitoring the constant need for additional accommodation. With only a few exceptions, buildings were owned by the end-users (Hart, 1987, p. 13). Corporate growth, speed of construction, and economies of scale dominated corporate strategy and policy. The focus on growth, and the desire of corporations to allocate their scarce resources to their core activities, resulted in an increase in demand for rental space and in a professionalization of the real-estate market (Kohnstamm & Regterschot, 1994). Due to

1900	1920	1940	1960	1980	2000
– small family-run businesses – restricted to home country – accommodated in living quarters – CRE/FM part of activities owner	– growth corporations – establishment CRE/FM departments	– international growth – continuous need for accommodation – growth CRE/FM departments	– international expansion CRE/FM – professional real-estate services	– increase in cost of accommodation – ICS, computer, robots – decentralization of authority	– back-to-core business – outsourcing – shareholder value – proving added value CRE/FM
		reconstruction after WW II			

this increasing demand for rental space the investor became an important player in the real-estate market (Hart, 1987, p. 14).

Responding to the expansion of the organization, corporations transformed their traditional functional structure into a more geographically oriented one. Parallel with this structural turnaround, corporations started to decentralize responsibilities from corporate headquarters and central staff departments to national organizations and operating companies. This shift of authority led – in many cases – to a clash with the urge to provide added value. The need to provide added value was enhanced by the emergence of professional real-estate consultants and the growing corporate desire to allocate scarce resources to core activities. The transition from owned to rented/leased real estate meant that clients were less emotionally involved in corporate real estate and that the more economic outlook of the real-estate investor had greater impact. The rising costs of accommodation as a result of the 1973 oil crises, combined with the introduction of the computer and information technology in business processes, and the globalization of markets, sparked managerial interest in real estate and real-estate services.

The corporate recession in the early 1980s resulted in further pressure on staff and support departments to provide real-estate and facilities-management services. Back-to-core-business, downsizing, lean-production, outsourcing, or right-sizing were the buzz words and corporations laid off thousands of employees resulting in a surplus of office and production space. The rising number of vacant properties and the consequent decline in market rents resulted in a decrease of both – internal – rental incomes and the rate of return on the real-estate portfolio. Corporate real-estate and facilities management departments had to rub their eyes and wake up. In order to cope with the changes in the corporate environment, real estate has to be managed, just like other corporate staff and resources. Joroff (1993) and Ebert (1993) reason that real estate is a corporation's fifth strategic asset, after human resources, capital, technology and information.

Case study: Philips Electronics

In 1899, a few years after the foundation of the *Philips Gloeilampenfabrieken*, Gerard Philips employed the engineer A. De Broekert to supervise the construction activities of Philips. The growth of Philips was mirrored by the expansion of the engineering division 'Technische Bedrijven', which was involved in the design, construction and management of all Philips buildings all over the world. In 1908 Philips began construction of the first of a series of concrete buildings that would dominate the city of Eindhoven right up to the present day. This first building, located at Emmasingel, was five storeys high, occupied a ground floor area of 2000 m² GFA, and was the first completely concrete building in the Netherlands. Besides the fact that the buildings were constructed in concrete, in contrast with most other buildings, which were still made of brick, the size of the Philips buildings was unlike any other buildings in Eindhoven (Onna, 1997, p. 13). In the period between 1920 and 1930 Philips erected more than 160,000 m² GFA of factories and offices, one of which is the *Lichttoren* – designed by the Philips architects Roosenburg and Scheffer – which was completed in 1922 (Bekooy, 1991, p. 57).

In the construction of its numerous buildings Philips strove to achieve a certain degree of industrial architecture combined with a high level of standardization of constructive elements (Onna, 1997). This enabled Philips to modify the usage of buildings, if necessary. The concept of standardization was also applied outside of Eindhoven. As a result, it was often quite easy for insiders to recognize a Philips building anywhere in the world.

The organization of the engineering division up until World War II was characterized by:
– a strong focus on Eindhoven,
– a limited sphere of activities both in size and variety,
– a direct link to the board of directors,
– management and operation of the various functional activities were grouped together, and
– an organization based on technical disciplines.

After World War II Philips continued to expand its business activities. As a result, the engineering division established branches all over the world in order to supervise the design, construction and management of Philips factories and office buildings. In the time frame between 1951 and 1964 the total number of Philips employees grew from 99,000 to almost a quarter of a million world-wide. In order to accommodate its personnel the total amount of office and manufacturing space grew at a similar pace, rising from 1.3 million to 4.4 million m² GFA. As a result of the growing need for accommodation, the engineering division expanded as well and by 1966 employed more than 2500 people in a wide range of activities, including construction, accommodation, facility services, fire department, etc. In 1968 the engineering division was reorganized in response to the continued changes within the Philips organization. The division was separated into a local technical department serving Eindhoven and a global architectural and engineering department (AIB). Within this new organization the architectural and engineering department – employing more than 300 people world-wide – was responsible for managing the construction and design of Philips buildings.

In its centennial year Philips Electronics was faced with severe financial problems. One of the measures taken was to establish a Fixed Assets task force. This task force was responsible for solving problems within the corporate real-estate portfolio, and for addressing the question of how real-estate assets could be turned into cash. In the past five years the task force has released more than NLG 1 billion by reducing the amount of real-estate assets. At the end of 1995 Philips Electronics owned real-estate assets worth NLG 4 billion, equivalent to 8% of total corporate assets. As a consequence of a major reorganization programme:
– central services were delegated to the individual operating companies;
– Philips International maintained a small staff in order to provide the board of management with information and to administer the proceedings of Centurion;
– the Architects & Engineering Division was sold to a commercial consultancy firm in 1991, thus becoming DHV-AIB;
– the remaining staff involved with corporate real-estate affairs have now been re-located to the national organizations;
– in 1996, five years after the creation of the task force, the portfolio was reduced by almost 20%, freeing up almost NLG 1 billion.

Currently all decisions regarding the design, construction and management of real estate are decentralized to the operational business units within Philips Electronics. The 'central' real-estate department now merely acts as an internal consultant to the business units.

Corporate real estate and architecture

The evolution of the real-estate function within corporations and the general attitude of corporations towards real estate has consequences for both the architect and the valuation of architecture for corporations. The consequences of these changes are described on the basis of three issues that are often addressed within the field of CREM.

a. In-house versus outsourcing

Faced with corporate attempts to withdraw the company's activities back to the core business, support departments like CREM are under pressure. Many of the traditional products and services provided by staff and support departments are also available through external service providers. At the beginning of this century many corporations – such as Unilever, Philips, AKZO Nobel and ABN AMRO – employed their own architects and engineers. The emergence of real-estate service providers in the 1970s and the corporate tendency to contract out support activities have resulted in cutbacks in in-house staff. The increase in the number of people involved in the construction and accommodation process led to the disappearance of the powerful individual client, while at the same time offering opportunities for outsiders such as architects and consultants.

b. Own versus lease

Due to the lack of alternatives, the vast majority of buildings used to accommodate industrial and commercial activities were, up to the 1960s, owned by individual corporations. A shortage of capital in Dutch industry, a decline in the attractiveness of the housing market, and the emergence of British real-estate investors triggered the kick-off of a commercial real-estate market in the Netherlands. If buildings were to be rented or leased to corporations, they had to appeal to many potential users. Buildings with an expressive architectural image – linked to a previous user, for example the head office of the ING Group designed by Alberts and van Huut, which is still referred to as the NMB building – are difficult to rent out to another organization. The increasing proportion of rental/lease buildings in corporate real-estate portfolios makes it difficult to realize expressive architectural buildings for the commercial real-estate market.

c. Asset versus means of production

Parallel with the changes in the focus on real estate, the focus on interest in the analysis of competitive edge shifted at the end of the 1980s towards the internal aspects of the corporation. Competitive edge was seen as depending less upon corporate choices in market positioning and more upon the exploitation of unique internal resources and capabilities (Grant, 1995). Real estate is and can be one of those strategic assets. Contrary to the alleged decline in the market for qualitative buildings, the increasing attention to corporate resources may result in a growing attention to corporate architecture. Nourse and Roulac (1993) identify corporate architecture as one of the eight driving strategies for CREM. The physical image of a building may provide a way to advertise and attract attention to the firm's goods and services. When buildings reflect the purpose of the business and encourage important working relationships, they can become significant elements of corporate strategy (Seiler, 1984). Similar to the situation at the beginning of this century, corporations start to value the benefits of a corporate image through the use of architecture.

The objective of this paper was to increase awareness of the implications of the changes within corporations for architecture and the construction process in general. Hence, when the energy and skills of business leaders interact positively with the energies and skills of architects and designers, the results are beneficial both for the partners and for the larger community (Walton, 1988). The transformation of CRE departments – as a result of transitions in both the corporate organisation and in the corporate attitude towards real estate – also has implications for outside parties as architects and engineers. Awareness of the issues facing CREM may result in the conviction that managerial attention towards real estate is not to overpower good architecture but rather to ensure a professional client.

References

Bekooy, G., *Philips honderd 1891-1991*, Zaltbommel, Europeese Bibliotheek, 1991

Blanken, I.J., *Geschiedenis van Philips Electronics NV, deel 3*: De ontwikkeling van de NV Philips's Gloeilampen-fabrieken tot elektrotechnisch concern, Leiden, Martinus Nijhoff, 1992

Bowley, M., *The British building industry; four studies in response and resistance to change*, Cambridge, UK, Cambridge University Press, 1966

Ebert, L.P., "The future of corporate real estate", *The Digest of Corporate Real Estate*, Ernst & Young, 1993

Ferry, D.J., P.S. Brandon, *Cost planning of buildings*, 5th ed., London, Granada Publishing, 1984

Goold, M., A. Campbell, M. Alexander, *Corporate level strategy*: Creating Value in the Multibusiness Corporation, London, John Wiley & Sons, 1995

Grant, R.M., *Contemporary strategy analysis, concepts, techniques, applications*, Oxford, Blackwell Business, 1995

Gunst, D.D. de, T. de Jong, *Planning en ontwerp van kantoorgebouwen*: Typologie van gebouwen, Delftse Universitaire Pers, 1989

Gunst, D.D. de, T. de Jong, *Typologie van gebouwen*: Handleiding bij het ontwerpen van bedrijfsgebouwen, Delft, May 1982

Hart, H.W. ter, *Commercieel vastgoed in Nederland, een terreinverkenning*, Deventer, Uitgeverij FED, Vlaardingen, Nederlands Studie Centrum, 1987

Joroff, M.L., M. Louargand, S. Lambert, and F. Becker, *Strategic management of the fifth resource*: corporate real estate, report no. 49, Industrial Development Research Foundation, May 1993

Kohnstamm, P.P., L.J. Regterschot, *De manager als bouwheer*: De rol van de bestuurder bij de realisatie van nieuwe huisvesting, Ten Hagen & Stam, 1994

Krumm, P.J.M.M., *Pinpointing added value of CRE/FM*, presented at the EuroFM Research Forum, World Workplace – Europe Maastricht, The Netherlands, 7-10 June 1998

Krumm, P.J.M.M., "Case description: Philips Electronics", *Module M4 "Beheren" 1997-1998 Reader Philips*, H. de Jonge, P.J.M.M. Krumm, en J.C.H. Vredenbregt (eds.), 1997

Nourse, H.O., S.E. Roulac, "Linking real estate decisions to corporate strategy", *The Journal of Real Estate Research*, Fall 1993

Onna, N. Van, *Architecture in Eindhoven*: impressions of an urban landscape, Eindhoven, 1997

Schulitz, H.C., *Constructa-preis 1990*: industrial architecture in Europe, Hannover, T. Schaffer Druckerei GmbH, 1990

Seiler, J.A., "Architecture at work", *Harvard Business Review*, September/October 1984, p. 118

Staal, G., *Between dictate & design*: the architecture of office buildings, NIA Publishers, 1987

Walton, T., *Architecture and the corporation*, New York, MacMillan Publishing Company, 1988

Culture, recreation and religion

'Through' - line transformer

Marc Neelen[1]
graduation project Architectural Design

mentors
Daan Vitner, Leen Hulsbos, Prof. Jürgen Rosemann[2]

This project sets out to provide a stimulus for the deserted inner periphery of Belgrade, a vast area in the physical centre of town. Because of the clash between the town and its CIAM extension, the two parts of town approach each other awkwardly, leaving an undefined area in the middle. This design proposal may be viewed as a scenario in its own right.

The site can be seen as a series of zones between the two parts of town. The starting point for this project was to accept the shortcomings of the area and its assembly of fragments (zones) as a positive condition providing the necessary complexity, and to retain the existing confrontations (physical/social/utopian) as far as possible. The change has to come from the introduction of elements, which generate activity in the area and serve as a binding structure between the two parts of town.

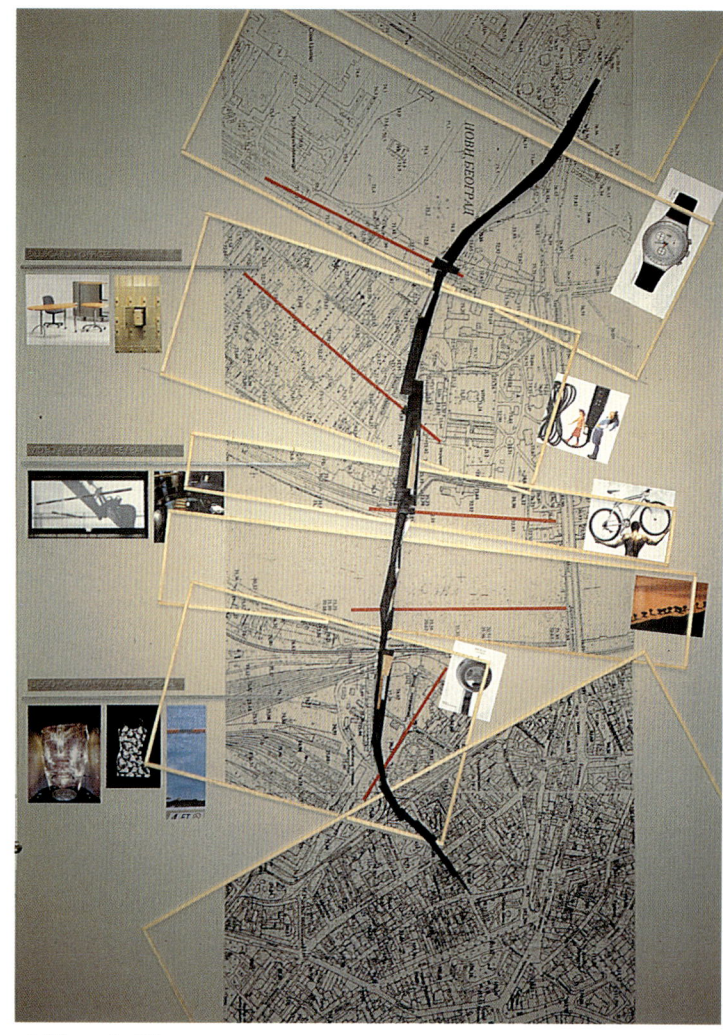

billboard offices
video/performance - bar - outdoor cinema
disco - catwalk - swimming pool

[1]
'Through' - line transformer was created in close collaboration with Ana Džokić (Belgrade), who also designed the East Gate Building.
[2]
Prof Darko Marušić was involved in the project as a mentor from Belgrade.

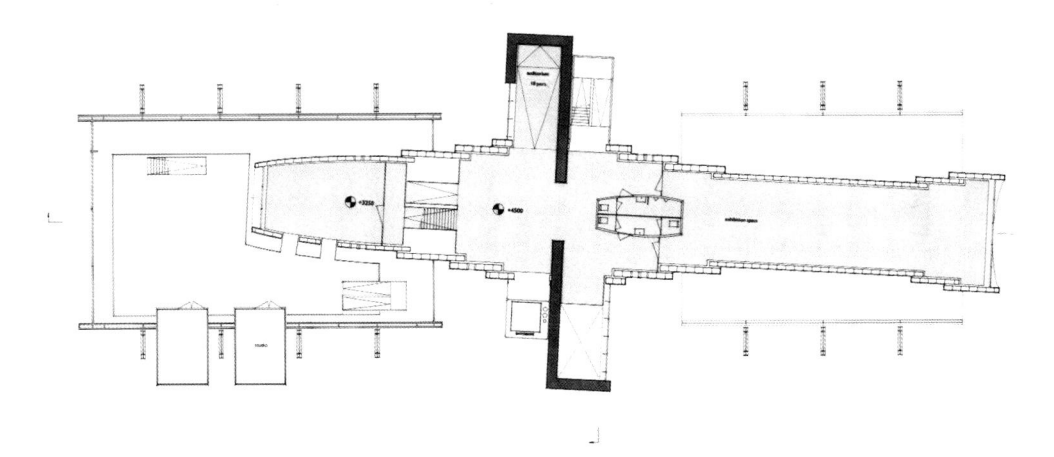

The introduction of a strip creates a coherent system on the scale of the city. The strip is a vector-like circulation space, containing transit and attraction functions. It provides visual and programmatic unity and forms part of the public cityscape. Along the strip are structures in various densities; these use the strip in horizontal and vertical directions, intensifying its vector effect.

Various programmatic elements are accommodated along the strip to provide a network of semi-public functions. These form a spatial system and a podium for both metropolitan and local functions. As time goes by, the nature of the strip will change in response to new demands, and it will lose its pioneer status.

In the scenario the highest density of elements is generated around an existing bridge on the route over the river. Two gate buildings mark the entrances to the bridge. These are vital elements in the scenario, on the one hand functioning as occupants of a deserted area, and on the other hand fulfilling a tenuous role, due to their function and the shortness of their existence. In both buildings the flow along the line of urban intervention is used as a characteristic element, together with a strong core featuring as a landmark on the riverbank. The core represents the character of the building. Even when the building decays, the core will remain as a sculpture in the future cityscape.

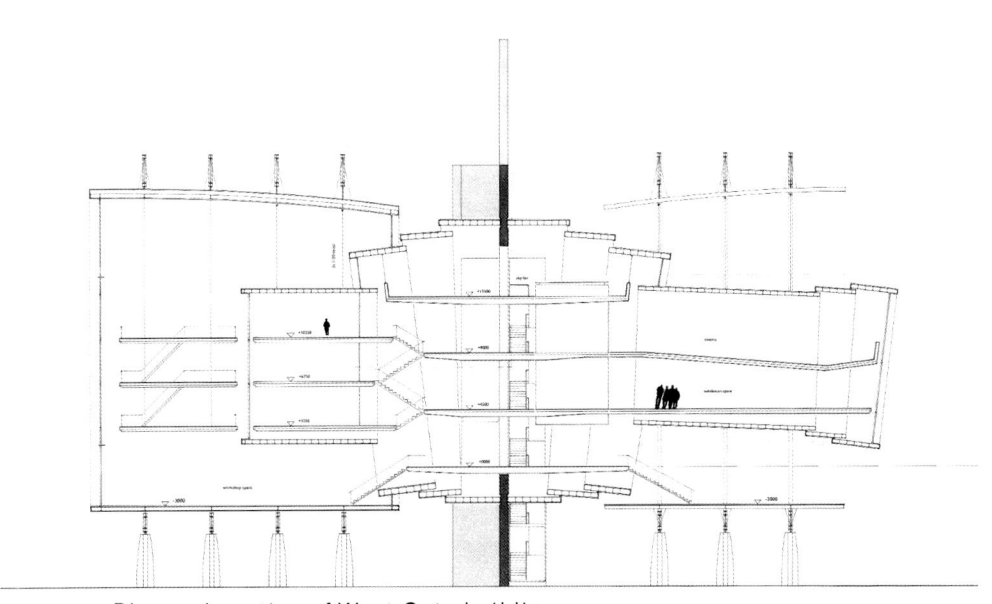

Plan and section of West Gate building

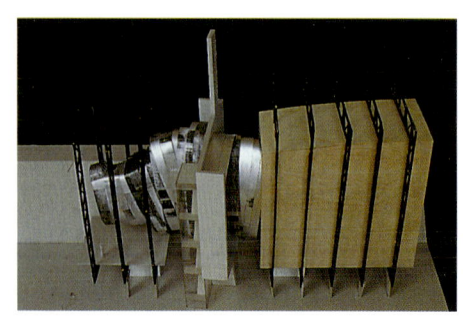

'Through' - line transformer

Model of West Gate building

West Gate building

The western bridge entrance provides a workshop space for unstable media forms. The usual concept for this type of building has been turned inside-out, with the most private functions situated in the skin of the building, while the most public functions form a continuous flow through the building. The use of materials is closely connected with this concept: except for the core (a concrete element), all parts are detachable, non-polished in appearance, and contained in large, open-frame structures.

East Gate building

The building at the eastern bridge entrance contains a discotheque, radio station and diving tower. In view of its limited lifespan (due to the unpredictability of the site and the dynamics of the cultural scene), this building has been constructed in such a way that it can be dismantled without losing its role as a landmark. Its core is a strong refractory element with a vital function (diving tower) which will survive after dismantling. It is the inverse of the West Gate building, as its continuous element is extremely smooth and closed, while the space necessary for the most public function is openly situated in a transparent box.

In a highly unstable area this design proposes a flexible and temporal solution which is capable of responding to a changing environment. It focuses not on trying to fill the gap but on using emptiness as an advantage, thus representing a departure from existing approaches to similar conditions.

The strip connecting the two parts of Belgrade

Dance and theatre college in Arnhem

Nienke Ettema
graduation project Architectural Design

mentors
Prof. Arne van Herk, Jan van de Voort and Peter Lüthi

The College of Arts is planning to concentrate its four dance and theatre study programmes, with some three hundred students in all, around the Rietveld Academy in Arnhem. There are plans for them to come together on a narrow strip of land next to the Roermondsplein roundabout, beside the River Rhine. The location is the beginning of a green belt near the centre of Arnhem of which the park-like nature should be preserved. The route over the Rhine embankment is being extended, with a wooden bridge running past the college and its theatre café, and ends at the municipal museum. This creates a recreational promenade, bringing the town in closer contact with the river.

The main features of the programme are studios of different sizes, classrooms and a theatre. The four departments will be housed in one building, so that they can make use of each other's accommodation and knowledge. The theatre is in the inner angle of the building.

The building, which has been sunk into the dike, rises slowly out of the ground. The building is low on the Rietveld Academy side, where the buildings behind are also low, and high on the town side of the Roermondsplein. On the side facing the road the building has a high, regular back which is hemispherical. On the side by the river the roof slopes down to the water, with a wall that undulates as a result of the trees and the theatre further along "pressing" themselves against the building.

The hemispherical shape creates an enclosed inner area without cutting off the view of the river. At the lowest point on the site, where there is a risk of flooding, the building is on stilts, giving the impression of a gateway to the inner area. The entrance is below this overhang. Mooring posts in the water protect the building against accidents and drift ice. They can also be used to construct a stage; the theatre roof can function as a stand.

The building has been divided up into four different segments, each with its own structure. This provides the college with a wide variety of studios in terms of size, height, orientation, view, natural lighting, etc. After all, every theatre is different.

Section

Dance and theatre college in Arnhem

The segments are connected by the roof, which is visible wherever you are, because a gap has been provided between the partition wall and roof throughout the building. The roof contains skylights, so that daylight can penetrate deep into the studios. Another connecting element is the ramp, which runs parallel to the roof towards the main floor in each segment and ends in a terrace. This is not the main access route but a kind of promenade from which you can look into the studios from a distance without disturbing the occupants. The studios are accessed from the central hall, which functions as a sound buffer with respect to the road, and there are horizontal corridors running past the studios, from which your gaze is directed outside. Wedges containing the vertical traffic, toilets, emergency exits and informal meeting places separate the different segments.

The internal structure of the college is made of concrete, partly to prevent the building rising by the ground water. Where the building is above ground, it has a lighter wooden structure covered with a thin layer of zinc. The sloping south wall by the water has extra protection from the sun in the form of zinc grids, which will be covered by climbing plants. On the side by the road, the grids are horizontal, providing the transition between the closed roof and the relatively open outer wall. These walls have been worked out carefully, bearing in mind that it was important to find a good solution to the rainwater discharge, because the roof and outer wall are continuous.

Floor plan + 4.3 metres, ground level

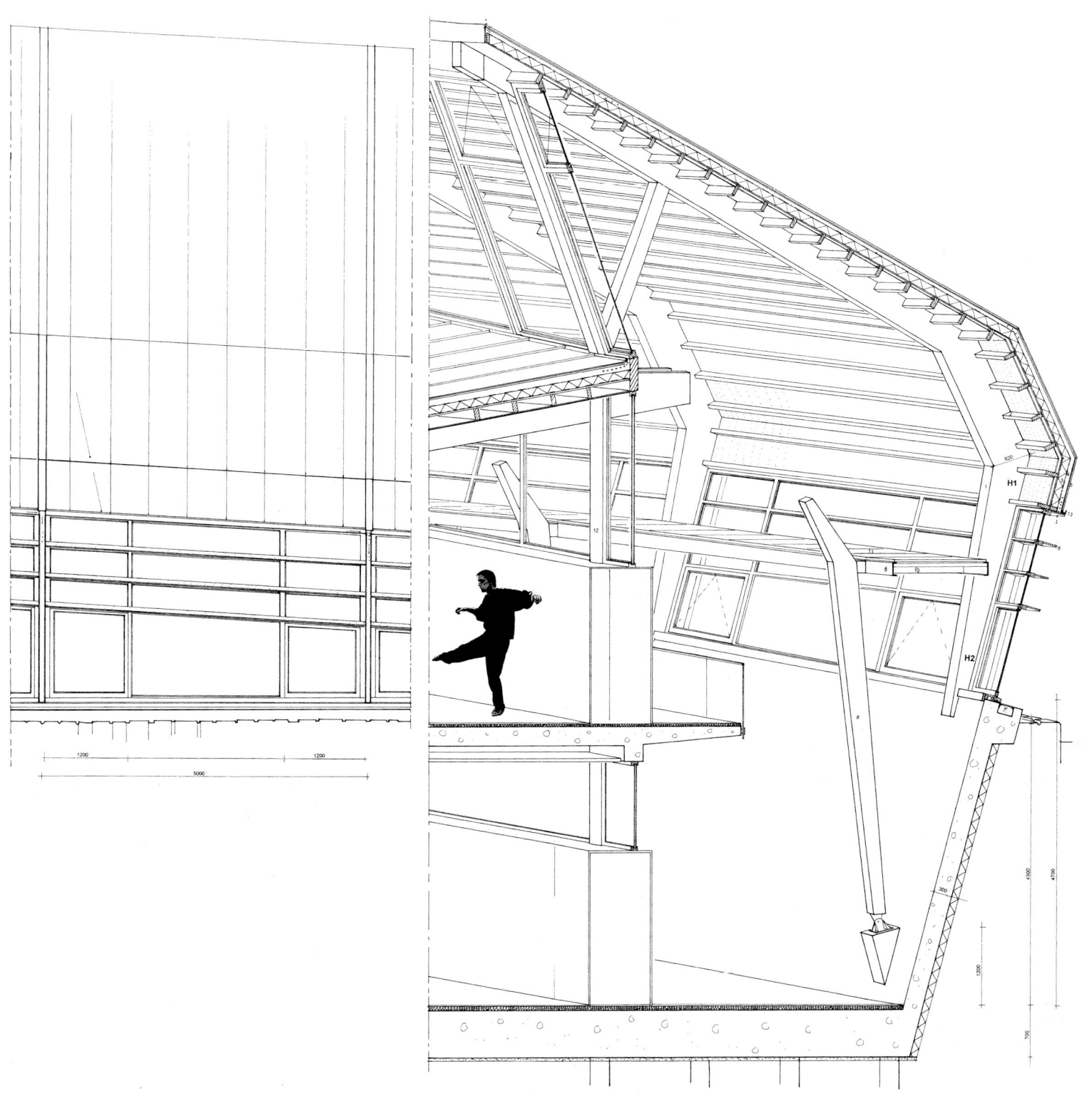

Section 2nd segment, detailed drawing of north and south walls

Culture, recreation and religion

Everyday temple

Lidewij Lenders
graduation project Architectural Design

mentors
S. Umberto Barbieri, Peter Lüthi, Jan van de Voort

In today's society, religion plays an ever-diminishing role. Nevertheless, many people need a place to commemorate important events in their lives in accordance with their own religious conviction.

This place does not have to be tied to a particular religion, but should have a hallowed atmosphere. An attempt has been made to design a spiritual location, where birth, life and death, the three inextricably bound stages in a person's life, can be celebrated.

The building is closely intertwined with its surroundings and with everyday life. It is precisely in everyday things that spirituality is visible: a ray of sunshine, a waterdrop or a spider's web are wonders if you take the time to dwell on them. The architecture of the building is the same: it is quite natural at first sight and exceptional upon closer inspection. Details and materials are very important in this respect. The interior is unpretentious and shows how beautiful pure materials can be.

The project is situated on the Müllerpier in Rotterdam, a location in the centre of the city with a high scenic quality, the open location on the river Maas. The urban development plan takes advantage of these two qualities. By creating fairly narrow streets and enclosed squares, the openness on the quayside is emphasized.

Two tree-lined avenues and an alleyway access the area. These paths are interrupted by seven squares: the welcome square, the sport square, the arts square, the entertainment square, the knowledge square and finally, the square on the Maas.

The buildings lining the streets consist of street-level three-storey houses.

Public buildings are situated on the squares. They are removed from the rigid urban development structure.

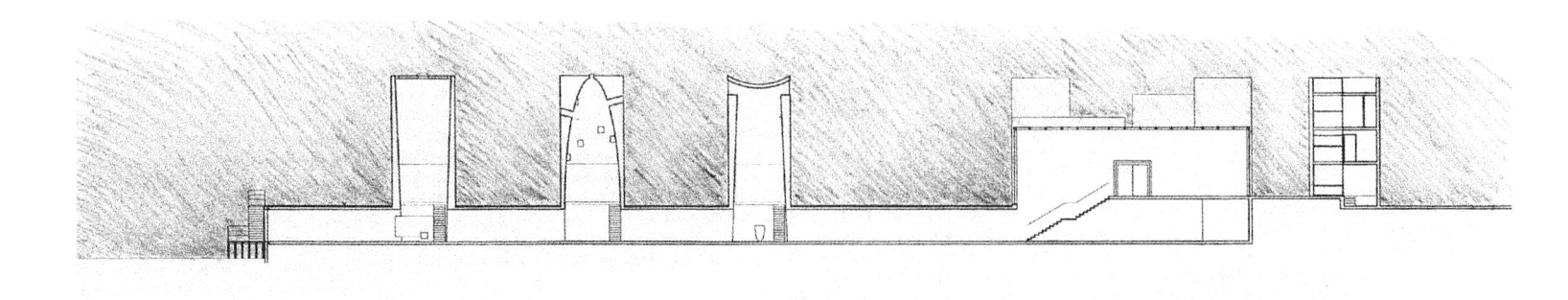

Cross-section of square and chapels

Sketch of the entrance
A small stream of water flows in through a small opening in the facade.

Chair, made from a single sheet of birch multiplex

The temple is situated on the latter square, the square on the river Maas. The building appears to merge into the housing structure. Inside, however, two connections are created with the Maas.

The building is divided into different zones. Louis Kahn has articulated this principle as follows:

> First you have a sanctuary and the sanctuary is for those who want to kneel. Around the sanctuary is the ambulatory, and the ambulatory is for those who are not sure but who want to be near. Outside is a court for those who want to feel the presence of the chapel. And the court has a wall. Those who pass the wall can just wink at it.

The building comprises three volumes. The two on the flanks accommodate the general functions like conference rooms, lodging rooms, a crèche and a restaurant. The volume on the side of the square is the ceremonial area. The main ceremonial room consists of a light central square surrounded by a gallery, with a staggered ceiling. The temple has an exit across water, for instance to the graveyard on the opposite side of the river. A water street enters the building on one side. On the other side an underground corridor connects the temple with a jetty on the water. The birth, life and death chapels interrupt the corridor and tower above the square.

Square and building seen from the Maas

Culture, recreation and religion

Everyday temple

Main ceremonial room

Gallery

170 The elements of light and water are just as important as the tangible materials. On account of the triangular roof construction, the light enters the interior in various ways, depending upon the time of day. Rainwater is transported in a stream through the interior.

The acoustics also play an important role in the individual perception. This can partly be regulated by means of the sliding/revolving panels that separate the main room from the gallery. Plain materials are used; materials like concrete blocks, Belgian bluestone and birch multiplex for the interior; recycled bricks, concrete slabs and natural stone boulders for the exterior. The chairs, made from birch multiplex, are specially designed for the interior.

Some materials

Sports centre, sailing school and sports hotel in Hoorn

Hans Konijn
graduation project Architectural Design

mentors
Richard Foqué, Jan Bos en Prof. Dr Clemens Steenbergen

The programme of this graduation project consists of a sports centre with a wide range of sports facilities. On account of the unique location of the centre on the banks of the IJsselmeer, the programme includes a sailing school with a harbour. To enable the public to stay at the centre for several days, a sports hotel is also linked to the centre. With the total programme, the centre is one of the largest sports centres in the Netherlands.

The project is situated in Hoorn. It occupies an interesting position in terms of landscape and urban development due to its central setting within a very diverse landscape. The location consists of a green area on the banks of the Hoornse Hop, a basin-shaped inlet on the IJsselmeer lake. To the east is the mediaeval town centre of Hoorn, while residential areas, built in the nineteen sixties, are situated to the north and west.

The most important basis for the project was that the centre should respect and reinforce the landscape features of the location, such that a relationship would be created between the building and the landscape. In this way a building was created which was specifically suited to the spot. The landscape features that were important for the creation of the concept were the bend of the adjacent dike, the elongated shape of the green belt and the immediate proximity of the water.

The sports centre is situated in a kink in the bend of the dike. The entrance to the centre, which faces an important traffic intersection on the edge of the old town centre, can be accessed on foot and by bicycle via a route along the water and via a bridge from the Westerdijk. Motor traffic is directed via the Westerdijk to the parking garage, which lies under the pedestal on which the entire centre is built. The harbour is situated behind the sports centre and is shaped to the contours of the building.

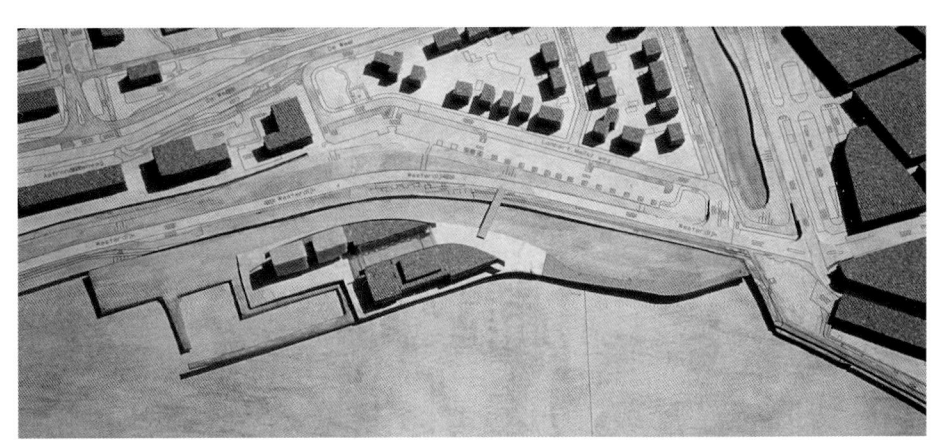

Draft model of building and landscape

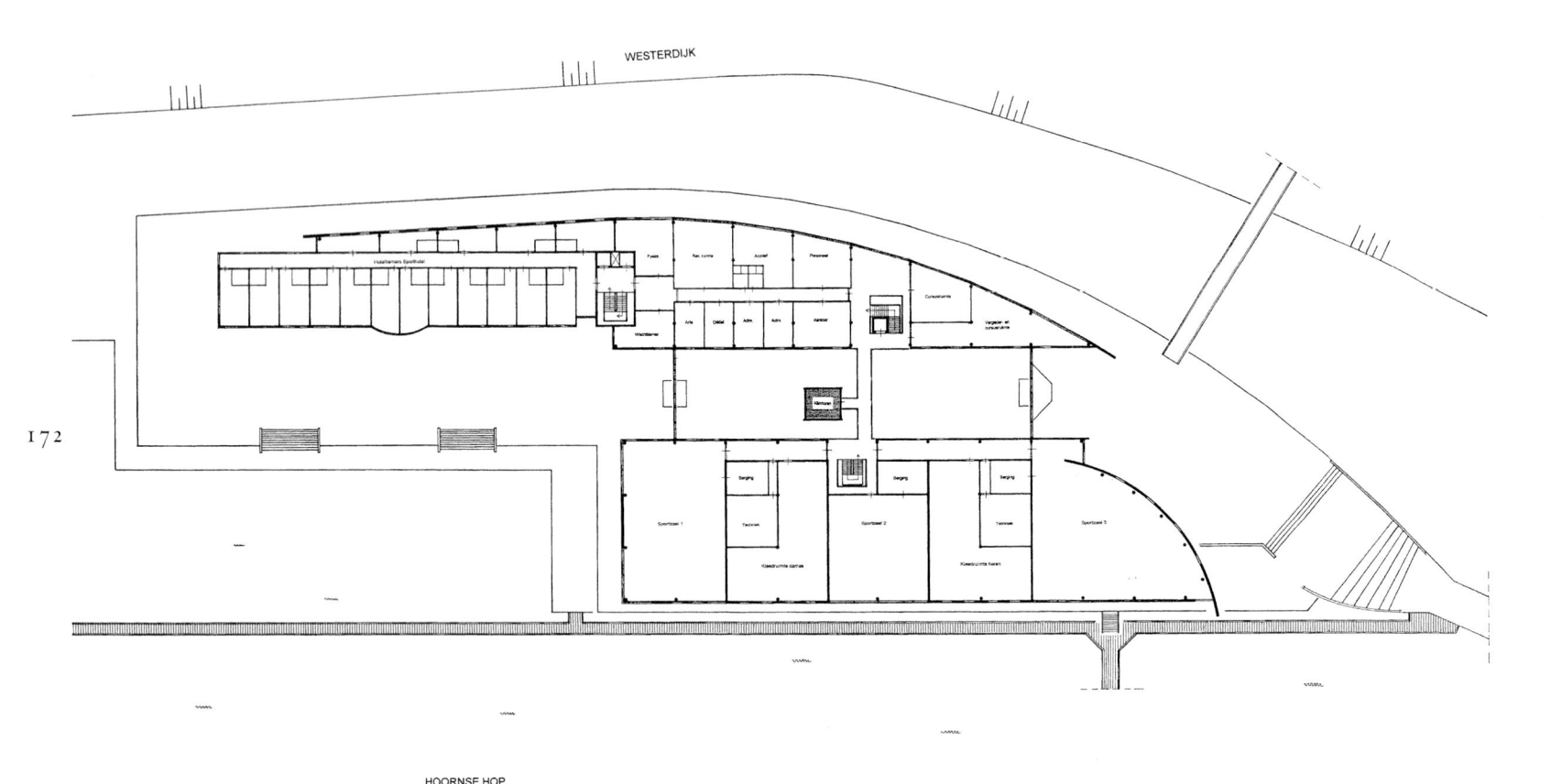

Plan of the first floor

The sports centre on the pedestal is composed of two main volumes. The first main volume is elongated and is located along the body of the dike. It contains the functions that do not require a direct relationship with the water, such as office spaces and the rooms for the general public. The volume follows and accentuates the curve of the Westerdijk. The powerful form thus created expresses the dynamic character of the sports functions in the building.

The curved volume accommodates the sports hotel, the rooms of which have a view of the harbour and the Hoornse Hop. The sports hotel is elevated on columns, so that it is possible to see the harbour and the water of the Hoornse Hop from the Westerdijk underneath the sports hotel. The second main volume lies directly on the water and contains all functions that should have a direct relationship with the IJsselmeer. These are the sailing school and the restaurant on the first floor and the various sports rooms on the second and third floor.

The two main volumes are connected by means of a transparent atrium with two important functions. Firstly, the atrium facilitates the desired open structure of the centre, so that the various functions can be shown to the public, from both inside and outside the building. Secondly, it provides for a (sight) relationship between the harbour area behind the building and the grounds in front of the centre. This ensures that there is coherence within the entire location and that the site is not split up into clearly defined areas.

The dominant feature of the centre is the climbing tower in the atrium. The climbers climb to the highest point of the centre where they are rewarded for their efforts with a magnificent view over the IJsselmeer and the surrounding district.

Section through sports centre

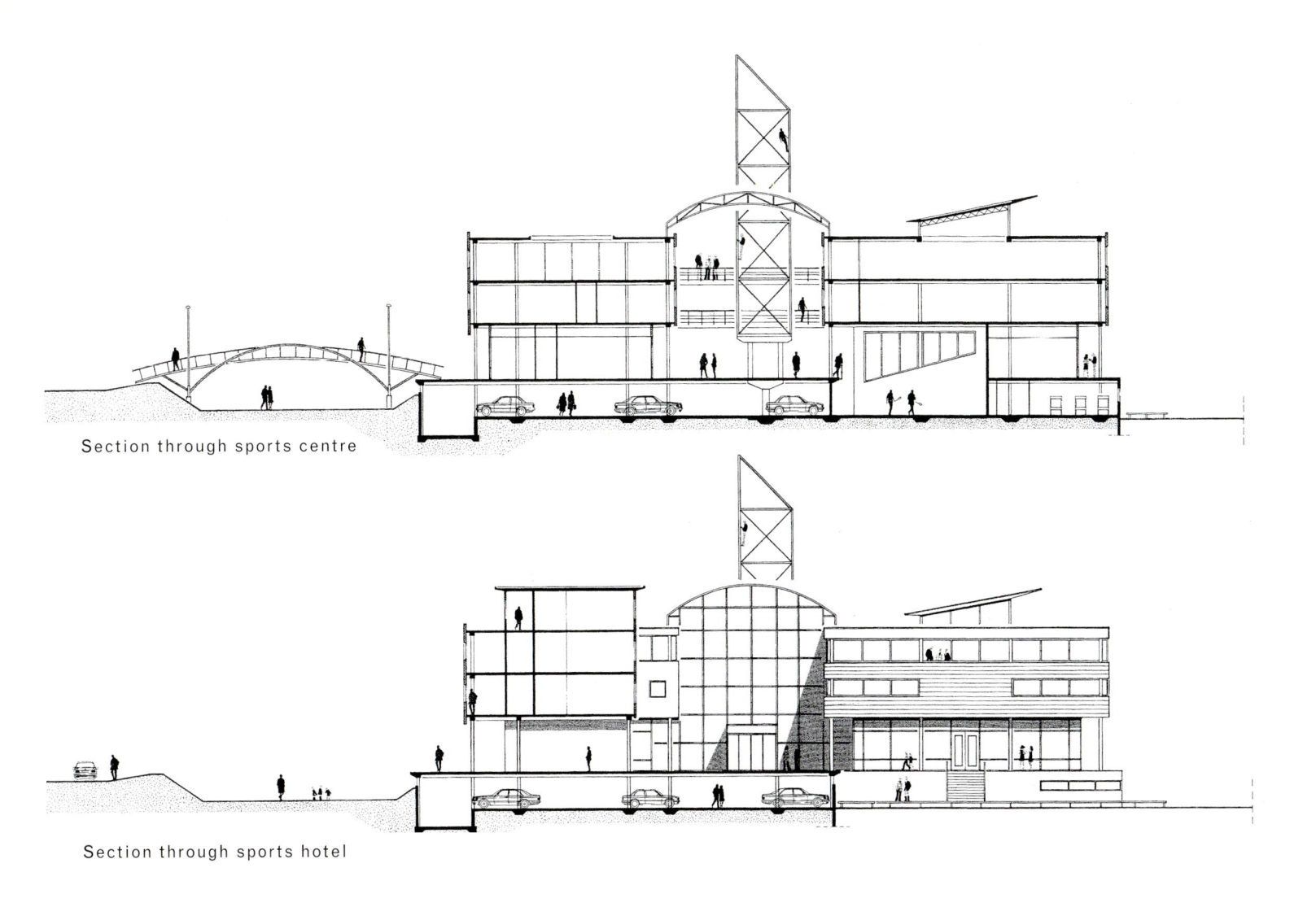

Section through sports hotel

West side, with the sports hotel to the left and the sailing school harbour in the foreground

Culture, recreation and religion

Punto de Encuentro
Spanish cultural centre on the Boompjes

Huib van Zeijl
graduation project Architectural Design

mentors
Prof. Leen van Duin, Rogier Verbeek, Dr Han Meyer

The design specification for the Spanish cultural centre takes up a recent trend among such organizations: the consolidation of activities currently dispersed throughout the country, thus enabling them not only to greatly improve their financial basis but also project a distinctive image nationwide. The centres are used as a medium for introducing these organizations to the world or even as diplomatic intermediaries between countries and cultures, without ceasing to be valuable as leisure centres. Here the cultural values of society are reflected.

The Rotterdam Development Plan indicates various key issues and areas for intensive transformation or programming in the city centre. These include a number of potential locations for cultural and recreational institutions. The three vertices of Waterstad (the area by the river) are among these. In recent years there has also been a growing realization that the Boompjes boulevard – the centuries-old Waterstad riverfront – occupies an important position as an urban space. But the current fragmented approach to this location fails to do justice to its exceptional spatial and programmatic potential. That is the main reason for deciding on a project that goes a step further than the Development Plan's conservative approach to the waterfront – a project that provides the Boompjes with a programmatic stimulus. At the same time it is important to create a strong relationship between public space and the additional programme. A cultural centre is just what is needed to achieve this close fit between the urban space and the building, so that both serve a clearer purpose.

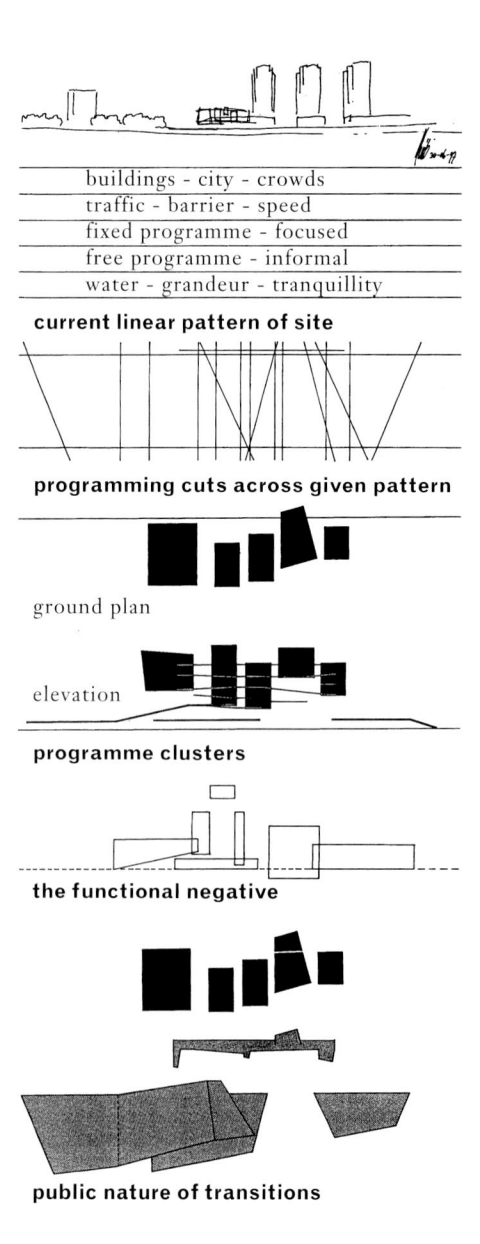

buildings - city - crowds
traffic - barrier - speed
fixed programme - focused
free programme - informal
water - grandeur - tranquillity

current linear pattern of site

programming cuts across given pattern

ground plan

elevation

programme clusters

the functional negative

public nature of transitions

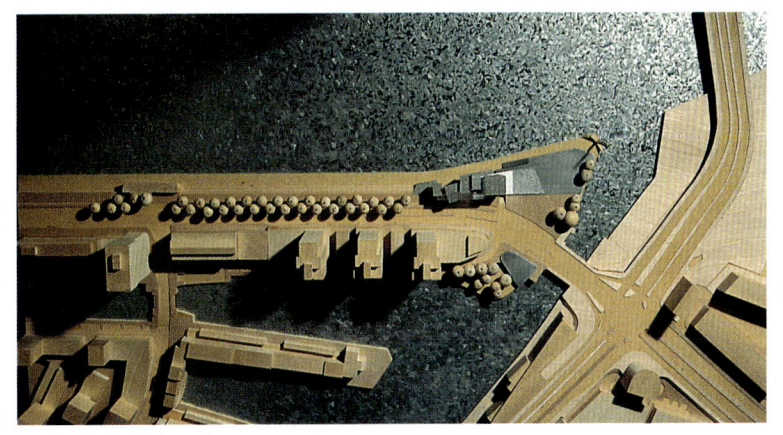

Model of the site

The Boompjes has a very linear pattern of land use. In addition this quay is cut off from the city by the busy main road. There is a lack of elements to break through this pattern, inviting passers-by to rediscover the quay. By programming the building to cut across the given pattern, one creates a clash that constantly reveals different aspects of the programme or setting. In order to emphasize this clash, all the building's components appear as independent masses. They maintain sufficient distance from each other to prevent noise pollution, to keep the lines of sight open or even accommodate other programmes. The differences in height create a dynamic play of ramps connecting the programmes with each other.

The transition from public space to specific programme is not abrupt but flowing, so that programmatically the design is also firmly embedded in its surroundings. The horizontal concrete surfaces play an important role here. They also form the architectural basis for the building, holding together the composition of masses floating above it. At the head of the building the tables can be turned, creating a programmatic jump in scale, intensifying the experience of the building in its surroundings. At first sight the square is the stage of urban life, while the refreshments area is the hall containing the audience. On summer evenings the large surface of the outside wall becomes a projection screen, with the building as the background and the square as an open-air auditorium for the crowds of visitors...

Theme collage: programme and surroundings

Culture, recreation and religion

Punto de Encuentro

176 Scale model

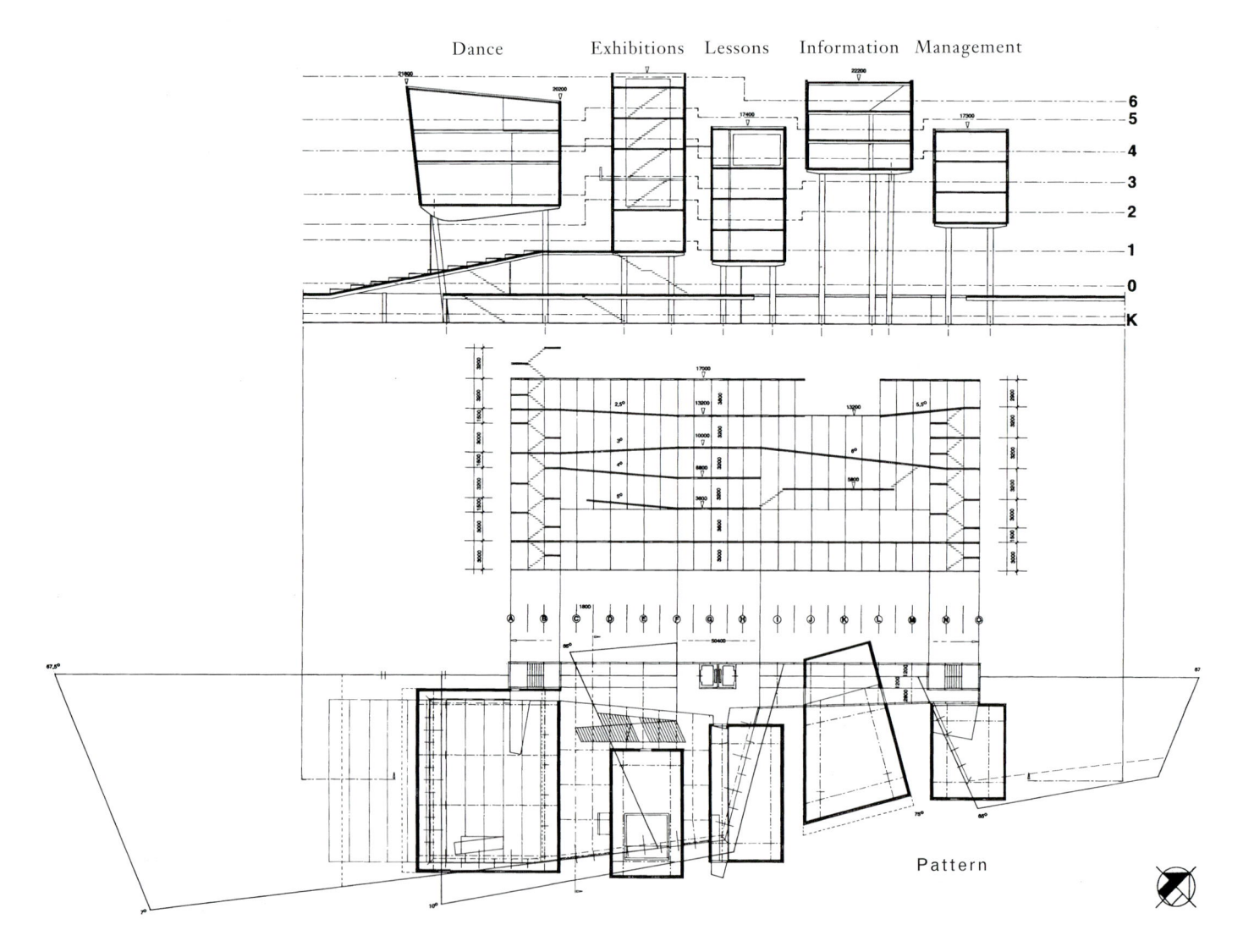

Dance   Exhibitions   Lessons   Information   Management

Pattern

Instead of closing up completely and meekly complying with the prevailing linear organization of its context, the building reacts to the grandeur of this space on the waterfront. The design has grown out of the programme and its setting, but also provides every freedom for the visitor's subjective interpretation. Mediterranean villages, the composition and division of a surface, use of material, colour and texture, parading, long-gone port industry or perhaps an abstraction of the Boompjes – with the fusion of many different references, the architectonic building acquires a powerful identity of its own. But above all, in its individual components linked by a separate traffic system, this is a design that reflects the dynamism of this city at the River Maas.

Techniques and technology

A design research experiment in brief: the Imaging Imagination Workshop

Martijn Stellingwerff, Jack Breen

Introduction

The third biannual conference of the European Architectural Endoscopy Association (EAEA) took place in August 1997 in Delft. The conference was chaired by Professor Jan van der Does of the Media section and hosted by the Faculty of Architecture. An international group of experts on simulation and presentation techniques attended the conference and gave presentations on the following subjects: current developments and use of endoscope and computer techniques, research involving simulation and architectural representation, and teaching, planning and the adaptation of visual media for the benefit of architectural design. The faculty's new endoscope laboratory was presented at the conference and new digital simulation techniques were examined.
A design/research workshop was held on the second day of the conference.

In this article we focus on the rich exposure of ideas and intense exchange of knowledge that took place in the conference workshop. We describe the way the workshop was organized and the response we received from participants. The combination of a strictly defined design task, early and constant guidance of participants, a questionnaire that investigated the techniques used and participants' attitudes and preferences, and a systematic documentation of the results led to a number of interesting proposals and significant findings.[1]

Development of the Imaging Imagination Workshop

The title of the conference workshop was *'Imaging Imagination, exploring the impact of dynamic visualization techniques in the design of the public realm'*. The theme was inspired by the term *imaging*, introduced by John Zeisel as a characteristic ingredient of design in his influential book 'Inquiry by Design'[2]. Zeisel argued that imaging is an essential design activity, as the designer has to steadily create design images throughout the different phases of design. These images communicate the *intentions* of the design as far as they are known at that point to the critical designer and his or her team, as well as to others involved in the design process, such as the client(s) and various other actors influencing design *decision-making*.

We were curious how endoscopic imaging techniques might be able to stimulate the *imagination* in the design process. Again, this might involve both the stimulation of the *designer* and the commitment of the *other disciplines* concerned. We hoped a workshop situation might provide insights into this essential aspect of creative design. Another point of interest was how different *optical* endoscopic approaches might compare with emerging *computer visualization* techniques.

The method adopted for the workshop at Delft was inspired by a previous EAEA workshop held in Vienna. A design task would once again be set beforehand and forwarded to the participants, who would then prepare a contribution *prior* to the conference. This time the model would not travel from one institute to the other, however, but a relatively simple model set would be sent to each participant separately. The object of the workshop was to include – and confront – both *optical* and *digital* endoscopy techniques. The decision was made to use a 1:200 scale model in addition to a computer model, which was created making use of

---

[1]
The papers presented at the conference and the workshop results can be found in the Conference Proceedings: Does, J. van der, J. Breen, M. Stellingwerff, (eds.), *Architectural and urban simulation techniques in research and education*, Delft University Press, 1998

[2]
Zeisel, J., *Inquiry by design*: tools for environment-behaviour research, Cambridge University Press, 1984

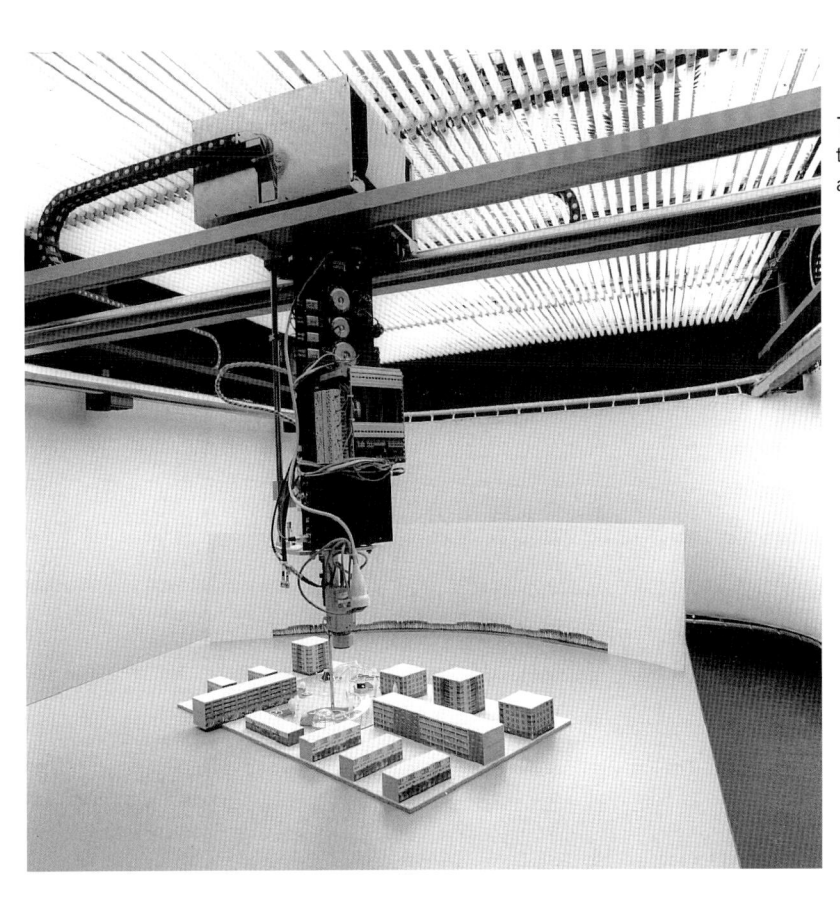

The workshop scale model in the new endoscopy laboratory at the Faculty of Architecture

Each of the institutes that had shown an interest in the workshop was sent a set, consisting of a model for either optical or digital visualization. In addition, each received a written text with plans, amounting to the rules for the workshop exercise, plus a questionnaire designed to gather data on the technical aspects of the presentations and specific experiences or suggestions.

The workshop contributions

The input for the conference workshop consisted of thirteen different entries, eight of which were prepared using optical visualization techniques and seven using computers. At the beginning of the conference, the participants handed over their material: the stills which had been requested for the workshop exhibition, videotapes and computer files. Using the still images taken from predetermined positions in the model, a wall of images was made, which could be viewed during the afternoon of the workshop session at the conference. During the project presentations, additional images on video or slides were presented and some of the design models brought to the conference were viewed in motion, either using the Faculty's endoscope or by means of VRML software. Each of the contributions was presented on a web site and in the conference proceedings in the form of a project file. Each project was presented in the following format: basic information, an overview and a series of images from the pre-determined viewpoints, a short description of the project and specific information from the workshop questionnaire accompanying the project.

texture-mapping techniques. The idea was to keep the design task relatively simple, with a clearly defined set of constraints, in the hope that this would facilitate the comparison and evaluation of contributions, on the level of the quality of *design proposals* as well as the specific *technical solutions*.

The design task chosen was a variation on one of the regular form studies exercises. The site is an imaginary one on the edge of a Dutch city. To suggest a proper sense of place and a basic level of realness in the model of the surroundings, a texture-mapping technique was adopted which had been developed by the Delft Media Group in the Vienna workshop. This entails the sampling of images and their subsequent application as a kind of urban 'wallpaper' onto the elementary geometry of the building blocks. The facade textures were taken from real buildings on the new housing estate in the south of Delft, called the *Tanthof*. On a bicycle trip through the area, images were collected using a digital photo camera. A selection of images was made and these were 'straightened' using photo editing software. The flattened elevations were then applied as texture mappings in the computer model and used as 1 : 200 elevations for the scale models.

The workshop projects were presented at a plenary afternoon session. Prior to these presentations two senior members of the EAEA, Antero Markelin from Stuttgart and Wolfgang Thomas from Essen – both pioneers of Endoscopy – were asked to follow the sessions critically and report their findings at the workshop discussion after the presentations. During the first part of the meeting, all contributions were presented separately, with a brief round of questions and comments for each project. After all the projects had been presented, the meeting reconvened for a group discussion.

The Imaging Imagination Workshop

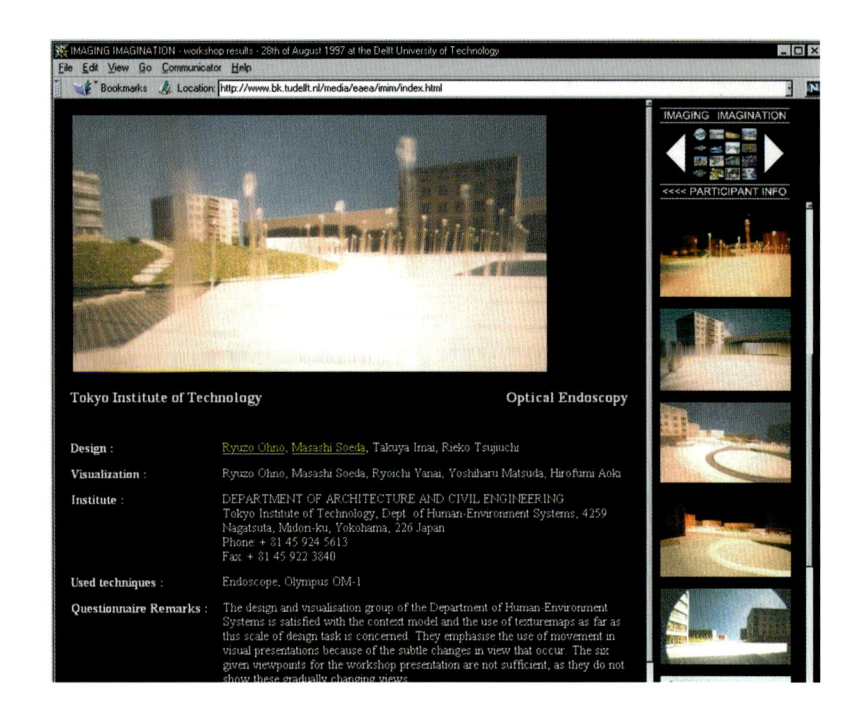

The Imaging Imagination web site

Workshop discussion

Markelin stated that he had seen many interesting and fascinating works, where the idea and technique fit together in very different ways. Some plans were realistic (and could be built tomorrow), others less so. From the presentations one could learn about the ideas behind the projects. The focus was almost always different. There were examples which had concentrated on finding the 'right solution', where the presentation was less important, and there were others where the presentation itself was seen as the main task, the central problem. As regards the issue of whether CAD or Endoscopy is better, Wolfgang Thomas felt optimistic about the way both techniques were being used. It is not the particular type of technique that matters but the production of the right image and the level of validity in relation to the design being presented.

There is a need to differentiate between realism and simulation. The acceptance of a simulation is often greater if the audience is aware of the fact that it is only a limited simulation and there is a model involved. There is always a reduction, even though we may include non-visual information, such as acoustic input.

At this point, lighting in an optical endoscope model still seems to have the edge over a computer model but there are situations where using CAD is better. CAD makes it easier to do things which are normally not possible and CAD is tempting, even seductive.

A number of participants have sought solutions beyond architecture – looking further...

Working with the computer is still very different from working with a scale model. The use of different tools can possibly stimulate different design solutions and at present it still appears to lead to different kinds of images and use of 'camera' motion. Computers are steadily developing and gradually becoming more sensitive, both in their user interfaces and visual expression potential. At the same time traditional techniques are relying more and more on computation, and will probably continue to do so.

As regards the texture-mapped context model, the Dresden group were impressed how well this worked: "a good and cheap technique". Amin Amin, from the Delft Building Technology Group, stated that his group had been challenged by the model to find texture maps that would fit in.

Another good aspect of the workshop, according to Thomas, was that as well as the more academic presentations, it provided an opportunity to bring together the conference participants, who came from very different cultural backgrounds, on the level of Imaging, so that they could get to know each other and share each other's enthusiasm, creating a miniature global village.

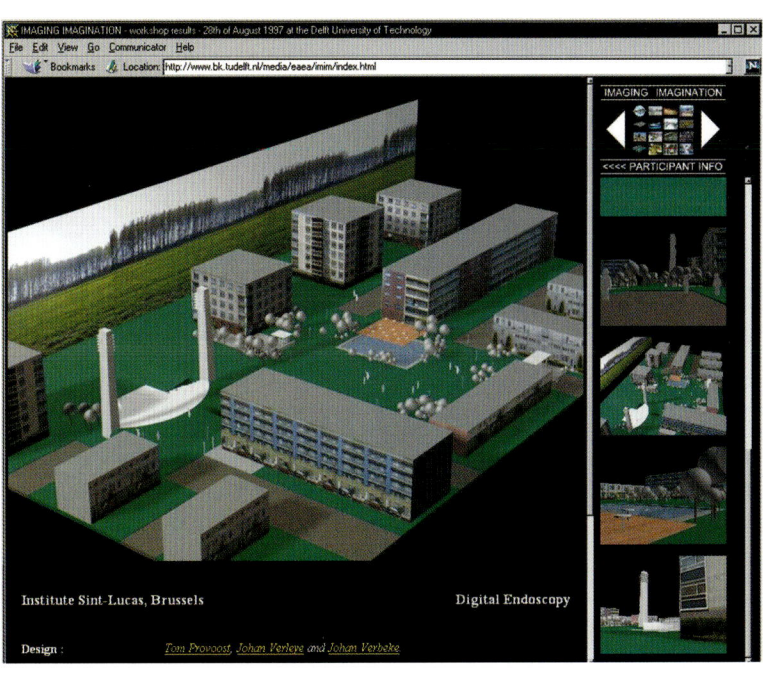

Questionnaire results

The texture-mapped models were generally received very positively. This can also be seen in the various designs, which attempt to fit in with and react to the surroundings. During certain decisive moments in the design process, some participants would have preferred a less detailed model, with only the abstract forms of the building blocks (without facade textures) in order to focus on shaping the building volumes and proportions of spaces. The facade textures provide a great deal of information, even though the projection is totally flat. More 3D geometric details could be provided in the balconies and gardens, because these elements are most distorted when projected on a flat facade.

The question of which view – eye-level or bird's-eye view – is more appropriate for visual checking during different design tasks provided considerable insight into and confirmation of the use of endoscopy and certain graphic user interfaces in computers. Most primary urban design decisions, such as the placement of masses and finding an appropriate urban scale, are done in bird's-eye view. The more detailed decisions (visual checks) and decisions about height are made in eye-level view (e.g. details on the ground, choice of texture and material, light adjustments, camera placements, finding the appropriate human scale and proportions of spaces).

The comparison, after taking the average of the answers in all questionnaires and for all design tasks, shows some preference for the use of eye-level views (60%) over the use of bird's-eye views (40%). There was remarkable consistency on this point among 8 participants (all between 54% and 64% for eye-level use). Only two participants seemed really devoted to perspective eye-level views, with a score of only 25% and 10% for the use of bird's-eye view.

The simultaneous combination of both views is very important, however. In most endoscopy laboratories this combination is almost natural, as the designer is standing next to the scale model and looking through the endoscope pipe or looking at a video monitor. When the views are separated through enhanced technology (as happens when electronic camera navigation tools are introduced or in most full immersion virtual reality applications), the need emerges for the insertion of a second view-frame to provide an overview. In a video or an earlier computer animation of a route through a model, the same need for an overview may arise. If a small overview image is not provided, one can easily become disorientated.

Techniques and technology

Conclusions

Essentially, what endoscopy does is create images from a design model, from an imaginary eye-level. This is an effective way of presenting a completed design to others. However it also has potential for creative use in the design process. This workshop was intended to explore the uses of endoscopy as a design instrument.

As part of the overall conference arrangement, the Imaging Imagination Workshop attempted to bring together experts from different institutes within the framework of a creative exercise, to stimulate the comparison of results and lead to an exchange of ideas. From this point of view the workshop can justifiably be called a success. Although the number of participants was limited, the task led to contributions of impressive quality (on the level of both design solutions and technical implementation and innovation) as well as considerable diversity.

Although it is impossible to generalize, we were able to recognize the following themes running through the different projects:
— a 'scenographic approach' (emphasizing the changing visual qualities of the design as perceived from different viewpoints and experienced through motion)
— an 'atmospheric approach' (making conscious use of selected stimuli such as differences in lighting conditions and the use of background sounds to convey a sense of presence)
— an 'experimental approach' (using the instrumentation in a search for the 'correct' form for the design, or an attempt to shift the existing boundaries of design media).
 These categories are not inclusive in the sense that any one comprehensively sums up a specific project. Indeed, a number of workshop participants will probably recognize more than one of these categories in their design visualization project.

The decision to include both optical and digital endoscope techniques has worked out well. It is increasingly a question not of either/or but both/and. An optical approach may be better in some cases and a computer approach in others. Much depends on the personal preferences of the designer. Working with the computer is still very different from working with a scale model. The use of different tools may stimulate specific design. The two media still appear to lead to different kinds of images and use of 'camera' motion. Computers are steadily developing and gradually becoming more sensitive, both in their user interfaces and visual expression potential. At the same time traditional techniques are relying more and more on computation. New opportunities lie ahead for the combined use of digital and optical techniques.

The general impression at the conference was that optical endoscopy is very much alive and kicking. At this meeting it once again became clear that international endoscopy groups are not conservative in their approach, but look towards imaginative solutions and innovative applications.

For the full documentation of the workshop, including all project files and images, we invite you to look up the Imaging Imagination web site:

http://www.bk.tudelft.nl/media/eaea/imim/

A strategy for the use of simulation tools in building design

Pieter de Wilde, Marinus van der Voorden and Godfried Augenbroe

Introduction

The use of computational tools for the simulation of the performance of buildings has become widely accepted in building research. However, in spite of the clear merits of these tools and a number of successful projects demonstrating their use, they are not yet entered in widespread use amongst architects. Although many research projects have had the intention of bridging this gap between the world of building design and the world of building simulation there has to date been little success in achieving this objective. A number of plausible reasons have been established for their limited use (such as the unavailability of appropriate models, the costs involved in simulation, and the knowledge required to use these expert tools); nonetheless it has proven difficult to provide practical answers to these problems, which consequently still constitute a barrier to the use of simulation tools.

Conversely, building practice is confronted with continually increasing stringent quality requirements. One such area is the level of energy consumption, where standards are continually being tightened. Diversity in the design of buildings and the dynamic aspects of their performance means that it is almost impossible to predict the performance of a building without making use of computational tools. As a consequence, the practical application of simulation tools during the design of buildings is becoming increasingly urgent. Simulation tools offer the possibility of predicting the performance of buildings and of comparing the performance of different variants under identical conditions. However, it is far from clear when the use of simulation tools is appropriate, or which *design decisions* can be supported with simulation tools.

Consequently the general goal of our approach is to develop a strategy to stimulate the implementation of simulation tools as a routine design support instrument during the design process.

One area of building design in which the use of simulation tools is generally accepted as being extremely useful is *energy-conscious design*. For the purposes of this paper, energy-conscious design will be limited to energy-saving components.
Energy-saving components can be defined as components that are integrated into the building with the intention of making a contribution to lower energy demands. Examples of energy-saving components are sun spaces, solar walls, advanced glazing systems, and photovoltaic arrays.
Energy-saving components are tangible additions to the building that attest to the architect's ambition to achieve an energy-conscious design. In spite of the architect's good intentions the actual energy savings achieved by these components frequently proves to be lower than was expected; moreover the use of these components might in fact result in malfunctioning buildings.

Integration of energy-saving components in existing building concepts is the title of a PhD project currently in progress at the Faculty. This project is focused on bridging the gap between building design and building simulation. The choice and design of energy-saving components is used as a concrete and actual application domain.

Approach

The first stage in the development of the strategy was to make an inventory of the current utilisation of simulation tools in building design. The following impediments to their use have been observed.

Complexity and the uniqueness of design processes and simulation processes

Designing a building is a complex process, since it is comprised of a large number of decisions with partly cyclical and partly sequential dependencies on each other; each individual decision may require careful consideration of a number of aspects. Each subsequent decision is partly dependent on the previous decision; however attention shifts randomly from one aspect or context to another. This means that no two design processes are similar to each other. The simulation process (or, more correctly, the simulation procedure) is more organised, but depends greatly on the design process in which it is used. Once again the number of decisions to be made is large, and the decisions are interrelated.

Difficulty of describing the two processes

It is difficult make an adequate description of these processes. The large number of decisions that require consideration makes the description complex; but an additional problem is that an adequate description also needs to include a number of thought processes that cannot be readily observed (the mental processes of those involved and consequently dependent on chance, personal preferences, etc.).

Absence of well-defined points for the implementation of simulation tools

There are no general guidelines for the most appropriate time to implement simulation techniques in the design process. Usually they are introduced when the designer is confronted by a question that requires additional information before a well-founded decision can be made. However it is very well possible that these questions are encountered at a point in the design process that is not the most appropriate phase for the use of simulation tools.

Lack of guidelines for the selection of tools

Although a wide range of computational tools with a great variety of specific uses have been developed the availability of these tools is still a problem. The selection of a simulation tool appears to depend largely on the tools that happen to be available, and on the preference of the person who is to carry out the simulation.

Lack of guidelines for adequate modelling

Decisions made during the translation of the design into input for the simulation have a great impact on the computational results that are obtained. Nonetheless the actual modelling often depends largely on the perception of the person making the simulation. However it should be noted that recent work[1,2] deals with this problem.

The gap between simulation and design evaluation

A typical simulation tool generates data, which can then be used to obtain answers to design questions. However the simulation will not be able to answer questions about the design without some form of post-processing of the data it generates.

The second stage in the development of the strategy was to classify these observations. Improvements in the guidelines for the selection of tools and for modelling are to be anticipated since these constitute the objectives of some international research projects currently in progress, such as IEA Annex 30 *Bringing simulation to applications*[1] and the CIBSE *Application Manual for building energy and environmental modelling*[2].

Although research currently in progress is working on the issues shown below, they will nonetheless require further attention:
– The definition of well-defined starting points for the use of simulation tools in the design process and the specification of successive interaction points;
– The structuring of the process of designing the building with an emphasis on *building simulation intervention points* linked to design decision points;
– The structuring of the design information;
– The improvement in the efficiency of the evaluation process (largely with respect to the interaction between *design* and *simulation*).

A strategy for the optimal deployment of simulation tools in the design process that emerges from this inventory and classification will be reviewed in the next paragraph.

---

[1] IEA Annex 30, *Bringing simulation to applications*, http://www.ecbcs.org/annex30.html

[2] Bartholomew, Hand, Irving, Lomas, McElroy, Parand, Robinson and Strachan, *An application manual for building energy and environmental modelling*, Proceedings of the 5th International IBPSA Conference, Prague, Czech Republic, 8-10/9/1997, Volume II, pp. 387-393

[3] *Energy performance of dwellings and residential buildings*, part 2: Examples, pp. 10-36, Nederlands Normalisatie Instituut, NPR 5129-2, July 1995

[4] Capsol version 2.0, Program for multi-zone transient heat transfer Physibel, Belgium, Maldegem, 1998, http://www.physibel.be/VON2CP.HTM

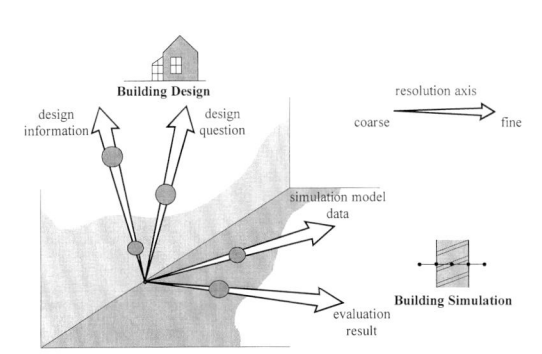

Figure 1 Visualisation of the data categories and resolution axes

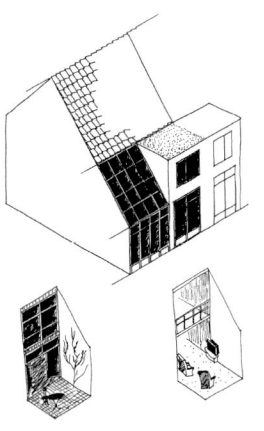

Figure 2 Omega house with sun space (draft)

Strategy

The objectives of the strategy as described below is to provide a framework that:
– allows the positioning of design decisions in the design process;
– identifies decision points for which support is both desirable and effective;
– defines evaluations that would be able to provide this support;
– specifies the level of detail needed for these evaluations;
– indicates the type of simulation (tool) to be used.

The following steps will be taken to meet these objectives:

1. Design decision moments:

The specification of *design decision moments* will result in the definition of identifiable intervention points for the use of simulation tools in the design process; design decision moments can also be used to designate successive steps in the interaction between *design* and *simulation*. Design decision moments can be identified from an examination of the relevant operation at any given point in the design process.

2. Information categories:

Once the process of the design of buildings has been structured and the different types of building simulation as part of that process have been identified it becomes possible to distinguish four different categories of data, as the main information carriers: two are inherent to the flow of information in the design of the building, i.e. *design information* and *design questions*, and two are inherent to performing a particular type of building simulation: *simulation model data* and the *evaluation results* (see figure 1).

3. Resolution axes/ resolution space:

The level of detail of each of the above four data categories varies from coarse to fine, though not necessarily in a monotonic fashion in time. At any given point in the design process each data category can be plotted on a *resolution axis*. It then becomes possible to represent each design decision moment in the design process in a four-dimensional *resolution space* (see figure 1). Each of these points represents a specific description of the interaction granularity between *design* and *simulation*, which may be considered to be a specification of the depth of the information provided by the building simulation process.

Within this framework the efficiency of the design process incorporating simulation techniques can be improved by:
– refinement of the direction of the evaluation process by increasing the sensitivity of the evaluation for the relevant design context;
– enhancement of the control of the simulation process, for instance by sensitivity analysis or by searching algorithms;
– increasing the significance of the simulation results for the design process by processing the results, such as by arranging them in sequence, indicating the consequences, etc.

Example

The strategy will be demonstrated by means of an example from real design practice. This example comes from a design project currently in progress at the Netherlands Energy Research Foundation (ECN), the objective of which is the development of an energy-conscious housing scheme, known as the *Omega house*. The basis of the Omega design project is the reference house for the Netherlands[3].
One particular case has been defined within this Omega project; this case is restricted to an integration of a *solar area* energy-saving component into the original reference house (see figure 2). The particular subject of the study is the quality aspect of energy consumption, in which air temperatures will be used as (global) indicators of thermal comfort.

The example shows how *design decision moments*, *information categories* and *resolution axes* can be used to describe the interaction between design and simulation, and how this description could enhance the use of simulation tools in the design of buildings. The example also demonstrates where a further elaboration of the strategy is required. The dynamic thermal simulation program Capsol[4] was used for the calculations in this example.

A generally accepted rule in energy-saving design is that first of all the energy demands of a building should be minimised; secondly, maximum use should be made of renewable energy sources; and finally, fossil energy should be used as efficiently as possible.
In the Omega house design process this general rule has an influence on all phases of the design and on all design decision moments. Some design decision moments related to the energy-saving component *solar area* are listed below. The link between the design phase and design decision moment is arbitrary.

Phase of the design process	Design decision moment
Conceptual design, early	1: To what extent should the building be insulated, and be airtight?
Detailed design, halfway	2: Should an open sun space be incorporated in the building?
Detailed design, final	3: Should ventilation openings or sunshades be included in the sun space?

Number 2 of these three design decision moments has been chosen for further examination

Design decision moment 2 is characterised by the design question: "Would the integration of an open sun space be a suitable decision with respect to the conservation of energy?"

The following information is of relevance to this question:
– The typology of the design decision series: an orientation on a specific energy-conservation component (sun space).
– Information with respect to the context:
objective: the reduction of the energy demand of the design by using solar energy;
constraints: a possible conflict between energy savings and thermal comfort;
conditions: a design for the Netherlands; no precise location as yet;
design phase: detailed design;
design process: top-down design (increasingly explicit).

The data available at this design decision point is as follows:

Design information:
A description of the reference house for the Netherlands; the functions and dimensions are deemed to be definitive, although the further details may be amended as desired; the choice of the installation is left open; two possible options can be considered for the integration of a sun space in the building (see figure 2).

The design question:
Would the integration of an open sun space be a suitable decision with respect to the conservation of energy or would other measures, such as improvements to the insulation or the airtightness, be more efficient? This question includes sub-variants as to whether an open sun space would be compatible with the design and which variants would be worth an initial examination. The evaluation of the following three variants on the reference house should give an initial insight into promising alternatives:
– reference house, U_{facade} = 0.35 W/m²K
– extra-insulated/airtight house, U_{facade} = 0.25 W/m²K
– reference house with 'open' sun space, with double glazing
– reference house with 'open' sun space, with high-efficiency glazing

This *design question* also relates to evaluation criteria. In this case the variant with the lowest energy consumption will be chosen, subject to the condition that the temperature in the house does not exceed 25 °C for more than 5 hours a year.

Simulation model data:
The geometry and materials are derived from the specification of the reference house; climatic data is simulated by the test reference year for the Netherlands; ventilation is in accordance with Dutch regulations; heating is provided by a heating unit (3000 W for the ground floor and first floor, 1500 W for the attic) when temperatures fall below given set-point values; external sunshades attached to south-facing windows are used when the temperature in the house exceeds 22.5 °C.

Evaluation of the results:
The following results were obtained from the calculations:

variant	energy consumption	$T_{gr.\,floor}$ > 25 °C	$T_{first\,floor}$ > 25 °C	T_{attic} > 25 °C
reference house	27,66 GJ/year	0.8 hour	0.5 hour	0 hour
extra-insulated/airtight house	14.68 GJ/year	1.2 hour	0.6 hour	0 hour
house with open sun space (double glazing)	25.46 GJ/year	1.0 hour	0.7 hour	0 hour
house with open sun space (high-efficiency glazing)	24.90 GJ/year	1.0 hour	0.7 hour	0 hour

According to the criteria improvements in the insulation and airtightness of the house should be given preference above the incorporation of an open sun space.

The resolution of the available data (see figure 3):

Design information:
The resolution of the design of the house may be described as fine; however the resolution of the operation 'the addition of an open sun space' is fairly coarse.

Design question:
The design question is still rather undecided, and needs further refinement before commencing the evaluation; consequently this can be considered to be coarse.

Simulation model data:
An advanced computational tool has been used in which a detailed model of both house and sun space have been simulated; this can be ranked as fine. However, other detailed tools and models are available.

Evaluation of the results:
The intrinsic nature of the data obtained from the simulation is very detailed; nonetheless the conclusions based upon this data (the 'real' answers) should be considered as coarse as these answers give only an initial impression and provide information for only two sun space variants.

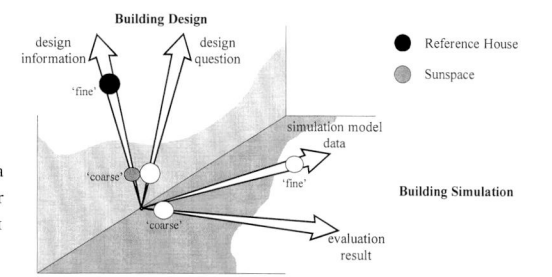

Figure 3 Positioning of data on the resolution axes for design decision moment 1

Conclusions for the next step in the design process:

On the basis of this evaluation of the results, the design team should reconsider the insulation and airtightness of the house. It may be concluded that of the two variants with an open sun space that were examined, the variant with high-efficiency glazing performs slightly better than the variant with standard double glazing.

Feedback to the design

The design decision moment described in the example confirms the general rule in energy-conscious design, i.e. that priority should be given to improvements in the insulation and airtightness above contemplation of the addition of passive solar elements. A study of a broader range of sun space variants can provide clearer support for decisions with respect to the 'addition of a sun space to the Omega house'.

When converted into *data categories* and *resolution axes* the evaluation process is likely to continue until a higher (fine) resolution of the evaluation results can be achieved. The resolution of the design information with respect to the relevant operation will need to be refined to attain the required resolution of the results. This can be achieved either by considering one solar area in detail or by considering other variants representative of a certain type of sun space.

A universal approach that would be advantageous to the design process in general (and not just the design of the Omega house) would be to create a framework prescribing a specific order of design decision moments. Rules should be established for the resolution of the four data categories for each design decision moment. This is necessary to ensure that the simulation process generates precisely that data needed to carry out the correct evaluation. These rules will also indicate which data is not yet needed, and consequently which decisions may be postponed.

Conclusions and closing remarks

This paper presents a strategy for the use of simulation tools in the design of buildings. The strategy consists of a framework for a more explicit and efficient interaction between *design* and *simulation*.

The definition of *design decision moments* is dependent on the processes involved and on the information available at these points. The paper demonstrated a process-based approach; however further study of *design decision moments* is required.

The positioning of the data on each of the four resolution axes is still very global. These resolution axes should be equipped with some sort of calibration to provide more detailed information on the resolution required when using simulation at specific design decision moments.

The quest for Zappi

An introduction to Zappi
Prof. Dr Mick Eekhout

The quest for the new and the unknown is something I have been consciously and unconsciously engaged in since starting my architectural studies in 1968. During the last decade I have enjoyed the privilege of having my own design and production company in Delft, with a motivated staff who have allowed themselves to be misused to realize exotic ideas and to perform unusual experiments.

Zappi represents the ultimate in the new and unknown. The term Zappi was invented by the former town architect of Haarlem, Thijs Asselbergs, at a forum discussion in January 1992 in which Professor Jaap Oosterhoff was my opponent. We were asked to describe an ideal building material that was as yet unknown to either of us. After the discussion the term Zappi lived on as a form of special epithet. Originally launched as a term for a new building material that possesses superior qualities but is yet to be developed, it also symbolises the adventurous quest. It represents that which is unknown, mysterious and challenging. It is both a material and an idea, simultaneously tangible and abstract. It is a mentality that cares little about the apparent senselessness of ideas, nor of the practicality of inventions.

Zappi has left its mark on my work in four ways. Firstly, Zappi as it began: a long-term fundamental research project with the objective of the development of a strong, stiff and tough glass-like engineering material that does not fail suddenly on overloading. This research project was begun under the supervision of my Chair of Product Development in the Faculty of Architecture. The project is being carried out in conjunction with the Faculties of Aerospace Engineering and Applied Sciences (the Materials Science program).

Secondly, Zappi represents not only objectives but also a mentality. Zappi is a friendly and rather comical bulldog, with a character combining intelligence and perseverance. This mentality is needed to generate the motivation needed to maintain the process of design, research, evaluation and development. And who is best suited to the search for this new product? An individual has as many disadvantages as a team. An individual needs a soundboard and subservient assistance; a team can choke the creativity of its members.

In my opinion the search for Zappi may take an entire lifetime. I am someone who enjoys designing and building, but who also enjoys research. The process of design, manufacture and construction usually gives more satisfaction than the void experienced after a building has been completed or a new product has been manufactured and launched. The ultimate goal represented by Zappi may, like the horizon, always remain just one day ahead; but it is, nonetheless, just as noble a goal as the Holy Grail was for King Arthur's Knights of the Round Table.

Thirdly, Zappi is always close by. Each step towards Zappi is also Zappi itself, simply because of the pleasure one can derive from achieving a definitive step on the road towards Zappi. An example of such a step forward is the frameless glazing of the early nineties. Each further development towards a perfect structural glass material is also part of Zappi. Each result is achieved because Zappi takes immediate advantage of every new opportunity, although at the same time it never forgets that the achievement of the ultimate objective also involves a number of discreet steps. That is the reason why this article contains Zappi in its title: its publication marks one step that has been taken, to be followed, hopefully, by many other equally successful steps.

Fourthly, Zappi represents the infectiousness inherent to the development of new products for the building industry. Zappi wants to see the entire audience laughing with it at its jokes, to win applause with its clever feats, and to stimulate the larger circle of parties who are actually involved – all those who, in one way or another, are engaged in product development for the building industry. This is achieved by disseminating new ideas and products amongst professionals with the motivation to upgrade the technology of materials and products for architecture and for the building industry. Zappi's answer to the question 'Would you ever do it again?' would always be 'Yes!'

A proposal has now been drawn up for the fundamental materials research required for Zappi, which is one of Zappi's objectives. However, information about the initiative has already been published – and the pull effect of marketing has resulted in the first collaborations.

Zappi, designing a material
Dr Fred Veer

The concept of designed materials is new to materials science. Traditionally a new material was developed, and then it was up to designers and engineers to find ways to use it. The modern discipline of materials science has made it possible to design materials that are tailored to the demands of designers and engineers. The materials science research constituent of Zappi is an experiment in the design of a material that satisfies the requirements of the architect needing a combination of the mechanical properties of steel and the transparency of glass.

Glass in architecture

For centuries glass has been used as a transparent barrier to preserve the interior climate of a building whilst allowing daylight into its interior. Experience has shown that it is the most stable transparent facade material available. However glass has very poor mechanical properties. This has resulted in a material conflict. The glass window, so essential for the inhabitation of interior spaces, is in structural terms no more than a hole in a wall. From the beginning of this century onwards large glazed openings played a major role in the development of Modern Architecture. Glass was used in the construction of tall buildings as a facade cladding for steel or concrete framework structures. Increasingly stringent requirements from the 1960s onwards created a need for the enhanced performance provided by the use of coatings and advanced double-glazing systems. In the last decade the use of ultra-transparent glass facades and roofs to contrast with closed walls has become an accepted architectural practice. Yet glass remains mechanically unreliable. In modern applications the glass panels are fully pre-stressed to allow them to bear greater stresses. But although special laminates are available, they do not offer a significant improvement on glass as a structural material.

The design of the Zappi material

In essence Zappi should combine the following properties:
- The mechanical properties of steel
- The transparency of glass

In physical terms this is an impossible combination in one single material; the first property requires the dense metallic crystalline structure of a metal, whilst the second property requires the microstructure of an inorganic amorphous solid. These are mutually exclusive structures.

Some answers to the problem can be obtained by combining existing materials and techniques in novel ways. What we have at our disposal are transparent materials such as glass and polymers. Pre-stressed glass possesses the required strength and E-modulus, whilst polymers such as polycarbonates have the required ductility. The combination of these materials in a composite should provide us with a structural material that possesses enhanced properties in

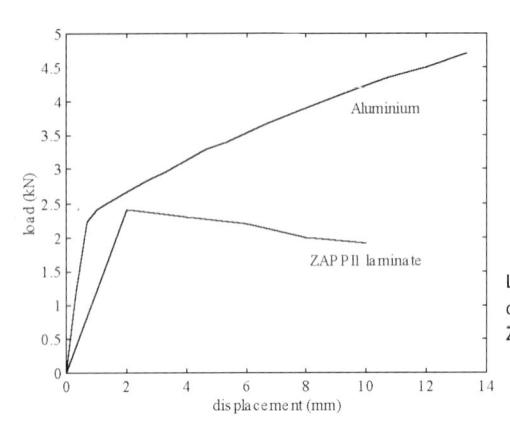

Load displacement diagrams of Al 1010 and Zappi1 laminate beams

comparison with its components. But a number of obstacles remain:

– Pre-stressed glass fails as a result of extensive unstable crack growth with multiple multi-directional crack branching, leading to total decohesion of the material after global or local overloading.
– Amorphous polymers such as polycarbonates have very low surface energy values, which render them highly unsuitable for conventional laminating processes.

If we are to make a suitable composite then the cracking behaviour of glass will first need to be modified in such a way that the glass will fail in a controlled manner. Next we have to bond this modified glass to a suitable polymer.

There are several possible approaches that could be used to modify the glass. The most logical approach would be to develop a new glass "alloy" with the required properties. However the development of a new type of glass is a complicated process, requiring extensive technical facilities. Another approach is to modify the fracture behaviour of existing types of glass, which can be achieved with existing surface modification techniques. The further development of these techniques for standard glass may not provide an optimum solution, but it will result in a demonstration of the technology.

Two years of preliminary research have resulted in a scientifically-verified concept for a material that combines the transparency of glass with the mechanical properties of aluminium. As a result of the complexity of this work many aspects are not yet ready for publication.

The Zappi graduation studio
Dr Fred Veer,
Prof. Dr Mick Eekhout

In the past few years glass facades and roofs have become increasingly common in architecture. All these glass constructions require an amount of structural metal that detracts from their transparency and sometimes dominates the overall impression. The reason is simple: glass is unsuitable for structural applications as it cannot be subjected to stress, because it can fail spontaneously as a result of its inherent brittleness. And transparent plastics that do fail in a safe manner do not possess the rigidity needed for structural use.

The Zappi material must provide the answer to this problem. This is a transparent material that *is* suitable for structural purposes. The Zappi design and research studio in the Product Development Laboratory was set up to create this material. This is a studio in which graduation students have accepted the challenge to design and make use of transparent materials. The students are supervised by scientific staff from the product development, materials science, building physics and adhesion disciplines.

The cross-fertilization achieved between physics and design leads to results that are innovative in both scientific and design terms. The teamwork and team spirit of students and staff resulted in the mentality needed to tackle the complex problems posed by Zappi.

Within two years 10 engineers have graduated from the Zappi studio. They have made a great contribution to the studio's work, both individually and as a team. Working prototypes of a number of Zappi components have been designed, manufactured and tested in the Product Development Laboratory. The following sections review the results of these first 10 graduation projects.

Hinged nodal bond

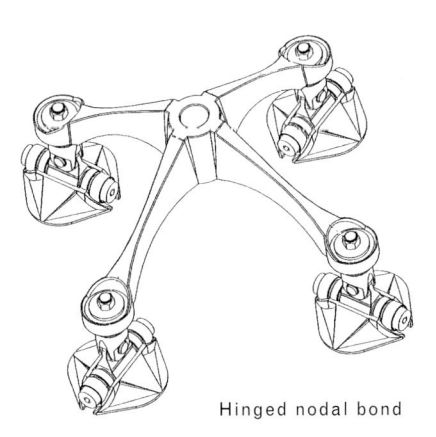

The prototype Zappi beam after the trials

The nodal bond, Barbara van Gelder

Connections between glass and metal have always been a problem. One possibility is to drill holes in the glass, and then harden it. Subsequently bolts are passed through the holes to attach the glass. However this is not always desirable with modern double glazing panels as this may lead to leakages into the air cavity, with all the concomitant problems that this causes. One alternative is to bond the double glazing panels to the metal: a new technology, about which relatively little is known at present. Barbara van Gelder carried out research into glass-metal bonded joints, and came to the conclusion that one of the greatest problems involved in this technique is the rigidity of the joint, which caused substantial localized forces in the glass and ultimately resulted in fractures adjacent to the bond. In order to solve this problem she designed a hinged nodal bond that prevents the build-up of excessive forces in the glass and which results in a safer form of construction. A patent application has been submitted for this design.

The glass bridge, Michiel Niens

In the past few years the use of transparent atrium bridges in buildings has attracted the interest of architects. But most of these designs are unsafe. In cooperation with the Octatube Company Michiel Niens has developed a glass bridge with a span of 20 metres, intended for pedestrians. The design made use of existing state-of-the-art materials and techniques, which were used to the limits of their capabilities. Although this design has not yet resulted in a commercial product, the study has demonstrated the limits of the technologies and materials currently available.

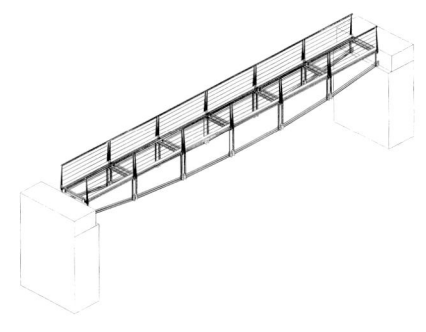

Glass bridge for pedestrians

The safe beam, Monique van Liebergen

The present concept of the Zappi material is as such pointless unless it can find applications in structural components. Monique van Liebergen accepted the challenge to design a beam based on the laminate concept. The beam must be constructed in a way such that it will not fail when overloaded, but will instead exhibit gradual deformation. After a long period of research she succeeded in making a prototype of a transparent Zappi beam possessing the desired properties: a glass beam that merely deforms slightly on overloading, rather than collapsing. A patent application has been submitted for this design.

The mastic seal, Kim Duyvestein

Mastic seals are often used in modern glass structures. However in scientific terms the humble mastic seal is a *terra incognita*. So mastic is used, but apart from its chemical properties we know little about its structural properties or its performance, and they are always ignored in the design phase. Kim Duyvestein was assigned the task of carrying out research into the constructional opportunities offered by mastic. After this research into mastic's possibilities she designed a Zappi structure in which the components were bonded using mastic. All details of the structure have been subjected to an experimental investigation into their structural properties and performance.

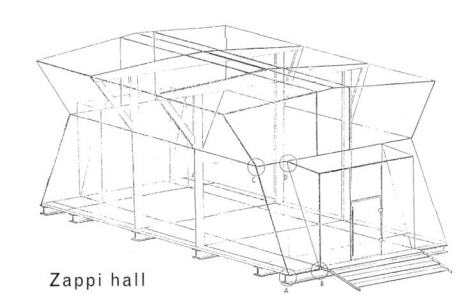

Zappi hall

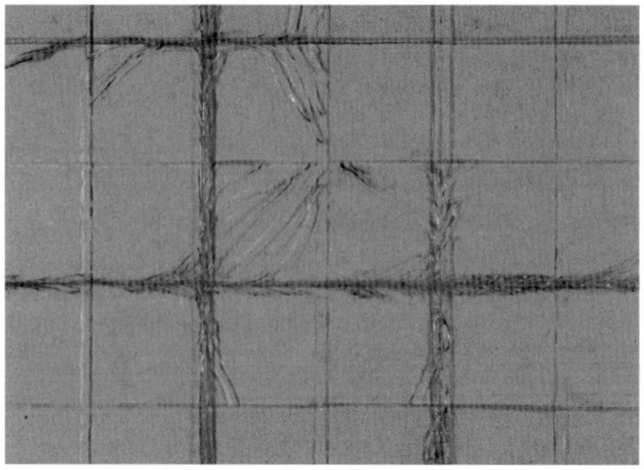

Cracks in the pane subsequent to the trial

The unbreakable pane, Saskia de Vries

One of the several problems encountered when using panes of the present types of glass in horizontal applications is that the entire pane fails when struck by a large object. Saskia de Vries was assigned the task of designing a Zappi pane that would still have sufficient residual strength to be structurally loaded after it had been damaged. After the construction and evaluation of a large number of prototypes she succeeded in making a prototype capable of withstanding being struck 50 times by a falling pointed block of steel. A patent application has been submitted for this design.

The large facade, Menno Gijrath

A new material also requires new design methods. Menno Gijrath designed a Zappi alternative for the existing glass facade of the Ministry of Housing, Spatial Planning and the Environment. By designing a 7.2 x 3.3 metre Zappi box a facade can be constructed with a much higher degree of transparency, and which performs much better in terms of building physics. A prototype of a segment of the Zappi box has been constructed, and an investigation has been carried out into its thermal insulation properties. The investigation demonstrated a significant improvement in the thermal properties, which would result in a reduction in the heating costs.

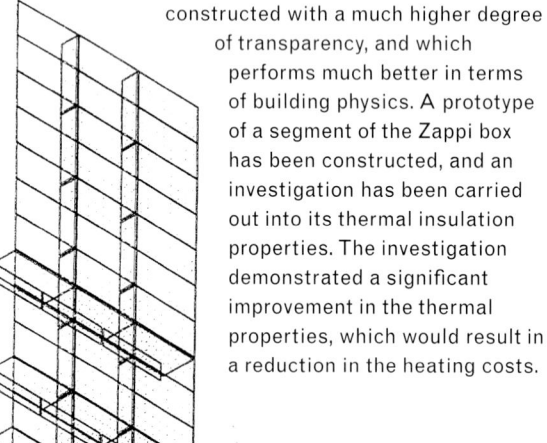

The design for the Zappi facade

The glass music box, Ameike Weijers

One of the Netherlands best-known glass buildings is the *Glazen Zaal* (Glass Hall) in the Beurs van Berlage (Stock Exchange) that was completed in 1990, a design of the architect Pieter Zaanen and the structural designer Mick Eekhout. Ameike Weijers was given the assignment to transform this design into an alternative Zappi design – a design that was to make no use of any non-transparent material whatsoever above ground level. After a prolonged cycle of design and redesign she succeeded in making a design that would meet the structural requirements. However the acoustics of the hall would be a problem; in the alternative design the reverberation time would be excessively long. In order to perfect the design Ameike developed a translucent sound-absorbing panel. The translucence of the panel retained the architectural effect of the overall design. Tests carried out on a prototype demonstrated the acoustic properties of the translucent panel.

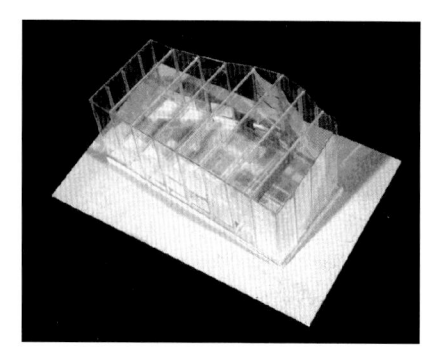

Model of the new design

The sound-absorbent panel, Kees van Kranenburg

Existing glass structures often exhibit major deficiencies in terms of building physics. The glass construction increases the architectural expression of the building, but at the expense of the comfort it provides. One of the problems is noise. A large glass facade possesses only limited sound-absorbent properties, which is not beneficial to the comfort in the rooms behind the facade. Kees van Kranenburg accepted the challenge to design a panel that had good structural properties and was transparent, but which possessed much improved sound-absorbent properties. A long period of research into the acoustic properties of the Zappi panel was required, followed by a series of designs and the construction and testing of the prototypes.

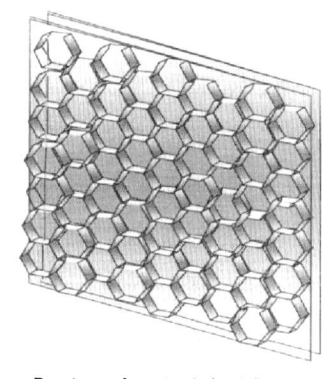

Design of material with a high acoustic impedance

The transparent column after the trial

The design of the Zappi spiral staircase

The transparent column, Joost Pastunink

The column is one of the basic elements in framework structures. In the past glass columns were used only extremely rarely, as their inherent brittleness makes them unsuitable for structural purposes. A transparent column capable of transferring invisible vertical forces would offer unprecedented opportunities. Joost Pastunink has laid the foundations for this type of column. By designing a process to make a laminate using two concentric glass cylinders he was able to manufacture a prototype that did not fail spontaneously when subjected to an overload, but which gradually crumbled in safety under the load that was imposed. Even after a considerable amount of fracturing the column still exhibited a substantial residual load-bearing capacity. The total load-bearing capacity of a column 40 mm in diameter and with a wall thickness of 3 mm is 10 tonnes – equivalent to a roof surface of 100 m^2, including the own weight and the useful load. A patent application has been submitted for this design.

The invisible stairs, Rene Stratenus

Once the first prototypes of structural components had been finished the question arose as to what other possible uses there might be for the Zappi material. Rene Stratenus made a study and suggested the idea of a Zappi spiral staircase. This is an interior feature with an extremely complicated construction, and which largely determines the appearance of the interior in which it is located. After a preliminary study Rene drew up the details of a design for a completely transparent spiral staircase that made no use of metal or other non-transparent materials. A prototype of the critical parts of the structure was made for testing. These tests demonstrated that the design functioned as expected.

Zappi as a product
Jan van der Woord

Engineering materials, i.e. materials that can be used to make objects, all have a number of properties that can be of greater or lesser benefit to the products that are manufactured from them. Moreover those properties are always present to no more than a given level, and specific properties may have a detrimental effect on the product in which the material is used. In every design one has to make an optimum choice from the existing materials, for which one needs to weigh the advantages and disadvantages of each material. This choice is a task inherent to every engineering design process. Product specifications then serve as guidelines. However, they can be of a nature such that it is impossible to make a satisfactory choice from any of the known materials. This problem is frequently encountered in technologically advanced industrial sectors such as the aerospace industry. As a result of the increasingly stringent requirements imposed on this industry, designers have long been unable to meet the needs of the design by using existing materials. New materials have had to be developed. Metallurgists make great efforts to design metal alloys with continually higher quality, alloys that are continually more suited to the objective for which they are intended. The polymer industry is as regular as the clock in the introduction of new materials onto the market that able to meet the new requirements. Aerospace technology makes a particularly large contribution to this process. The similarly-named Faculty at the TU Delft carries out a great deal of research in the field of high-grade composites in which the favourable properties of each of the components from which they are made, reinforce each other. It will be obvious that this all involves extra costs: the price per kilogramme is rapidly increasing, but "you get what you pay for".

The development of new materials is very similar to the design and development of new products. Both

Visualization of a
transparent building
(Monique van Liebergen)

processes depend on the determination of the specifications, creative moments, evaluatory investigations, and market research. Engineers, proficient in the technology, can perform well in both fields.

In technological terms the demands made on architecture are of a very different nature and of a much less stringent level than those made by the aerospace industry. The fact that a plane must fly and that a building must remain upright on the ground is not just a 'fundamental' difference in terms of the technology; it is also a very substantial difference. In functional terms a building is actually many times more complex than an airplane. And also in contextual terms. Buildings do not have merely an intrinsic value; they also make a permanent contribution to the quality of the city. Society maintains a long-term and intensive relationship with the buildings it produces. This is one reason why the cultural significance of buildings is of an entirely different order of magnitude than that of other engineering products, and why the design assignment for a building has such a very specific character. It is much more than the sum of a system of technological procedures. An insight into the interaction between people, and between people and their surroundings, is indispensable for the successful design of buildings. It is almost impossible to express this in terms of performance specifications; it requires both cultural substance and imagination from the designer. Here too, as in advanced technological environments, there is a process of material selection, of choices for existing materials for use in structures that are redefined in each design that is made. And here too, it is possible that there is dissatisfaction with the existing materials that are available, with the restrictions imposed by the properties of those materials. There may be a demand for a material that "can do everything", or is in any case able to combine the properties of two or more dissimilar materials. Zappi is such a material.

Architects can give a name to Zappi and work on the further details of its specifications. Moreover they will be able to make use of it in designs, when they draw up imaginary plans. Since architects have virtually no tradition of developing new materials, unlike technological designers in the aerospace industry, the development of Zappi will at the very least require a multidisciplinary approach. Creative technological ingenuity supplied by materials science must go hand in hand with architectural perceptions. A one-sided technological approach is not effective in architecture.

The Product Development section has included the realization of Zappi in its research program. At present work is being carried out on a compartmentalized twin-material laminate concept, originating from the materials science discipline. This concept constitutes the indispensable basis for the entire Zappi development process. It is based on the bonding of alternate layers of glass and polycarbonate to combine the strength of brittle glass with the toughness of relatively weak polycarbonate to yield a material better than either component; it also makes use of the compartmentalization of alternate sheets of glass to stop any fractures in the glass at the inner edges, and thus prevent the further growth of fractures through the layer, resulting in the subsequent failure of the material. Moreover the compartmentalization of the glass will make it possible to manufacture sheets of material that are larger than the maximum size of commercially-available sheets of glass.

Specific aspects of the concept are being tested by a number of graduation students, and possible applications of the material are being examined in structural designs in architectural situations. This work has resulted in the first refinements of the construction and manufacture of the material.

The development process is actually a process of product development. The formulation of a concept, possible applications, the performance, the feasibility of its manufacture, and the revision of the original concept follow each other in a cyclical development process. The first scale-models of prototypes have been developed and tested, leading to the first phase of the scaling up of the designs.

Whether all this work will ultimately result in a product ready for the market is still debatable. The project certainly has led to a tangible result in so far as that a discipline has been developed that will be able play a pioneering role in the use of promising new materials in architecture. At present Zappi still represents the development of new materials for a gradually evolving architecture. Its expansion into the development of the full range of new technologies of relevance to architecture is a possible future perspective. If Rietveld and Duiker had come into contact with such forms of Zappi at the time they were making their designs then they would perhaps have been able to realize their architectural ideals in a more durable manner.

Postscript
Prof. Dr Mick Eekhout

Although Zappi is still a long way off, the research and development program is an exciting and convincing process. What is so stimulating is that the various projects make it possible to achieve *incremental* results. Factors of major importance for each incremental result are its orientation to constructional value, its practical application, and its contribution towards the improvement of architectural quality. Zappi prefers its high-tech product to be used in good buildings – which it makes even better. This means that the significance of the development of a new product cannot be assessed on its own. As is always the case in research and development, real satisfaction is derived from the victories you win by the skin of your teeth. Perhaps the best remedy for the disease of sterile architecture is joy in design, joy in performance, vigour and wit.

Overview

Activities

The city and the periphery

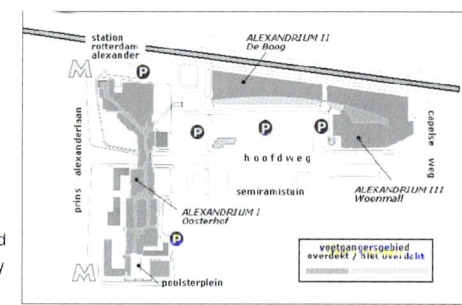

Inaugural lecture
19 September 1997 *Prof. C. van Weeren* The wealth of design

Doctorates
4 November 1996 *S.P. Tjallingii* Ecological conditions: strategies and structures in environmental planning
16 September 1997 *J.L.H. Renckens* Technology and organization of aluminum/glass facades
21 October 1997 *L.J.M. Tummers* The country in the city: the urbanism of the large agglomeration
21 October 1997 *J.M. Tummers-Zuurmond* The country in the city: the urbanism of the large agglomeration
11 May 1998 *P.P. van Loon* Interorganisational design: a new approch to team design in architecture and urban planning
26 May 1998 *R.A.J. van der Bijl* Precedent-based systems: research into an implementation in the knowledge domain of built environment and safety
23 June 1998 *G. Wigmans* The enabling city

Conferences, symposia, seminars, lectures, workshops and excursions
September 1997 *Netherlands Institute of Land Use Planning and Housing (NIROV)*, conference

The city and the periphery
   An interdisciplinary graduate urban development studio, commissioned by the NIROV and dealing with the competition between town/city centres and peripheral centres, started in September 1997 under the title 'Mobility and Spatial Planning'. Participants included transport specialists and town and regional planners from both the Delft University of Technology and the Catholic University of Nijmegen.
To investigate this competition in terms of mobility aspects and urban development quality, two cases were examined: Rotterdam with the peripheral location 'Alexandrium' and Nijmegen with the peripheral location 'Brabantse Poort', a key project from the early 1990's. A NIROV working group studied a number of large foreign mega-stores. The city centres and their peripheries were extensively analysed and compared in terms of their spatial and functional characteristics. The question is how you achieve the right function in the right place, with the right urban development quality? To this end, a conceptual framework was formulated to match the function profile, location profile and urban development profile. The accessibility of the centre locations appears to play an exceptionally important role. In addition, large-scale suburban centres may compete with the city centres, but a very important factor is whether the cities are large or small. In Dutch towns and cities, the centre remains at the top of the services hierarchy and, compared to the situation in other countries, there is no immediate threat of its role being undermined, partly on account of the existing meticulous sector-oriented zoning policy. Proper vigilance continues to be essential, however.
Final report: Bousema, Van Heun, Hotze, Keijzer, Rooij, Van de Wetering, *De stad en de rand, een interdisciplinaire studie naar een gespannen verhouding* (The city and the periphery, an interdisciplinary study of the tensions between them), Delft, Publicatiebureau Bouwkunde, 1998

October 1997 *25th Anniversary Volkshuisvesting* (Public Housing specialization)
1 October 1997 *Designing sustainability*, symposium Research School of Design and Computation
14 October 1997 *The future as a magnifying glass for the present*
24 October 1997 *The making of architecture*, symposium

'What's the matter with a glass box?'
   A symposium on architecture and glass facades with lectures by Hinrich Reyelts (Lehrstuhl für Gebäudelehre und Entwerfen, Universität Karlsruhe), Michael Schumacher (Schneider und Schumacher, Frankfurt) and Jouke Post (Post Ter Avest Architecten, Rotterdam). Subject was the B2 assignment to redesign the facade of the glass office wing of the Netherlands Architecture Institute (NAi). Students presented their plans to a panel

Erasmus intensive project

of experts: Mick Eekhout (professor of Product Development, TU Delft), Just Renckens (Renckensadvies Malden) and Bert van de Linden (Scheldebouw BV). The symposium was chaired by Jan Brouwer (professor of Building Technology, TU Delft), and was organized in conjunction with the Booosting foundation.

27-29 October 1997 *Utopia versus utopia*, workshop
13 November 1997 *Le Corbusier 's Maison Currutchet*, seminar
19-20 November 1997 *Urban morphology and conservation*, seminar
21 November 1997 *Functionalism*, seminar
28 November 1997 *Giorgio Grassi*, symposium
8-9 december 1997 *Collaborative Design Studio*, workshop
January - March 1998 *Limits of spatial design*, lecture series
6 January 1998 *The production of the built environment and the position of the architect*, seminar
23 January 1998 *A symposium in memory of Donald Schön*
30 Januari - 1 February 1998 *Object & Space*, workshop
4 February 1998 *Feasibility: a tricky problem*, seminar
18 February 1998 *Rotterdam: city and harbour*, symposium
14-16 April 1998 *'Woon-werk-woningen'*, seminar

18-30 April 1998 *International workshop Atelier Européen: 'Technologie de l'Architecture'*
An international workshop organized by the collaborating universities l'Ecole d'Architecture Paris-Tolbiac, Universität Karlsruhe, University of Venice, University of Liège and Delft University of Technology. Around sixty students from the five universities joined the workshop, the subject of which was the design of a residential building on the banks of the Seine with special attention being paid to the development of the facade. Lectures were given by William Vasal (Renzo Piano & Partners), Claude Vasconi (architect in Paris) and M. Bedel (Gartner France). There were excursions to the head office of the RATP, the Musée de l'Histoire et de Sciences Naturelles and the Bibliothèque de France. This annual workshop will be held in Venice next year.

18 April - 3 May 1998 *Comparing contradictions*, lecture series

May 1998 *Erasmus intensive project*, workshop
Within the terms of reference of the Erasmus programme, a three-week workshop is held each year with the focus on a current problem in the city. In the 1997-1998 academic year the project took place in Nancy, France. Faculties from Nancy, Porto, Barcelona, Thessaloniki and Delft participated.
The project group from Delft worked on a comprehensive approach to the future design of an area in the north-east of France that is undergoing change. The main emphasis was on finding a new essential structure to prevent the uncontrolled proliferation of urban sprawl. The constant interaction between the various scales played an important role in the design. It proved possible to present both large-scale and small-scale solutions that would enable the zone currently being transformed under economic, social and political pressure to retain and strengthen its own identity.

4 May 1998 *Intimate strangers*, lecture series
12 May 1998 *'Werk aan de winkel': development of demand and supply on the shop premises market until 2015*, symposium
14 May 1998 *Bridges: construction and architecture*, symposium

24-29 May 1998 *INDESEM '98*, seminar
The International Design Seminar is held once every two years at the Faculty of Architecture in Delft. It was an inspiring week, attended by around a hundred students from all over the world and well-known architects appearing as lecturers and critics. This year's theme – Operation NL, the experiment ahead – included an assignment focusing on a densely populated area in the centre of Rotterdam. For this week the faculty building had a special interior, based on the winning design from a competition held in March to select participants for the workshop. The design had the same enigmatic nature as the workshop. An airborne grid formed the basis for the interior. This was combined with a guiding line and superb lighting effects, creating a unique atmosphere appropriate to this special event.

28-29 May 1998 *Design methodology*, symposium
29 May - 12 June 1998 *Design strategies: Dutch architecture in the 20th century*, symposium
11 June 1998 *Architecture in Israel, 1948-1998*, conference

Exhibitions

1-26 September 1997 *Rietvelds Ranke Ruimtedieren*
1-30 September 1997 *The National Renovation Award*
3-30 September 1997 *Projects NRP 1997*
1-31 October 1997 *CASAS, ceramics by Arthur Meijer*
19-27 October 1997 *Raumplan – Plan Libre*
24 October - 28 November 1997 *Functionalism: Scharoun versus De Opbouw*
7 - 28 November 1997 *Giorgio Grassi – works*
7 November - 5 December 1997 *Le Corbusier: Maison Currutchet, La Plata, Argentina, 1948*
December 1997 *Baustelle: Tschechische Republik*
January 1998 *St. Petersburg: city on the waterfront*
April 1998 *Auf dem Weg zum Neuen Wohnen: die Werkbundsiedlung Breslau 1929*
9-30 April 1998 *Van caritas tot zelfbouw*
21 May - 2 June 1998 *Old cities in Morocco*

Competitions and awards

September 1997 *Housing Generator competition*

11 December 1997 *Rotterdam-Maaskant award 1998*: DBSG Stylos
The 1998 Rotterdam-Maaskant award has been given to the architecture student association *Stylos*.
"The 'major' prize is awarded in recognition of activities that publicize, instruct, stimulate or steer, which serve to clarify or reinforce the cultural significance of architecture or landscape design or serve to promote the conscious perception of design in these fields."
From the jury report:
"The fact that *Stylos* has been awarded has more to do with the character of a particular period than with the way of thinking and working of this architecture student association over many years. This continuous reflection and deepening stimulates and revitalizes the discussion and opinion forming about architecture and urban development. Exceptional in this respect is the continuity of these results, taking account of the annually changing composition of the governing bodies... An important aspect is that the organization does not only reach the students, but also the entire professional community in the Netherlands and beyond."

From the *Stylos* response:
"The independence of *Stylos* facilitates the organization of activities in addition to those provided by the education system. The direct individual input generates great commitment such that students are time and time again willing to spend time organizing activities."
Stylos has decided to spend the prize money on a project with the working title *Image and Language*, which brings up the subject of communication about and within the field.

26 March 1998 *PRC Bouwcentrum award 1998*: Pity van der Schaaf
15 April 1998 *Environmental award higher education*: Prof. Cees Duijvesteijn

Bending or breaking

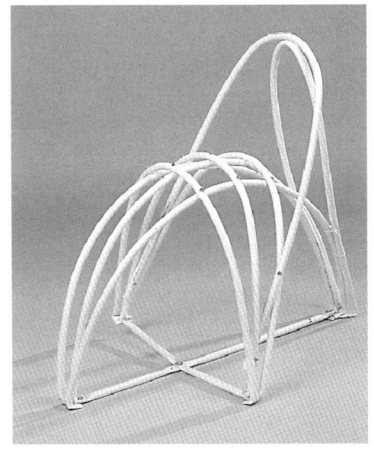

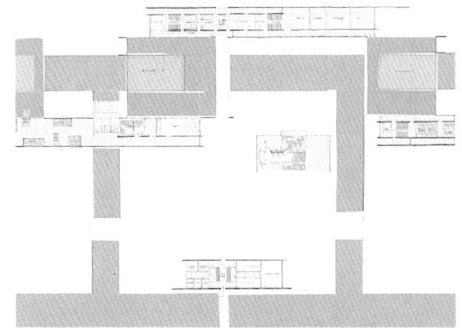

The 'other' baths in Bergen

D6/AV-Small House Big Space project

The D6 module was presented in the past academic year, together with an Architectural Design/Public Housing variant. The link-up between two design periods gave students the opportunity to do research and design work in slightly more depth.

The research that was the key feature of this design project involved the combination of living and working in an urban environment, the location being the Wilhelminapier in Rotterdam. The project was set up in such a way that it was possible to switch straight over from a study to a typological design, in which the specification was examined from the perspective of the smallest unit, the home-cum-workplace. The first period concluded with a week-long workshop at which our students worked closely together with students from the Technical University of Berlin and the Weissenseeschule Berlin to produce an urban planning scenario for the Rotterdam dockland area. In the second period of the project, the typology of the first period was combined with the scenarios from the workshop. This led to a master plan for the Wilhelminapier, a section of which was finally developed in detail. A joint final presentation took place in Berlin.

D5 Urban Design

During the period January/February 1998, the D5 Urban Design module was devoted to the task of creating an urban design for one of the islands in the new urban district of IJburg in Amsterdam, known as 'Strandeiland'.

There was a "hidden agenda" when the module was developed. First of all, the module aimed to impart the students with methods and skills with respect to development designs at the urban level. At the same time, an attempt was made to design the module in such a way that part of the research of the Urban Design chair could be performed by the students. The research used a systematic analysis and documentation of basic types of urban open spaces.

Important reasons for choosing the Strandeiland as design location were the topicality of this assignment as well as the character of the location as 'clean slate': we saw the lack of an historical foundation as a favourable condition to compel the designer to investigate the usability of existing instruments and typologies for the production of a new spatial composition. There is maximum cause for reflection on existing instruments and typologies, and thus for performing research into it.

Bending or breaking, workshop

A two-day workshop was held within the scope of the B2 module. The purpose of this workshop was to become creatively and experimentally acquainted with linear materials and to learn to deal with their limitations.

The assignment was to design and produce a chair using recyclable PVC construction pipes, glue, pop rivets and binders. The chair concept, which had to be produced on a scale of 1:1, was developed on the basis of the testing of materials.

To complete the workshop, the students gave a presentation and a professional jury evaluated their work. Besides being properly proportioned and composed, the chair had to be practicable and well-constructed. Furthermore, criteria such as originality, use of materials and connecting mechanisms were important. The workshop was concluded with a dinner at which everyone was expected to sit on their own chair.

The 'other' baths in Bergen

In the electronic era the 'real' experience is increasingly problematic. In the architecture of Peter Zumthor and others we see a movement that is critical of this development. With his almost minimalist architecture Zumthor explicitly focuses on the entire sensory perception of look, feel, sound, smell and, in his design for the thermal baths in Vals, even taste.

For us, this design and a wider interest in the manipulation of the architectonic skin was the pretext for devoting a special design project and seminar to the subject, in the context of the women's studies module *Manipulated skins*. Students examined, in both theoretical and design terms, the possibilities of a 'sensory' approach to architecture and the way in which the human body is staged in it. Visiting critics/lectures: Beatriz Colomina, Hilde Heynen, Heide Hinterthür, Peter Zumthor

Curriculum

With more than 3000 students and 300 staff members engaged in teaching the Faculty of Architecture is the largest technical faculty of the Netherlands. The curriculum offers opportunities for in-depth study of a wide range of scientific questions. Every year some 250 foreign students enrol in the international courses of the faculty.

Graduates have acquired a thorough scientific, technical knowledge and design skills; they have built up an ability to contribute effective and practical solutions to design problems. The study takes five academic years. Students acquire the necessary basic knowledge and skills during the first two years. In the third, fourth and fifth year they choose one of the five specializations: Architectural Design, Building Technology, Public Housing, Real Estate and Project Management, Urbanism. Graduates may use the title 'ingenieur' (ir.). The degree of engineer is internationally recognized as being equivalent to a Master of Science degree (MSc).

The curriculum of the faculty is characterized by various teaching methods, the most important of which are problem-based learning and project learning. Students work in small groups using feedback from a tutor. The subject matter is divided thematically. One theme is highlighted for a period of eight weeks. The study of theory and practice, learning to design, and acquiring skills are all adapted to the theme. Theoretical and practical skills can thus be directly incorporated into a design exercise.

Basic programme

Block 1 Space
Block 2 The building process
Block 3 The town
Block 4 The building and construction
Block 5 Kitchens and bathrooms
Block 6 The region
Block 7 Assignment, situation and programme
Block 8 Form and function
Block 9 Technical services
Block 10 'Imago': Integration of Environmental Aspects in the Built Environment
Block 11 Obsolescence and re-use
Block 12 Imaging and materialization

Specializations

Architectural Design (core modules)
A1 Architectural studies
A2 The architecture of mass housing
A3 The building
A4 History and design
A5 Concept and detail

Building Technology (core modules)
B1 A box of building blocks
B2 The drawing board
B3 The workplace
B4 The laboratory

Real Estate and Project Management (core modules)
M1 Capital investment
M2 Development
M3 Construction
M4 Management

Urbanism (core modules)
S1 Patterns
S2 Processes
S3 Society
S4 Site

Public Housing (core modules)
V1 Design and management of housing
V2 Housing, physical planning and environment policy: the housing market and VINEX
V3 Urban renewal and restructuring
V4 Public housing (study group)

Combined modules

AB Structural design
AM Architecture, technology and management
AS Architecture of the city
AV Residential building
BM High-rise
BS Mobility and flexibility
BV Building technology and housing management
MS Location development
MV Accommodation management
SV Urban residential areas

Differentiation modules

D1 Restoration
D2 Interior
D3 Landscape architecture
D4 Building in developing countries
D5 Urban design
D6 Architectural studies of residential areas
D7 Design methodology and applied informatics
D8 Design and cost control
D9 Integrated design
D10 The laboratory
D11 Media
D12 Renovation and re-use
D13 Technology transfer

Research programme

The five-year research programme (1994-1998) is divided into seven fields of research which correspond with the faculty's seven clusters: Architectural Design; Building Technology; Urbanism; Real Estate and Project Management; Public Housing and Urban Renewal; History, Media and Theory; and Computer Science. Research proposals are submitted to the Standing Committee on Science Policy for approval. The research themes of the clusters are listed below:

Architectural Design cluster
Architectural design: Design methods; Architectural design: Housing; Architectural design: Non-residential buildings; Architectural design: Restoration; Architectural design: Interior

Building Technology cluster
Structural design; Load-bearing structures and applied mechanics; Building physics, Services, Environmental design

Urbanism cluster
Urban design; Physical planning; Landscape architecture & environmental aspects of design

Real Estate and Project Management cluster
Project management; Real estate management and development

Public Housing and Urban Renewal cluster
Public housing; Urban renewal and housing management

History, Media and Theory cluster
History; Media; Theory

Computer Science cluster
Technical design and computer science; Computational design

The Faculty of Architecture participates in the research programmes of the following post-graduate schools and research institutes.

1. Netherlands School for Advanced Studies in Construction (BOUW)
Participants: the Faculties of Civil Engineering and Architecture, Delft University of Technology; Faculty of Building and Architecture, Eindhoven University of Technology; School of Management Studies, University of Twente.

The Netherlands School for Advanced Studies in Construction researches and develops technology for the planning, design, production, realization and management of structures. Research is based on an integrated interdisciplinary approach involving materials science, construction, applied mechanics, building physics, computer science and technology and management. Research themes include high-rise development, underground construction, new infrastructure and offshore construction. In addition, attention is paid to process organization, information technology, quality management, logistics and industrial construction.

2. Netherlands Graduate School of Housing and Urban Research (NETHUR)

Participants: University of Amsterdam; Delft University of Technology; Eindhoven University of Technology; Utrecht University

The research and education programmes of the Netherlands Graduate School of Housing and Urban Research focus on urban dynamics and housing. Research themes are the 'built environment', 'users of urban space', 'urban administration and policy' and 'models and instruments'. A recent research project is concerned with 'Social and economic reorganization, government regulation and the city'.

3. The Netherlands TRAIL Research School

Participants: Delft University of Technology; Erasmus University, Rotterdam

Transport, logistics and associated infrastructure are essential for the functioning of society. The research programme focuses on the transport of persons and goods. The projects deal with a variety of subjects, such as relocation activities, transfer, transhipment, storage and distribution.

4. Underground Space Technology Subsurface Construction

Participants: The faculties of Civil Engineering, Mechanical Engineering, Marine Technology, Applied Earth Sciences, Architecture, and Systems Engineering, Policy Analysis and Management, Delft University of Technology

Subsurface construction not only relates to traffic, transport and infrastructure, but also includes underground storage, buildings, public functions and utilities. Research focuses on alternative solutions in the field of design and construction. The main research themes are: infrastructure for traffic and transport; infrastructure for utility services and communication systems; storage of materials.

5. Delft Interfaculty Research Centres (DIOC)

Delft University of Technology has selected ten technological themes under which twelve multidisciplinary research programmes are conducted: the DIOC programmes. They have a laboratory function in developing technological innovations. Research is based on two lines of approach: to come up with innovative solutions ('the excellence aspect') and to provide solutions to issues of a socio-economic urgency ('the relevance aspect'). The Ecological City research project of the Faculty of Architecture comes under the theme of Sustainable Environment.

6. OTB Research Institute for Housing, Urban and Mobility Studies

Participants: Faculty of Geodetic Engineering, Faculty of Architecture. Delft University of Technology

Founded in 1985, the OTB research institute is an independent interfaculty organization. OTB carries out housing and urban policy research. For fundamental and applied research it draws on the technical sciences, policy analysis, management science and informatics. The main emphasis is on policy-making issues related to housing, urban renewal, building and real estate management, urban policy and environmental planning, land use, environmental protection, infrastructure, traffic and transport, construction policy, and land information.

Acknowledgments

Delft University of Technology,
Faculty of Architecture
Berlageweg 1
2928 CR Delft
The Netherlands
phone ++(31)152784237
fax ++(31)152784727
www.bk.tudelft.nl

Photographic acknowledgements
Aeroview BV, Rotterdam, p. 65

Design
Fred Inklaar, Amsterdam

Printing
Snoeck-Ducaju & Zoon, Gent

©1999 The authors and 010 publishers, Rotterdam [www.ArchiNed.nl/010]

CIP/ISBN 90.6450.358.3